WHICH WAY DID THEY GO?

ANDREW BENNETT

Trafford
PUBLISHING

Sections of *A Stewards Enquiry*, *Taking the Biscuit* and *Mad about the Guy* have appeared in the annual *'Rundown Events'* books.

Parts of various chapters have previously appeared in *'Footnotes'*, newsletter of Ackworth Road Runners & Athletics Club.

Order this book online at www.trafford.com/07-1155
or email orders@trafford.com

Most Trafford titles are also available at major online book retailers.

© Copyright 2007 Andrew Bennett.
Cover Design by Stephen Ward.

Note for Librarians: A cataloguing record for this book is available from Library and Archives Canada at www.collectionscanada.ca/amicus/index-e.html

Printed in Victoria, BC, Canada.

ISBN: 978-1-4251-3147-0

We at Trafford believe that it is the responsibility of us all, as both individuals and corporations, to make choices that are environmentally and socially sound. You, in turn, are supporting this responsible conduct each time you purchase a Trafford book, or make use of our publishing services. To find out how you are helping, please visit www.trafford.com/responsiblepublishing.html

Our mission is to efficiently provide the world's finest, most comprehensive book publishing service, enabling every author to experience success. To find out how to publish your book, your way, and have it available worldwide, visit us online at www.trafford.com/10510

www.trafford.com

North America & international
toll-free: 1 888 232 4444 (USA & Canada)
phone: 250 383 6864 ♦ fax: 250 383 6804
email: info@trafford.com

The United Kingdom & Europe
phone: +44 (0)1865 722 113 ♦ local rate: 0845 230 9601
facsimile: +44 (0)1865 722 868 ♦ email: info.uk@trafford.com

10 9 8 7 6 5 4 3 2

May you all achieve your targets and goals but perhaps more importantly, enjoy your running.

CONTENTS

Acknowledgements

To all those featured in the book and others on the West Yorkshire running scene and beyond who have provided storylines, incidents and inspiration.

Members and friends at Ackworth Road Runners & A.C and the Wednesday evening splinter group who put me through my paces each week at Pontefract.

My dearly loved Dad, the late Alf Bennett for his support and encouragement.

Roger Cope for the superb title, Stephen Ward for the cover photograph, Ian Wilson, Roy Young, Ann Sinar, John Bell, Cyril & June Jones and others for promoting my first book and trusting they will do the same for 'Which Way'

My Mum, Selina Bennett, Caroline Tempest and Claire-Marie O'Grady.

Introduction

HEN I finished my first book 'Middle of the Packer' in 2003, It was my intention to put down my notebook and retire my word processor for good, but I was soon press ganged into contributing articles and short stories for the newsletter at my running club. A loyal band of followers kept asking when the next book would be published so 'Which way did they go' has evolved from there.

My first race was at a local half-marathon in 1983 and I literally haven't stopped running since. I should complete my 900th race sometime in 2007 with 75 Marathons included in that total. Most of my running has taken place in West Yorkshire and the North of England but I have occasionally travelled further a field and overseas to pursue my interest.

On my travels I have made many friends and visited many places that only running would have taken me. Each race is so different with many providing new experiences, amusing incidents and different angles for stories. In 'Which Way' I try to capture some of these races, events behind the scenes and anything loosely connected to running while trying to maintain a humorous theme throughout.

CHAPTER 1

I've Started So I'll Finish

As MORE and more people began to stream through the concourse, I began to wonder if I would spot Les, but true to his word, he arrived dead on the stroke of seven 'o' clock. We had arranged to meet in Charing Cross Station intending to catch one of the early trains to the London Marathon start at Greenwich. Many of those heading towards the platform were wearing lycra in bright colours and making me feel scruffy and out of place in my cagoule and track suit bottoms. Several were leaving nothing to chance and were already stripped for action with their numbers pinned neatly in place.

I grabbed some breakfast in the hotel at crack 'o' dawn. The management had been kind enough to open early especially for the marathon runners but only three of us had taken up the offer so far. We sat strategically around the breakfast room in an attempt to make the place look full.

I had cereal, tea and toast but had promised myself a celebratory full English Breakfast tomorrow upon successful completion of the race. I wished the other two hardies the best of luck before wandering out onto the street to flag down a passing cab.

The main party from my club, Ackworth Road Runners were down for just one night, Les was staying in his caravan for a week near Crystal palace while I had opted to come down for three nights. I generally like to take in a couple of attractions and had been amongst the first in the queue at the British Museum on Saturday morning with the intention of seeing the Magna Carta. On Friday evening I went for a drink with a work colleague at

Plaistow in the east End of London.

I joined running friends, John and Kevin on Saturday lunchtime to see a useful QPR side thrash hapless Grimsby at Shepherds Bush. The Grimsby supporters carried inflatable haddocks and sang 'We only sing when were fishing'. On Saturday evening I met up with friend Rebecca to see 'Joseph', so with the Marathon Exhibition included, I had already had a hectic weekend before even a stride was taken in anger.

The train was less than full, unlike some of the later ones I had caught in previous years to Blackheath where packers had to be employed to squeeze in as many people as possible. I can remember one poor sod clambering onto the overhead luggage rack to lay down. As if it wouldn't be bad enough once the race started.

We were soon underway emerging into the daylight across the Thames where pleasure boats were gently bobbing about in anticipation of another busy day's trading on the water. There were glimpses of St Paul's and other notable landmarks in the distance on the London skyline. Back to back terrace houses with chimney stacks, satellite dishes and masses of aerials lined the approach to Waterloo East where more would be marathoners joined the train.

'Houses to Let at affordable prices' was emblazoned on a gable end while the slogan on a bill board stated 'Take Courage'. This seemed fairly appropriate under the circumstances. The train slowed down beyond the Market Porter Pub into London Bridge Station.

Into the suburbs with tower blocks and three or four storey tenements lining the route close to the New Den, home of Millwall Football Club. Graffiti was daubed on walls, bridges, parapets and virtually any surface that was possible to spray. When do these idiots carry out these mindless acts and why aren't they stopped. Deptford was next and then our stop, Greenwich.

Les had been here before, done it and knew the ropes but it seemed simply a matter of following the flow. A friendly face from a Doncaster running club was making a call on his mobile. He walked along the platform with us and said he was just checking in with the missus. Apparently he had been ill and his better half was having reservations about him running today. He had promised to run with his mobile, check in from time to time and keep her up to date on his progress.

We were among the first customers in the station buffet and enjoyed a mug of steaming hot tea. I fancied a toasted tea cake or a muffin but reluctantly refrained.

Greenwich High Street consists of gift shops, restaurants to suit every taste and shops with a nautical theme. We followed the signs past the appropriately named Gypsy Moth pub to Greenwich Pier and the Cutty Sark. Built in 1869, the tea clipper set a record time in bringing wool from Australia. In a couple of hours we would revisit this very spot six miles into the race when I trusted I would be feeling fine and moving along quite nicely. The wooden ramps were down to cover the steps and barriers in place where hundreds of people would gather in anticipation of catching a glimpse of their friends and loved ones.

We leaned against the rail gazing out across the river to the Isle of Dogs. The stairway to the Thames Pedestrian Tunnel starts here emerging at Island Gardens at around eighteen miles into the race. I would be able to save myself considerable time and passage through here but would probably find myself in the lead on rejoining the race. I imagined people taking this easy option in some of the early editions of the race and probably hopping onboard the tube for a couple of stops too.

By now, a steady procession of people were making there way past the Maritime Museum and Naval College towards the start. 'The First Shop in the World' stands proudly on the corner at oo oo' 24' degrees. The window display consisted of ships bells, compasses and seafaring figurines. We made our way along The Avenue, through the spectacular gates into Greenwich Park and up the considerable hill to the tented village.

The area was already crowded with people sitting on the grass in small groups and generally milling around. Time for another drink so we queued for a complimentary cup of Brooke Bond P.G. Tips at the dedicated marquee. I paid a call at one of the long line of por-taloos before the queues really started to build. Already a pungent smell presided, the cistern wouldn't flush properly and Thames Water technicians were working frantically to restore the water pressure. Portable pipe work was everywhere to be seen.

We bumped into club colleague Mick, exchanged notes and found out about the word on the street. I perched on the end of a Kippax Harriers photo shoot but decided at the last minute that it wasn't such a good idea. They didn't want my mug shot spoiling their team photo on the big day. More club mates joined us in Kevin and John as our little band steadily grew.

Billboards and hoardings were plentiful advertising the main race sponsor, Flora, along with ancillary sponsors such as Unisys, Asics, Isostar, BUPA and Renault.

The changing marquees were pretty heaving, but we managed to commandeer a park bench to complete our final preparations. I secured my number with four safety pins making sure my club name was visible. Kevin used six for extra stability only to be ridi-culed for doing so and immediately being burdened with the new nickname 'Six pins'.

Announcements were continually being made to remind compet-itors of the impending departure of the baggage trucks. There was a sizeable queue here and even bigger ones now for the portaloos.

Girls in sponsors uniform were handing out bottles of Aqua-Pura Water and whilst drinking from one of these, a crown came away from my tooth. Fortunately I managed to catch it before I swallowed, so decided to tuck it away in a small pocket inside my shorts for the duration of the race. I trusted that it would make it around safely as I didn't fancy forking out a hefty price for a re-placement and the accompanying dentistry.

I would tell my lady dentist and trusty nurse Karen that the crown had come out during the race, in a vain attempt to make them think I was hard and macho. I would say that each time I gulped cold air, the pain was excruciating.

Despite been dubbed as the 'Worlds Longest Urinal' the queues at the portaloos still hadn't subsided and there would be a lengthy wait for sure. With the three of us now bursting for a final pee before heading to the starting assembly area, we made our way over to some bushes against a temporary fence in a secluded corner of the park.

Many people obviously had the same idea in mind, despite directives in the race literature not to use bushes, shrubs or peoples front gardens for such purposes but desperate times call for desperate measures. Looking around to ensure the coast was clear, we each got into position and made a start. However our cover was blown when a police officer appeared out of nowhere. There's never a copper around when you desperately need one.

"There's plenty of toilets, you've no need to go there" he bellowed from a distance. "Have you seen the queues mate" responded Mick. "You shouldn't have left it as late as this" he retorted still walking towards us.

Saving the best until last, Les replied. "I've started, so I'll finish".

CHAPTER 2

Bohemian Rhapsody

THE FIRST time I visited Prague, we travelled overland, overnight. My travelling companion Jonathon, was keen to give a good account of himself in the marathon so was anxious to have some rest. He slept on the train down to Kings Cross and again on the Euro star to Brussels. He made himself comfortable for the long haul on the overnight train from Cologne missing the most scenic leg of the journey. The flickering of lights from the fairytale castles and chocolate box villages reflected on the surface of the water along the River Gorge in the late evening darkness.

I was able to sneak to the buffet car for a beer and sandwich but soon returned. Things must have livened up later on as a noisy conga made it's way along the corridor and back. But unperturbed by all of this, Jonathon slept on. When I awoke on Friday morning, the outlook was of the gently rolling Bohemian countryside and we duly arrived in Prague around 8-00 'O' clock.

After a coffee in the station, we had to establish how to reach the hostel at Kacerov on the Metro train. Unsure of our bearings, we caught a taxi from the suburban railway station to the hostel. On arrival, a gust of wind blew Jonathon's door out of his grasp and a car travelling in the opposite direction crashed into it, inflicting small damage.

The lady driver who could do little about this was none too pleased and remonstrated with the taxi driver. He in turn vented his anger on us and seemed to be asking for some compensation. We paid him only the money for the taxi fare and disappeared inside the hostel. While we were checking in, the taxi driver reappeared with the woman hotly in pursuit. The argument continued and the taxi driver then made a call using the pay phone.

Jonathon tried to tap up the receptionist for information as to what had been said but nothing was forthcoming. He didn't appear to be having a great deal of luck. Our room was basic with three single beds between the two of us but much better than I had anticipated although we had to share bathroom facilities with the incumbents next door. Jonathon was well used to back packing and hostels on his many travels but I was more of a four star man myself.

We took a leisurely stroll back towards the Metro station, mindful of looking out for our taxi driver and giving him a wide berth should we spot him at the rank. Alighting from the metro train at Muzeum, we walked down the slope into the long expanse of Wenceslas Square.

Wenceslas Square came to world prominence in the Autumn of 1989 as the scene of protests and rallies. Vaclav Havel took over from communist Alexander Dubcek in what became known as the Velvet Revolution. Back In 1968 The Square also made world headlines as Soviet tanks suppressed Czech student protestors.

Likened to a busy tree lined boulevard rather than a square, Wenceslas Square is the hub of city life. We wandered the narrow streets beyond here into Old Town Square, crossing Charles Bridge and returning to the hostel in time to wash and change for the evenings activities.

Jonathon would gladly have settled for a 'Big Mac' but I was having none of it and was adamant that I hadn't come all this way to be deprived of my Bohemian Dumplings. We ate in a suitable vaulted cellar establishment and had three generous courses and a pint of pilsner for little above three quid apiece.

On Saturday we took a boat trip on the Vltava River in bracing conditions and were amongst the first in the queue for the pasta party which kicked off at midday.. With race day fast approaching we retired to the hostel early.

The race started in Old Town Square with prolonged early stretches on the cobbles while care had to be taken not to tread in the sunken tram lines. At two miles we crossed Charles Bridge, again running on cobbles. Apparently the only occasions the bridge is closed to pedestrians is when the marathon and half marathon races take place. As soon as the last runner is through, it's back to business as normal.

Most of the course consisted of an out and back along dual carriageways with two short sections towards half way forming a Y shape through forests. Jonathon had started quickly but emerged from the bushes at the side of the road ahead of me at five miles after obviously paying a call of nature. He was in front for some time and I acknowledged him as he returned down the opposite carriageway shortly after the first turnaround point.

The final stages were through Kampa Island with yet more cobbles and into the historic town finishing in Old Town Square. Both Jonathon and I beat our targets of 3 hours 30 and 3 hours 40 respectively for a mornings work well done.

In contrast to the previous day, the weather was warm and Jonathon suffered unduly, first resting before falling asleep. He awoke not feeling too good probably putting it down to the celebratory ice cream.

I returned to Prague in 2002, this time staying for four nights. With only the half marathon as a distraction on Saturday lunchtime, I would be able to do justice to the cities many historical sights. Staying reasonably centrally, I set out after unpacking with a sturdy pair of walking shoes and clutching a map. I followed narrow cobbled streets, each looking pretty much the same, occasionally opening into a larger square. Miraculously I found my way to Old Town Square, the medieval town's main market place.

The beautiful Old Town Square is a hotchpotch of medieval and baroque structures and is the natural place for visitors to spend some time. The assortment of yellow, cream and green pastel buildings are reminiscent of a scene from a Grimms Fairytale and just how I would have imagined a historic Eastern Block city to be. I bought a steaming glass of Gluhwein, apparently made from red wine, sugar, cinnamen and orange peel, from one of the stalls. This resembled a hot toddy and really hit the spot on the cold early spring day. Other market stalls were selling roast chestnuts, sausages and gingerbread while a choir of schoolchildren and a band struck up on a temporary stage. The grey sky was filled with flakes of snow.

I joined the crowd that waited for the Astronomical clock to reach 2-oo clock. On the hour, the doors opened and figures of Apostles emerged. The show was unremarkably short and probably not worth the wait. The clock in Dads Army where one of the miniature figures kept poking Corporal Jones up the bum with a sword was far better.

Looming over the square are the twin gothic spires of the Church of Our Lady before Tyn. Making my way towards the large wooden doors, I found the church to be closed for visitors so decided it was perhaps time for a first pint. I called at Caffreys where a stag weekend appeared to be in full swing.

Prague is apparently the new stag weekend capital of Europe as both Dublin and Amsterdam had become heartily sick of these people and had started to discourage them. Not too long ago, a Pontefract man had been imprisoned for an offence during a stag weekend in Prague. He had apparently been detained after several of his mates were cleared. His mother had appeared on both local and national television pleading that he had done nothing wrong.

The stag party dominated the pub. They were rude, loud and foul mouthed and made for an uncomfortable atmosphere. One of them was drinking without a shirt despite the bitterly cold weather outside. After drinking up at least for the time being, the stag party suddenly upped and left much to the relief of the other punters. Almost as quickly as they had left they returned, probably two dozen strong, the man with no shirt sporting tattoos on his tattoos.

I made my way through the historic Old Town towards Charles Bridge. Here more stag parties easily stood out from the other tourists, shouting and balling, bumping and clattering into people despite the early afternoon hour. What had Prague done to deserve this lot and what would they have made of it all in the Cold War era.

Mozart look-alikes in powdered wigs handed out flyers for the many concerts within the city and the maestro's music sounded out through windows, down alleyways and across court yards.

Charles Bridge links Stare Mesto, The Old Town with Mala Strana, the Lesser Quarter and spans the Vltava River. The bridge is without doubt the most popular tourist attraction with hundreds milling around to see the many painters, musicians and jugglers or just to browse at the array of souvenir stalls. The stone bridge was built in 1357 after the original, Judith Bridge collapsed in the flood of 1342. In the seventeenth century, statues of 30 saints were added to the Gothic stone structure.

I enthused at the sheer number of tourists, wondering if such numbers were apparent in March, how many would be here over a hot July or August weekend. Apart from the anticipated Japanese, there were Arabs, North Africans and a whole host of others who had me guessing as to their nationalities.

On the way back to the hotel, I called at the much celebrated Kavarna for a coffee. Within the magnificently restored Municipal House, the setting has brass chandeliers, balconies and a resident pianist.

First stop in the early evening was the Radegast Pub, a typical Czech tavern close to Old Town Square. I enjoyed Goulash and dumplings washed down with one of the fine Czech beers albeit in something of a smoky atmosphere. I called at a couple of old style beer halls and on the way back enjoyed a frankfurter in a bread roll on the corner of Wenceslas Square. As I stood eating, I was approached by ladies of the night and observed club touts, taxi drivers and a whole assortment of unlikely individuals all competing for business.

Friday was to be my big sightseeing day. I set out early on a bitterly cold morning, taking to the picturesque winding streets and the steep steps leading to Prague Castle. Although admission to the courtyards is free, a ticket is required for the attractions within. These include the Powder Tower, St Georges Convent and the Toy Museum. I visited the Basilica of St George and with driving rain now adding to the cold, I took sanctuary inside St Vitus Cathedral.

Dominated by the two gothic towers, the cathedral was completed in 1929, a millennium after St Wenceslas was laid to rest on this very site. Inside the cathedral, tour parties had taken shelter from the rain and it was hard to move around even inside such a vast interior. As only an occasional worshipper, what would my parish priest have given for such numbers at Sunday Mass.

With trusty umbrella aloft I moved slightly downhill to Golden Lane, the most visited and photographed street in Prague. The tiny multi coloured cottages nestle tightly against the northern walls of the castle.

I headed back down to Mala Strana and to Kampa Island on the waterfront. This was where the race would start and finish and a temporary marquee had been erected to deal with the registration and administration. The girl at the desk inside was well wrapped to combat the cold and cringed every time anyone opened the flap to enter or leave. I collected my race number, tee shirt and literature and with little else to see, braced myself again for the weather outside.

I wandered the peaceful Kampa Island passing the medieval waterwheels in the shadow of Charles Bridge. There are wonderful photo opportunities here of the bridge, the arches and the many turrets and spires of the Old Town across the water. This low lying area was devastated in the terrible floods of 2002 when the great rivers of Central Europe burst their banks.

I called for a coffee in a trendy establishment and from my window seat observed passers by battling against the elements. With lunch time approaching, I headed back across Charles Bridge which formed part of the Royal Route taken by Bohemian Kings between Prague Castle and the City Gates.

The James Joyce Pub is described in 'Time Out' Guide as a Hooray Henry Hangout for the expat crowd. It stated that few Czechs could afford the prices which is partly the point of this oasis. Businessmen in suits and smart office girls made up the punters but trade was generally slow. I ordered a beer and bangers and mash in onion gravy and picked a quiet corner table.

The waitress was Colleen, a dark haired Irish girl with green eyes. She didn't say she was Colleen, I heard no one call her Colleen but that was her name. She spoke in a Donegal lilt, similar to a young Dana that sent men hopelessly weak at the knees and set pulses racing. I ordered another beer as much out of necessity to listen to her speak as to quench my thirst. I had a couple of sips from my new beer and topped it up with the residual from my first glass. Everyone has done this at some time in their lives and today was my turn. The froth surged to the top of my glass and the beer over-flowed onto the table. Colleen appeared out of nowhere in the nick of time with a giant cloth, to save the day and spare my blushes.

I thought how wonderful for a young girl like Colleen to be able to work in a place like Prague. When I was of a similar age, I couldn't even see a way clear for me to be able to visit such places. If only I had my time to come all over again.

I sat talking to a man from South London who was here work-ing on a film set. Prague is a much sought after location with the historic and atmospheric streets meeting the requirements of many films. He had been here for three weeks but his services so far hadn't been required. He would turn up each morning only to be told to come back the next day.

He was staying in a top hotel with everything paid for but said there was only so much food he could eat, beer he could drink and attractions he could visit. Most of his time was spent wander-ing around or kicking his heels. I told him of my experiences in

Wenceslas Square the previous evening and he said there were some-where in the region of 3,000 ladies of the night in Prague. He reck-oned many of these were gypsies who preyed upon likely looking punters in hotels, bars and on the city's streets.

After lunch I headed north of Old Town Square to the Jewish Ghetto in Josefov. Here the streets were strangely free of both tourists and residents and an atmosphere of tranquillity presided. Remains in excess of 20,000 people are believed to have been buried in the Old Jewish Cemetery over a 500 year period with as many as twelve deep in places. The headstones are a jumble of different shapes and sizes, leaning in all directions.

On one side of the cemetery is the Pinkas Synagogue where the walls are covered with the names of 80,000 people who suffered in the Holocaust. There are also drawings by children of life inside a concentration camp which I found to be very moving.

The main purpose of my visit was to run the Prague Half Marathon which would start on Saturday midday. After breakfast and a brisk stroll, I packed my running tackle and gathered my belongings. I established that tram No 51 would take me to within striking distance of the start and joined a sizeable queue at the stop. The weather was bitterly cold with the occasional snow flurry but I was wearing plenty of clothing and had packed a woolly hat and gloves.

The changing rooms were in a school at Mala Strana with the classrooms designated to various blocks of numbers. I was No 55 so was in a room next door to the elite athletes. There would be several Kenyans starting along with other useful African runners. To reach the kit storage area necessitated climbing several flights of stares and I wouldn't relish these after the race when I returned to claim my bag.

I warmed up by way of a gentle jog if only to keep warm. The start would be on Charles Bridge which had already been closed to pedestrians. Extra care would have to be taken on the cobbles as the 2,000 runners headed across the bridge towards the myriad of towers, domes and spires. A left turn below the Old Town Bridge Tower brought another problem with tram lines again adding to the cobbles.

The early stages followed the Vltava through the Jewish Quarter before heading back to the city. I shared my experiences with two Sheffield girls who had driven here stopping off for a couple of nights in Amsterdam on the way. I promised to look out for them in the Sheffield races at the end of April before pressing ahead.

The route skirted the Powder Gate, probably my favourite Prague building. I had purchased a model of the same which would take pride of place in my cabinet at home alongside other memorabilia from my travels. The course headed along Na Prikope passing the designer shops and fashion malls. Enthusiastic spectators had now replaced the prostitutes, gypsies and touts as we crossed the bottom of Wenceslas Square and beyond the National Theatre, back towards the waterfront.

The route headed out and back to the Vrosovice district and then along the river bank to Branik. Although the course was generally flat, we would have a stiff breeze to contend with on the return leg to Kampa Island. Not surprisingly, several Kenyans were battling for the honours as the leaders returned on the opposite side of the road shortly before the first turnaround point.

As in the Great North Run, bands provided entertainment along the way and these included the 'Dixieland Messengers' and 'On the Bubble'. I was glad to be wearing my woolly hat and gloves but was nevertheless feeling cold, tired and miserable. But despite all of this, I was still doing a damned site better than the previous Sunday at Redcar when I must have put my shoes onto the wrong feet.

In order to keep going, provide something to do and to break the monotony, I started to count the runners on the opposite carriageway who had still to reach the final turnaround point. I counted upwards of seven hundred with many more still to come as the course returned across the river towards Kampa Island.

At this stage I ran stride for stride with a schoolteacher from the Greater Manchester area and the conversation was a welcome distraction, enabling us to forget our woes at least for the time being. He was accompanying a group of boys who were playing football matches against local Prague schools and had managed to wangle this for race weekend. Good for him! I bumped into him again complete with his brood on Sunday in the Old Town and again at the airport. The final two kilometres cut through pleasant riverside parks and historic courtyards to the finish at Kampa Square in the shadow of Charles Bridge.

As I approached the finish I could see my likeness on a large screen which wasn't a pretty site. Clutching my medal, I made my way through tourists and runners alike, back to the school. As anticipated, the steps to retrieve my baggage felt like mountainsides, not recommended after running thirteen miles. With the stairs safely negotiated, I managed to change into warm clothing and grabbed a coffee.

The walk back over Charles Bridge enabled me to stop briefly to see some of the back markers safely finishing their own race. I caught the tram and was soon back in the warmth of my hotel room.

Washed, changed and still only 3-30, I set out in search of a bar where I had seen live sport advertised, mainly to see if I could catch the final scores. The place was packed to the rafters with among others, yes you've guessed, stag weekenders. Many appeared to be well behaved but others were outspoken, offensive and in everyone's face. Why is it that young, and not so young men fork out good money to booze in Prague when they could do the same in any British town, defies belief. The excuse of dirt cheap beer doesn't stack up because they only appear to frequent the English and Irish style bars.

One incident tickled me when a man in one of the stag parties moved away from his group to chat up a couple of women at another table. No sooner had he introduced himself and settled down, before one of his mates called across telling him that it was his turn to buy a round.

While all of this was happening, Scotland were thrashing it out with Wales on the big screen at Rugby Union. I waited for the final scores which saw Leeds United in much happier times, beat Leicester 3-0 and Ross County and Inverness Caledonian, draw nil apiece in the highland derby.

On Saturday evening I wandered the streets looking in shop windows and calling for a beer or coffee wherever took my fancy. I came into the illustrious company of an Englishman abroad who was drinking alone and apparently celebrating a divorce. He would have bought my beer all night if I hadn't decided to move on.

I visited the spectacular National Museum at the top of Wenceslas Square on Sunday morning, fascinated by the huge collection of minerals and rocks from all around the world. From here I meandered to the City of Prague Museum where the prime exhibit is a room size paper model of the city prior to the decimation of the Jewish Ghetto.

I called at Molly Malone's where the resident stag party were a rugby team dressed in black and white striped blazers resembling humbugs and sporting boaters. The next bar was showing live English Football by way of Liverpool versus Chelsea and the obligatory stag weekenders seemed already settled in for the long haul. I moved to a quieter bar in the Mala Strana Quarter and finished watching the match there with a group of friendly and impeccably behaved Austrians. I once again climbed the many steps to the Castle before returning to the waterfront as daylight faded.

A late flight on Monday afternoon provided the opportunity to retrace my steps, not least over Charles Bridge. I made for the statue of St John Nepomuk and touched the shiny gold spot on the lower right hand side. This would ensure that one day I'd return to Prague, hopefully in the not too distant future.. The priest was said to have been thrown from the bridge in 1393 as a result of King Wenceslas IV's anti-clericalism.

I purchased a print of a typical cold war scene which depicted

Charles Bridge on a grey murky Autumnal day. Intending to hang it on the office wall at work, it was still there when I left my employment two years later, in a box on the floor.

The rowdy behaviour of the boozy stag parties dominated the airport lounges, but fortunately my flight home passed off without incident. Let's hope that Prague is as far as these yobs decide to travel for a drink and that they leave the likes of Budapest, Vienna and Krakow to the proper tourists. I won't hold my breath!!

CHAPTER 3

Seaside Shuffle

"CAN WE go now" pleaded the lady, when she thought I was probably out of earshot. I had just passed the twelve mile post on the cliff top path beyond Sewerby. It would be plain sailing from here with the wind at my back and a gentle gradient down to the finish on the North Promenade at Bridlington.

Work colleague Julia and her family, spent most of their weekends throughout the summer at a caravan in Bridlington and for long enough I had hinted I would be running in the half marathon today. This would be the last weekend they visited before locking up for the winter.

Meandering through Sewerby Park, passing the children's zoo and cricket field before turning onto the cliff path, I had to step out of the way, to avoid the land train which uses this route to ferry passengers from the town to Sewerby. Some years earlier the train had almost ploughed into me here, on a horrible, murky, and drizzly day.

I spotted a small pocket of spectators huddled together, wrapped in scarves, gloves and hats to combat the freezing conditions. Among them were Julia and husband Barry who provided welcome encouragement and support as I approached. I thanked them while trying to put on a brave face, look good and smile. But overhearing the comment of Julia's friend, she was obviously none too impressed, having probably been made to stand in the very same spot for over half an hour. She no doubt had expected me to be up with the front -runners rather than back in 192nd place.

Back at work on Monday, I discussed the events of the previous day with Julia and remarked upon the comment made by her friend. She had no idea I had overheard and appeared to be slightly embarrassed. I told her we had tea and toast before the race and fish and chips and a waffle afterwards, with a couple of pints at Wetherspoons to wash them down. Listening to the conversation, Julia's workmate Janet chipped in, "I thought you were supposed to be runners?", no doubt imagining me to be on a strict all year round diet and fitness regime. "But I am a runner" I replied, "Not a fast one, but nevertheless a runner".

I have run at Bridlington for almost as long as I have being running. I can recollect on one of the early visits, my Dad locked the car keys in the boot while I was out pounding the roads. He had to call out the R.A.C. and didn't seem to understand why I appeared non too impressed on returning to the car. On a separate occasion, I afforded myself a 'Full English Breakfast' with the race still three hours away. Five miles into the race, I could feel the fried bread lubricating my system as it started to take effect.

The ride over the gently rolling Yorkshire Wolds is reason enough for entering the race and provides a feel good factor before you even reach the seaside. Once there, the smells of salt and seaweed and the cries of seagulls tend to lift the spirits even if the weather is cold and miserable.

Bridlington has experienced something of a boom in recent years with the renovation of the spa area and refurbished seafront. Fishermen repair nets and stack crab pots around the picturesque bustling harbour which is flanked by two stunning beaches. Shops sell buckets and spades, fishing tackle and shellfish served in little plastic pots. A proposed new £60 million marina providing berths for 600 boats has recently been shelved but an alternative low key project will be considered to include shops, restaurants, homes and apartments.

The impressive start to the race on North Promenade has runners lined up facing the stunning chalk cliffs of Flamborough Head in the distance. The headland juts out ten kilometres and towers 130 metres above the water with seabirds, gannets and guillemots fighting for space on the many windswept ledges. Erosion has demolished precarious paths leading to hidden coves and has formed hundreds of rock pools, providing a paradise for children when the tide is out. Rock arches and sea stacks tower high above the water.

Every year, the lifeboat is kept busy helping people who have been caught out by the tides. This is the most dangerous spot on the east coast and people underestimating the strength of the currents are swept out to sea.

The first half mile along the promenade is usually covered at breakneck speed before a short pull onto Lime Kiln Lane has me puffing and gasping for breath. A mini roundabout signifies the one mile marker and a pleasant residential stretch to Marton Gate where the race starts to settle down.

Undulating country lanes lead to Flamborough but nothing too serious for the average competitor. Caravans are sited to the left and the manicured lawns of Bridlington Links on the right hand side. From time to time, the pavement meanders above the road before a welcome downhill and a left turn beyond several rows of distinctive red roofed cottages.

The streets of Flamborough fan out towards the cliff tops and the sheltered North Landing where open fishing boats called cobles are harboured. The headland is only minutes away and the scenery is dramatic. Danes Dyke close to the village is a four mile rampart designed to cut off the headland from bronze and stone age invaders. Although clearly visible today, some parts form a beautiful wooded ravine.

The chalk tower built in 1674 is the oldest remaining lighthouse in England where a coal fire was lit at the top of the octagonal structure. The present lighthouse was built in 1806 without scaffolding and stands closer to the sea. It became electronically operated in 1985 with the flashing light visible 21 miles out to sea.

In February 1871, a violent storm known as The Tenth of February Gale saw seventeen ships wrecked. Seventy men lost their lives including six from the lifeboat crew. There were two lifeboat stations at either side of the headland in those days with Paddington serving the South Landing and Gertrude the North. In 1935, a motor lifeboat came to the North with the South Station closing but in 1993, the North Station closed with the South reopening. Since 1871, the fourteen lifeboats stationed at Flamborough have been launched on 644 occasions and have saved 538 lives.

This area was declared a heritage coast in 1979 with all building developments carefully being monitored.

The middle section of the race to Bempton and beyond is the toughest part of the course with several long hills to check out the fitness. To the right are Bempton Cliffs which mark the northerly tip of a chalk belt that runs from the Isle of Wight to this part of the East Coast. Throughout the breeding season, in excess of 200,000 seabirds take refuge here making it the largest colony in Britain. Kittiwakes were massacred for their highly prized feathers in Victorian times and eggs were gathered by 'climmers' who descended the cliff face by rope.

Club-mate Ken Barton and I were discussing the merits of the course along this section when two young ladies effortlessly pulled level, chatting away together. They exchanged pleasantries whilst trying to persuade us into signing up for their Driffield Mucky Duck Race. They drifted away into the distance when we made it clear that the way we felt, this would definitely be our last race.

A useful downhill leads to the picturesque village of Bempton where the natives are usually warm and receptive in their applause and support. The long drag from the village and past the seven mile post, can be hard and gruelling and can shape you're race depending upon how you tackle it. My best attempt at this section was on a foggy day in the late nineties when the lack of visibility managed to camouflage the impact of the gradient. Turning left here by the windmill into Bempton Lane, it should be all plain sailing with only niggling little pulls to break up the long downhill sections. The scene is of caravan parks with the town and the coastline beyond, but ten minutes of hard running fails to bring the sea any closer.

The stage along Marton Gate will look familiar because it is tackled twice but rather than head out to Flamborough, a right turn leads into Church Lane. Suddenly the road surface appears smoother and the going becomes easier with a bank of woodland sheltering any breeze.

Entering the grounds of Sewerby Hall brings back memories of when I trounced a group of workmates, graduates, team leaders and anyone else who was out to impress the management at pitch and putt on a team building day. I didn't fare too well at clay pigeon shooting with the kick back of the rifle butt, constantly pummelling my shoulder blade. They said that some of the clays were woodcock, some pheasant and others teal but they all looked like little round discs to me.

Being only an average footballer in my younger days and pretty awful at cricket and squash, I would look to exact my revenge over my piers by thrashing them at putting or pitch and putt whenever the opportunity arose. Senior workmates, affluent colleagues and friends on days out have all been put to the sword when I have a putter in my hand. For this I must thank my dad who played hours with me on holiday as a youngster and must have had the patience of a saint. Strangely enough, I've never played a full round of golf in my life and often wonder how I would have fared, had I taken up the sport.

A slight pull is negotiated which can hurt at this stage of the race, before the course meanders through the courtyard passing the Clock Tower Tea Rooms, The Children's Zoo and cliff top cricket field. The run in to the finish beyond the twelve mile post where Julia and her colleagues were gathered, is spectacular. The path drops gently providing views of the bay, the beaches and the Edwardian buildings of North Promenade. Beware of pedestrians, of families with push chairs and of the land train that uses this route on it's journey from town to Sewerby. The train caused a problem on that foggy day when runners were unaware of it approaching until the last minute with the driver steadfastly refusing to move over.

The final half mile to the finish near the Royal Crescent can be agonising to say the least with the crowd at the end clearly visible, but not apparently coming any closer. A glance around may be in order to ensure club mates or those who you wish to beat you aren't sneaking up on you're shoulder in a frantic dash to the line.

On returning to her caravan at Christmas, Julia was shocked to discover someone had been using it to sleep rough. He had gained access through the skylight, hadn't caused any damage but had made use of blankets, tea and provisions. On asking around, people had seen a vagrant or drifter in the area who now appeared to have moved on. The things some people will do to stay in Bridlington!

CHAPTER 4

Lager And Harry Lime

I was in my early twenties when I visited Vienna for the first time. I had travelled with four mates by car from Northern Italy and down through Austria, arriving in the capital after a couple of overnight stops up country. We parked the car and seemed to walk for miles, just to catch a glimpse of the Blue Danube.

It was wide, dirty and very busy with river traffic but certainly not blue.

We caught a tram back to the city and I inadvertently pressed the communication button instead of the button to indicate the next stop to the driver. A bank of lights started flashing and a klaxon sounded before the tram shuddered to a halt. I made my way to the front of the carriage and apologised to the driver, doing my utmost to explain that it had been an accident. My friends thought this was hilarious and didn't let me live it down. The driver had the tram quickly underway but throughout all of this, the other passengers just carried on unperturbed, some reading newspapers and others in conversation as if this was just an everyday occurrence.

We called for a drink at a pavement café but ended up having roast pork, dumplings and the full works. The waiter persuaded us to have his special pudding which was especially stodgy. Each time I took a spoonful, it appeared to come alive, reforming to it's original shape and size.

I remarked upon the fact that I wondered if we would see the tubular advertising hoarding which concealed the door in which Harry Lime continually disappeared into the underground sewers, while trying to shake off his pursuers in the film, 'The Third Man'. My mates unanimously agreed the film was shot in Paris and not in Vienna but I was sure of my facts and bet each one of them a tenner that I was right. "How will we find out" said Des. "Oh we'll find out" I replied. When we saw the giant Ferris Wheel in Prater Park where Orson Welles 'Lime' character rendezvoused with Holly Martins played by Joseph Cotton, Des said, "You know he could be right" but there was no backing out now as we had all shaken hands on the bets.

The film was set in post war Vienna when the city was under the control of four powers, with Austria not being liberated until 1955. Harry Lime was supposedly killed in a car accident but was still alive. He was an unsavoury character and black marketer who dodged in and out of the bombed out buildings and the sewer system. In reality the glow and smell of his ever- present cigarette would have surely given the game away, but he eventually died in a shoot out in the sewers. 'The Third Man' was enhanced by the constant background zither music of Anton Karas and ends with the memorable scene featuring the long walk through the cemetery.

The tubular advertising hoardings were all over the city but I couldn't spot any concealed doorways. When we called for a drink that evening my mates took the Mick by saying, "What are you having Andy, a lager and Harry Lime". Barely a week after we returned, Reagan and Gorbachev had a summit in Vienna during the Cold war era and the TV reporter said the proceedings had provided a touch of 'Harry Lime'. A couple of my mates had seen this, the other two quickly found out and they all duly paid up. I wasn't letting them off the hook so easily.

For this visit, I would be among a field of 10,000 competitors, running the Vienna International Marathon. I caught the train from the airport to Vienna South Station and a taxi to the Hotel Ananas, arriving shortly before midday on Friday. As I got to know the city better, I realised the hotel was actually located quite close to the station and therefore the taxi driver had brought me on quite a roundabout route, obviously ripping me off. The previous time this happened was when I caught a cab from Wakefield Bus Station to Kirk gate Railway Station. I would normally have walked but was pushed for time. The driver had spun the car around and set off in the opposite direction. I quickly told him that I wanted to go by the most direct route which didn't break any ice as he nonchalantly appeared to take unnecessarily right and left turns, edging his way ever closer to my destination. I lost my temper with the Asian driver and on reaching the station, told him that by acting the silly bugger had cost him a tip. Any excuse!

I had apparently two reservations at the Hotel Ananas but had booked the hotel through the race headquarters and told them I only needed one room. The hotel was situated on the busy Recht Wierzeille and after changing and unpacking, I crossed to walk alongside the River Wien, which flows through an unattractive concrete channel parallel to the railway lines. The Naschmarkt is situated on a long promenade beside the river and among the many stalls are fruit, vegetables, fish, meat and poultry. There are numerous restaurants and bars situated in small prefabricated buildings and it was at one of these that I stopped for a first beer. In the half hour spent here I alternated between people watching and reading the Insight Guide to Vienna.

I progressed across the busy Ringstrasse or 'Ring' around which many of the Public buildings such as Opera House, museums, Town Hall, National Theatre and Parliament Buildings are situated. The No 1 tram travels clockwise around the 'Ring' and the No 2 anticlockwise, and a journey on either of these will provide an early insight into the layout of the city.

I ventured into the pedestrianised inner city area around Stephensplatz, dominated by the gothic St Stephens Cathedral with it's impressive geometrically designed tiled roof. In the square were performers, protestors and touts handing out flyers, mainly for concerts while around the perimeter, the pavement cafes, bars and restaurants appeared to be doing a brisk trade. A board advertised 'The Third Man Walking Tour', approximately two and a half hours and sturdy walking shoes required. This seemed like a good idea, as long as we didn't venture into the underground sewers.

Anticipating a quiet Friday evening. I looked into the hotel bar and couldn't fail to notice Gus, a loud, brash, huge American from Alabama who reminded me of the outspoken author and producer Michael Moore. His mate Pete from England was much quieter and the two of them were here for business meetings which began on Monday. I told them I was running the Marathon to which Gus replied, "Say he's doing the Marathon" with the emphasis on the 'ON' part, which everyone in the bar would have heard.

Gus constantly guzzled peanuts and after each handful, he would dust his hands together and follow this with a booming clap that made everyone sit up and look across. I ventured outside to watch the masses of roller skaters pass by in an event that formed part of the marathon weekend. I ended the evening listening to live country music in one of the prefabricated bars in Naschmarkt.

On Saturday morning I set out for race registration but was distracted at Schwedenplatz by the pleasure boats moored on the Danube Canal. One of these would depart shortly and in my hurry and excitement, I failed to read the itinerary correctly. Trade was quiet and I chose to sit on one of the wooden benches on the top deck, next to the rail. At the last minute a party of American tourists, probably with a prior booking, joined the boat, immediately taking charge and engulfing anyone who was already onboard. When the boat departed, these people were up and down moving from port side to starboard and were constantly in everyone's face. With my relaxing cruise rapidly becoming a nightmare, I opted for a quieter life, moving to a seat on the lower deck.

Once out of the city centre, we cruised through pleasant parkland and past most desirable residences. The Blue Danube Waltz was played over the speaker system and the captain even had the boat rock from side to side, making quite a swell on the water. I was glad when he stopped doing this as I could imagine the flimsy vessel capsizing. We were raised through giant locks into the main stream of the Danube where we were constantly passed by a procession of small motor launches.

In my rush to board the boat, I had understood the notice to read the round trip to be an hour but we had already taken an hour to reach the first stop at Reichsbrucke. I would cut my losses and disembark here, have a look around and head back to the city on the Underground. The Reichsbrucke would be where the marathon started and was close to a leisure area known locally as Copa Cagrana. An artificial waterway had been built, running alongside the Danube for 25 miles to channel floodwater from the main river. The course of the Old Danube had been blocked off and now formed a giant ox bow with small tributaries and wetlands. The land in between had becoming a leisure area for water sports, cycling, jogging, nude bathing and a host of other activities and was home to the Vienna International Centre.

Registration took place in a series of conference rooms on the fringe of Prater Park which more accurately resembled a sprawling woodland with footpaths and forest trails. The impressive funfair had rides from the gentle to the high tech with the centre piece being the huge Ferris Wheel. I collected the race literature, number and freebies, but with people packed shoulder to shoulder inside the hall, I didn't stay long, instead meandering back through the funfair.

I paused to watch powerful go karts race around a mini Silverstone and picked out an older guy with similar looks to record mogul, Pete Waterman. Pete was struggling to make an impact against the boy racers and was continually being overtaken. They went round and round, over and over again and certainly had value for money.

I stopped for a cappuccino at a pavement café and began to read the race literature with a certain section drawing my attention. It read as follows:- The race number is not transferable. It has to be worn at the front, must be clearly visible and must not be changed in any way particularly the print. Disqualification may be applied if a runner participates using someone else's name, does not wear or alters the race number, behaves unfair, is accompanied by bike, car, motor bike, in-line skates, skates, is not registered at the time keeping check points, participates on roller or In-line skates, skate boards or similar or takes animals along on the course. No exceptions to the rule will be made. Well I never!

The Austrian culinary delights of puddings, sausages and dumplings were agreeable to my taste buds and starting to feel hungry, I enjoyed Wiener Schnitzel at the peculiarly named 'Scholars'. Back on the street I followed the crowds of immaculately dressed people, no doubt leaving one of the many afternoon concerts.

'Flanagan's' was apparently voted the best overseas Irish Pub or some such title with an all Irish bar staff and an interior said to be shipped over from County Cork. I had a pint of the black stuff, and caught the tail end of the European Rugby Final between Leicester and Munster. The Irish team were camped on the Leicester try line but much to the disappointment of the many punters, were unable to force the winning score.

Back at the hotel I bumped into Big Gus in the lift. "Have you done your Marath ON" he asked. "No it's tomorrow". "Is it a Marath ON or a Sem EYE Marath ON" he enquired. I told him it was the full distance and after asking several other questions, Gus wished me the best of luck as he departed the lift at his floor.

I reached race start on Sunday morning, courtesy of two Underground trains, disembarking at Alte Donau Station (Old Danube). There was no dedicated area in which to change so people just made best use of the grass verges or the woodland at either side of the Wagramerstrasse. The clothes bags were then transported by a convoy of trucks to the finish area in Rathausplatz.

My gentle jog filled me more with trepidation than anticipation. All the walking undertaken on Friday and Saturday hadn't been the ideal preparation and apart from this, I had done no great mileage in training. But there was no backing out now and in four hours or so if I was lucky, I would have finished and probably wondered what all the fuss had been about.

I took my place, making doubly sure to enter the correct starting block. Race instructions had stated that anyone starting from the wrong block would have ten minutes added to their finishing time. Unlike the Great North Run where runners converge from the embankment after the starting pistol sounds, security here was tight and numbers were checked before entering the various enclosures.

But on top of all the red tape and the do's and the don'ts, no map of the course had been provided in the literature and I hadn't seen one at the registration hall either. Not that I would have been much the wiser if I had looked at a map but I always like to know the points of interest to look out for on route or if it were the intention to run one large loop or two smaller loops. Big Gus had asked if we ran by the hotel and I didn't know. The answers to all of these questions would unfold later in the morning.

I didn't move for two minutes after the gun had fired, but once underway, the crossing of the Danube was pretty spectacular. I felt reasonably comfortable in the early stages with the cool temperature and the drizzle ideal for marathon running. The 10,000 strong field had an international flavour with runners from France and the Scandinavian countries along with a huge contingent from neighbouring Germany. Two runners in the Australian national colours glided by effortlessly, there was a guy in a Union Flag vest while others wore replica football shirts, mainly of Italian clubs.

Even though I wasn't breaking any pots, I began to enjoy the race, with the route varied and interesting. We ran through the city, through suburbs and through parkland and there were no hills to speak of. The spectator support was good but not solid as in some of the German city races. We ran past the Naschmarkt, not as busy as on Friday, the Hofburg and the Rathaus where the 17K competitors were already finishing their race. On hindsight I would have been better calling it a day here.

Going past halfway and still feeling good with no real concerns, I had the horrible sinking feeling that I was about to struggle and was unable to do anything about it. Sure enough after two and a quarter hours of running, my knees began to hurt. This slowed me down alongside the Danube Canal, through the City Park and past the Ferris Wheel, where I would have certainly hoped to have been running stronger. In past races when I have felt like this, I have sometimes been able to tough it out, but today clearly wasn't going to be one of those days. I started to mix painful jogging with walking, but the jogs became shorter with the walks becoming longer. Added to this, the kilometre posts seemed to be drifting further and further apart.

There were several of those irritating out and back stretches through Prater Park where you could see the runners in front, coming back towards you and with all of them looking in much better shape. Most of those behind looked in better shape today even after I had reached the turnaround point and a steady trickle started to overtake me. The path was flanked by woodland, straight as an arrow and monotonous. How easy it would have been to cheat by just stepping across on one of these sections, joining the runners coming in the opposite direction and saving myself a few kilometres or more importantly, some time. But you could bet your life that there would be one of those magic carpets to record the timings from the chip attached to my running shoe. Sure enough it was there as I reached the turn around point going bleep, bleep, bleep as dozens of pairs of feet trampled across it. I needed to concentrate, dig deep, get my running together and banish all thoughts of cheating.

Out of the woods and back onto the city streets for the final 5 kilometres and I would be well outside my target of four hours. I once again began to pick up my stride inside the final kilometre but had left it far too late now for heroics. I breached the tape at the Rathaus in four and a quarter hours, an all time slow or a personal worst depending upon which way I looked upon it.

My strategy in future for these events would be to arrive the day before the race and cut out all the unnecessary walking, leaving the sight seeing until after the race. Alternatively I could opt for the shorter distance race options and leave the marathons for home. Either way I didn't fancy putting myself through this ordeal again. Now those thoughts seemed all too familiar!

That evening in the hotel bar, Gus asked how I had gone on in the Marath ON. I told him I had struggled. "That's too bad" he said, shovelling down a hand full of peanuts, dusting his hands and producing a thunderous clap.

He was joined by an elderly American lady who wore tight fitting trousers on top of frighteningly high heeled shoes. Her hair appeared to be dyed blonde and she looked to have lip gloss on top of her lip gloss, eye shadow on her eye shadow and mascara on her mascara. She was looking forward to seeing the famous Lipizzaner Horses tomorrow at the Spanish Riding School. "Have you booked" I asked, knowing that reservations were imperative some time in advance. "I've worked with horses for 40 years, young man" she replied. "If they don't let me in, I'll break the door down". I must say that I was rather flattered that she had called me young man!

I was determined that Monday would be my big sightseeing day and wouldn't let the stiffness and lethargy from my Marathon exploits get in the way. I started at Prater Park with a trip on the Ferris Wheel. I was fairly early so had a gondola all to myself. The clear day provided far reaching views of the park, the surrounding forest, the Danube and the city, during the twenty minute ride. As with many attractions, the exit is purposely positioned into a souvenir shop, and while I didn't buy anything, I couldn't take my eyes off the fully working model fairground.

Next was the Musikverein, home to the Vienna Philharmonic. Best known as the venue for the New Years Concert on TV, the magnificent main hall has a hanging ceiling to allow for better acoustics. Tickets are purchased by postal application a year in advance while Saturday and Sunday concerts are regularly sold out.

I dragged my weary body up the 553 steps on the south side of St Stephens Cathedral for more spectacular views of the city but could have saved my legs by catching the lift to the north tower instead where an enormous bell is housed.

From here I walked the broad elegant thoroughfare, Graben, leading to the Hofburg Imperial Palace, home to the Habsburg Empire up until World War One. The Lipizzaner stables and museum are housed in part of this vast complex. Still only midday, I walked the narrow medieval streets to the north which were far quieter and I enjoyed a coffee at one of the many pavement cafes.

I had sausages for lunch in the Rathaus Kellar swapping tables several times to avoid circling wasps, before spending most of the afternoon in the Museum of Fine Arts and the Natural History Museum.

Back at the hotel I asked the Lipizzaner lady if she had been able to see her horses. "No cigar" she replied, "But I'll try again tomorrow". That reminded me I hadn't done 'The Third Man Walking Tour' so now I would definitely have to come back again.

CHAPTER 5

Lonely As A Cloud

ESPITE LIVING only a hundred miles from the Lakes District, I was well into my mid thirties when I visited for the first time. I tell a lie, as a small boy, I visited Windermere on a day trip from Morecambe. We crossed the lake on a pleasure boat, apparently I was none too keen on the idea and screamed my head off. Dad took me below deck and bought me a bottle of pop which appeared to work the trick.

I knew nothing of the Lake District other than it being an area of outstanding natural beauty. I knew there were sixteen main lakes because I was asked to name them in a pub quiz. Our table of four named thirteen but missed out on some of the lesser known ones such as Ennerdale and Rydal Water.

So it was in 1988 that I first ran the Keswick Half Marathon. As we approached from Penrith, steep and rugged mountains came into view eventually surrounding the town and any course around here would surely be arduous. Having never been to Keswick and not being too sure of my bearings didn't deter my mother from screaming, "Why didn't you turn right", "Why have we come down here", "You've missed the sign for the Rugby Club", "You've made a bugger of this". Oh happy days!

The first friendly face I saw on parking the car was Maggie, a girl from my home town of Rothwell. Originally from the Lake District, Maggie had returned to the area upon getting married. She remarked how much weight I had lost and how good I looked. This gave me a welcome boost and a feel good factor somewhat redressing the balance for me being a useless driver.

Maggie's husband was a member of Cockermouth Running Club but on comparing races done and times achieved, I was a flyer by comparison. I think that Maggie was amazed that a one time fat sod could now look so svelte, but it was simply down to the running.

It's chance meetings like these at out of the way places that would prompt my mother, and no doubt other mothers of that generation to say. "Have you got a clean pair of underpants and a clean handkerchief. The jewel in the crown would undoubtedly be, "Make sure you wash you're knees, for if you get knocked down and have to go to hospital".

Like Maggie, the Lake's most famous son, William Wordsworth was born in Cockermouth, in 1770, before attending schools in Penrith and Hawkshead. He secured a place at St Johns College in Cambridge but spent most of his time socialising and rebelling against the system. After finishing university, he travelled extensively, walking in France, Switzerland and Italy.

Deciding to learn French and become an English teacher, he moved to Paris and then on to Orleans where he met Annette Valon, four years his senior. Being a catholic and he a protestant, she gave birth to his daughter Caroline in 1792, by which time Wordsworth had returned to England. The war put paid to him returning to France and he spent most of his time in London.

His family more or less washed their hands of him as he became a staunch radical. A close friend, Raisley Calvert left Wordsworth £900 in his will, then a hefty sum. He lived in Dorset before moving to Somerset where he met another aspiring poet, Samuel Taylor Coleridge. Wordsworth returned to the Lake District in 1799, moving with sister Dorothy to Grasmere. Wordsworth had the inspiration to write his best known work 'Daffodils' at nearby Ullswater. The poem celebrated it's 200th anniversary in March 2004, commemorated with recitals all around the country.

Keswick is a bustling market town with a fascinating history which includes the founding of St Kentigern's Church, the 13th

Century Market Charter and local lead mining. Among today's industries are farming, forestry and the manufacture of pencils. Keswick is the centre or starting point for many walkers, ramblers and mountaineers. The historic Moot Hall is the most notable building in the Market Place and houses the tourist information centre. A busy high street consists of outdoor wear shops, gifts, art and craft galleries and plenty of pubs.

The course would be challenging and the spectacular glaciated scenery would range from rugged volcanic mountains to hills with altogether smoother contours. A Stretch in Newlands Valley beyond Braithwaite was followed by an undulating lap of Derwentwater with elevated views across the lake. Climbing from Stair along the lower slopes of Cat Bells, the course plummets to the picturesque village of Grange on the southern tip of the lake.

The second half is slightly gentler along the eastern shore of the lake. The route passes luxury hotels set in spacious grounds along the waterfront and sometimes meanders away from the lake through woodland. There is a well deserved downhill to the finish in Davidson Park.

I ran here in three successive years from 1988, each time on a scorching hot May day. In one of these races, I struggled badly and must have looked a sorry site at the finish on the obligatory lap of the rugby field. My mum remarked that rather than pump my arms, I had let them drop down by my side and I looked ridiculous. She hoped that nobody had realised that I was with her.

I wrote out an address label for a souvenir addition of the local newspaper containing a race results supplement. The girl at the desk remarked on my neat hand writing, particularly after just completing thirteen miles. I wish I'd a pound for each time somebody had told me this!

In 1989, the second placed runner complained about the winner, Les McVittie taking an unofficial drink, but never put the complaint in writing. McVittie, I suspect along with most runners, was unaware of any such rule existing. The fact that the fourth and fifth placed runners were both D. Dixon also caused the Keswick officials some minor confusion.

A similar complaint about the water was raised some years later in a local half marathon. The officials involved had to negotiate long and hard into the afternoon to resolve the minor placings in the ladies event.

Six tough looking lads from the King's Own Border Regiment, carrying full kit and backpacks, yomped around the course in two and three quarter hours. They finished to rousing applause and a rendition of John Peel played by their regimental band resplendent in red, white and black uniforms.

I returned to the Lakes in 1994, this time to the Langdale Half Marathon. A number of our members had previously run here and had dubbed the race to be a killer. There was even a marathon held in conjunction which constituted two laps and was advertised as the toughest marathon in the world.

Sixteen or thereabouts made the journey in a clapped out mini bus with several more making a long weekend and staying at a farm house. The driver didn't know the way and before pulling off, turned around to anybody in general to ask directions. At this point, despite not being the organiser, everybody turned to look at me. "A1 to Scotch Corner, A66 to Brough, turn off to Kirby Stephen and then through Kendal and Ambleside", I replied. That appeared to be good enough and we were soon chugging along through the outskirts of Pontefract towards the A1.

I never had difficulty with directions. I studied maps like others would read a book and Geography was the only subject in which I really excelled at school. In my footballing days, they would stand and deliberate which way we should go to away games when I couldn't really see the problem.

From time to time I would go to meetings as part of my job. I would simply get into my car and drive, usually with little regard for the map. I can only recollect coming unstuck once when I ended up somewhat out of the way near Bury St Edmunds while travelling between Rugby and Norwich.

It was doubtful whether this particular mini bus would make it to the lakes, constantly struggling on the inclines but gaining suitable momentum downhill. All throughout the journey, the drivers ashtray, one of those round ones you find in pubs, was placed precariously on the mounting between gear lever and handbrake, but remained steadfast throughout.

Banter was friendly and light hearted. A new member in discussion said that he thought Andy Bennett would have been running today. I put him out of his misery by telling him I was in fact Andy Bennett, which I immediately regretted. I should have strung him along and tried to find out the gossip and what they were saying about this Andy Bennett.

Two hours into the journey and not taking into account the capable speed of the mini bus, people started to challenge my choice of route. We should have come by the M62 and M6 was the cry. Why didn't he speak up before? Another dickhead implied we should have come through Skipton and Settle.

With Kendal and Ambleside now behind us, one guy was bursting for a pee. Undeterred by comments that we were only ten minutes away from our destination, he suddenly asked the driver to pull over, scaled a fence and disappeared into a thicket.

Parking was at the Great Langdale campsite, quiet on a cold October day, but somewhat bolstered by the race traffic. The proprietor asked us to line up for a team photograph saying that it would appear in next seasons brochure. We duly obliged but even though I considered sending off for a brochure, I never did see the photograph.

The course would be tough and apparently I would do well to break two hours. The mail out for the race stated that the course had previously measured half a mile too long, twice as much in the marathon. The organiser then stated, tongue in cheek, that any purist had his permission to follow the original route if they could remember where that was?

The race started at midday adjacent to the Old Dungeon Ghyll Hotel, a grand old building with tall chimneys and gables at the head of the valley. This had previously been a farm as was apparent from the sizeable out buildings and stables. The October day was damp and grey with a cool breeze blowing down the valley. As we waited to go, I remarked to Paul Herman that steady away would be probably the best tactics if the course was as severe as rumour had it.

But once underway, this advice fell upon deaf ears with Paul's race plan being to go out hard and to hang on for grim death towards the end. The route followed the floor of the valley between neat dry stone walls to Chapel Stile, known for gunpowder production and quarrying. Here a left turn towards Grasmere provided the first difficult climb against a rocky backdrop. Three of our none running ladies gave their support from a lofty vantage point on top of a giant rock, high above the road. At least this would ensure that our runners continued running when perhaps it would have been more tempting to walk.

A useful downhill followed to Skelwith Bridge and with four miles completed in half an hour, I began to wonder what all the fuss was about. The next section to Little Langdale brought narrow roads, deep wooded valleys and hairpin bends. Traffic on the tight and twisting lanes was uncharacteristically busy for a grim Autumn Sunday. When runners, ramblers and cars all emerged in the same spot at the same time, there was understandably congestion and tail backs of traffic.

This was the heart of Alfred Wainwright country, the man who had popularised and made hill walking accessible to thousands of city dwellers, through his newspaper columns and books.

The landscape became barren and bleaker replacing the woodland and greenery as we began to climb steadily and then more abruptly. When the going gets tough, apparently the tough get going and I was still going along quite nicely. This was my last long training run before the Dublin Marathon and in this shape I would have nothing to fear.

I caught up with a couple of other club mates on the long drag and eventually pulled level with Paul towards the head of Blea Tarn Pass. I patted him on the back and provided words of encouragement but he appeared shattered having given his all. This was the section where everyone resorted to a walk but still I kept running, albeit agonisingly slow at times. I received encouragement myself from club skipper Terry Sinar, who was here for the weekend but had decided to cycle around the course. It was debatable whether two wheels would serve him better than two legs on this unforgiving terrain.

At the summit, I was rewarded with views of the Langdale Pikes in the distance and The Old Dungeon Ghyll and adjacent buildings in the valley bottom where the race would finish. The last downhill mile signposted as 1 in 4 was exhilarating with a hairpin bend and a cattle grid thrown in for good measure. I passed a string of athletes on this section, taking care not to lose control on the tight corners and making sure I hit the cattle grid with the balls of my feet.

I live in fear of breaking my leg or at the very least, twisting my ankle between the metal rungs of one of these nasty contraptions. I am timid to say the least when approaching a cattle grid on a flat road, so dread to think what might happen when I am going hell for leather down a mountainside.. Our three lady non runners were apparently petrified, driving down this section in the car.

The momentum I gained on the downhill carried me along the final flattish half a mile, where I finished just outside 100 minutes. I had come away relatively unscathed, well inside the two hours that had been targeted for me and was the second man back for my club.

After changing and regrouping back at the mini bus and with the usual inquest into the race still ongoing, we trudged wearily to The Old Dungeon Ghyll.

The Climbers Bar was crowded with the two staff working tirelessly to serve the punters lining the bar, two and three deep.

Apparently every mountaineer worth his salt had quaffed here including Sir John Hunt and Chris Bonnington who had given lectures in this very room. After establishing time would be called at three 'o' clock, we had twenty minutes to drink up, so Trevor ordered us another pint apiece.

Banter was friendly with most of the talk being about the race and I could have gladly spent another couple of hours here.

A group of five locals sat at a table in the corner, by a window. "You're coach is waiting outside" said one of them, "You'd better drink up". "There's no panic", I replied, but a few minutes later he repeated the request, giving me the distinct impression they wanted rid of us.

The five ranged in age from perhaps early twenties to late sixties. They were all outdoor types with ruddy complexions and beards or facial hair. One smoked a briar pipe, another smoked a roll up, one wore a deer stalker and another sported a well worn flat cap. A variety of sticks were leaning in the corner against the wall and underneath the table were two dogs. One was a black and white border collie and the other a greyhound or whippet.

I had seen the spokesman stand up and he was one hell of a big man. If a fight broke out I would be right behind him. He was built like one of those Rugby League forwards who seemed to turn out exclusively for Whitehaven or Workington.

Surely they wouldn't kick forty or fifty other drinkers out to let these five have a stay back, but that's exactly what they did with the bar staff moving around the room asking people to drink up quickly.

Back on the mini coach, the driver wasn't taking any chances with directions, so took it upon himself to head north to Keswick, and then on to Penrith. We stopped for a tea high above Swaledale, while the driver refuelled. Distant lights flickered in the dusk and a far off train could be heard, probably on the scenic Settle– Carlisle line. We were left to reflect on another enjoyable and interesting day.

CHAPTER 6

Pistols At Dawn

"I 'LL SEE you all after the race", I said, "I'm going to move further forward". Aren't you alright here with us", asked Terry Gough". "No, I'm looking to break an hour and don't want to get held up", I replied. "It'll be steady away for me" said Ken Barton, "I'm doing the Sheffield Marathon in two weeks". I was doing the Sheffield Marathon too, but it wasn't going to prevent me from having a blast today.

I was quietly, if not extremely confident of breaking an hour in the Goole One-Third Marathon. Last year I had run an hour and just two seconds, I had been in good form throughout the summer and on Friday evening had managed 33 minutes for five miles. After Friday's race at Rossett near Harrogate, a group of us had ventured into town for a meal.

The Cattleman's Restaurant is one of those places where huge steaks are served on giant plates and if you can manage a 32oz, you can have it for free. Going along with the general consensus, I opted for the less daunting 16oz steak along with onion rings, fries and all the trimmings but had to wait while one of our colleagues agonisingly paced himself over a steak twice the size. The things some people will do for a freebie!

The drinks waiter on seeing me said, "Don't you live at Rothwell", to which I replied, "Can't I go anywhere without being spotted". He introduced himself and said that I knew his sister, which was greeted with a spontaneous roar of approval from my friends.

On Saturday morning my stomach felt like a brick. This however didn't deter me from going shopping with my parents and on the way back, Dad dumped me out of the car leaving me to run the three miles or so back home. Intending to enjoy a gentle jog, I soon found myself belting along, not the ideal preparation for running a personal best the next day.

The first time I ran at Goole, I vowed never to return again. Ready and waiting to start, I became aware of a man moving through the crowd of runners towards where I was standing. He was one of those untrustworthy people with no bounce or head movements to his walk, instead just gliding along with a still head as if he were travelling on rails.

When he stopped abruptly in front of me, I could see he was holding a pistol. Nobody had told me it would be 'Pistols at Dawn' and why hadn't anybody given me a gun. "Where's your number" he snarled in a tone that implied I was about to cheat or try to get away with it like the 'Rogue Runner' in another chapter. How he could see that I wasn't wearing a number from where he had been standing, I don't know but he had certainly sussed me out. Glancing at my watch and seeing there were barely two minutes to the start, I sprinted to my car, foraged for the keys in my shorts pocket, removed my number from inside the envelope and pinned it to my vest while jogging back to the start." That was a close thing", said Kevin, "I've never done that before", I replied. Almost immediately, the nasty man fired the starting pistol into the air rather than at me and a mad scramble ensued along the street and onto the river bank.

In the early days, The Goole River Bank Challenge covered fifteen miles, along the banks of the Ouse and Aire, alongside the parallel channels of the Don and Dutch Rivers, beside fields, along quiet roads and through the villages of Airmyn and Rawcliffe. That same day, the fine weather turned into a torrential downpour causing some of the paths to become wet and slippery. In the final stages, my neighbour Graham took a tumble down a flood bank, jarred his back and didn't seriously run again for over a year. We couldn't even win the cake that was on offer or any of the other raffle prizes for that matter. The tee shirt awarded for completion caused controversy as it showed a map of the course including the River Calder which is at least twenty miles west of here.

Some years later, the race was reduced to a one-third marathon when access and permission didn't materialise to run on certain sections of the course. Over the years, the route has changed slightly to accommodate sections of the riverbank under repair with careful planning to ensure runners aren't travelling both ways on the same section at the same time. On one occasion we were required to negotiate the huge lock gates in the Port of Goole which didn't seem ideal for those with no head for heights like myself. In recent times the race has moved out of Goole and is run over a similar course from Westbank Leisure Centre near Hook. Meticulously organised by the Viking Striders, the numbers have perhaps suffered in recent years due to clashes of dates with other events in a busy June schedule.

An hour for a One-Third Marathon was no big deal so why was it so special to me. Well I hadn't broken 40 minutes for 10K or gone below 90 minutes for a half marathon and wasn't likely to do so unless I embarked upon a dramatic training regime and change of lifestyle. But I believed that an hour for somewhere in the region of 8-75 Miles was distinctly possible and I was about to give it my best shot.

Despite moving forward, I was still well back at the start but quickly into my stride as we left the streets by way of a ramp onto the riverbank. The tarmac path besides the river wall is barely wide enough for two runners, so with the anticipated hold up, patience would be the virtue in the early stages. The grass flood bank was much wider and I started to pick up places, always careful to check my footing as I moved at times onto the rougher terrain alongside the well trodden path.

The River Ouse is wide here and still tidal well upstream from Goole. A telephone acquaintance from work for a company in this area, told me she walked her dog in the evening on these very same paths. She made a point of coming out when the tide would turn which was apparently pretty spectacular. The only tide that would turn today for me would hopefully be my fortunes.

I missed the first mile post, but running with Ken Barton who didn't appear to be taking it steady as he had promised and Diana Howard from the host club, we went through two miles in a shade below 13 minutes, probably a little too quickly. A drop down the banking to the lower tier under the railway swing bridge slowed me down before the climb back up the flood bank where we ran alongside a low wall.

One year, the path was under water here and we in fact had to run on top of the wall. Some time later a guy who was parked next to me at a subsequent race casually remarked, "I'm not running at Goole again, we had to run on top of a wall. The most pleasant stretch on the course is approaching Hook where the long gardens of attractive houses back down onto the river, some with their own private jetties. The homeowners usually ensure the grass is cut short here which provides for a fast surface.

I'd been dreading the next section over the stiles and would inevitably be held up, losing time in the bargain. I can't do stiles and am too awkward and cumbersome to leap over them like others do. Instead I have to step up, swing my leg over and step down the other side. But the key was to do this quickly and with this in mind I had been practising over a set of three near home. Sure enough, there was the anticipated queue at the first stile, which would cost me valuable time. I was much quicker across the second but hopefully there would be no hold up here on the way back.

One runner within our midst would stop his watch at stiles, gates or any other obstacle for that matter be it at a water station or to tie his lace. If only it were so simple. While all well and good on training runs, the race clock didn't stop to accommodate these peculiarities.

Harold Britton and Derek Laughton who were enthusiastically following the race on their bikes gave me encouragement in Hook where I passed the four-mile marker in twenty six and a half minutes, well on schedule. With the road section still to come, I would be sure to make up even more time.

The road and the river run parallel at this stage and as I glanced across, I could see the leaders returning back, high above the road along the flood bank. As the gaps narrowed and more runners streamed past, I counted only seven Ackworth vests ahead of me which boded well for scoring points in the club's Grand Prix. Not only was I running to achieve a personal best and to dip under an hour, but points were also up for grabs in the club championship.

As I scrambled up the banking it was now my turn to look down upon those who were behind me and see if anyone posed a threat or had to be shaken off. I waved at a couple of colleagues like you do and jokingly shouted down to Ann Rhodes, 59-59, my much sought after time.

Dipping under seven minutes apiece for the fifth and sixth miles, I started to noticeably slow around the long wide-open river bend and into the stiffening breeze, even though I appeared to be still passing runners at will. I found the last couple of miles over the stiles, alongside the wall and under the railway bridge to be very tough and had to dig deep with the strengthening wind threatening to blow me off course. My time at the eight-mile post indicated I had five and a half minutes in which to cover the final part mile and to break an hour.

While this was well within my capabilities, I have never trusted part miles. Some can be short, some can be long and others can be very long. With this in mind I would give my all as I didn't wish to fall short again after doing all the hard work successfully. Still passing the occasional runner, I came down the ramp onto the street and turned the corner for the considerable run in to the finishing clock. Last year, I sprinted along this stretch only for the clock to tick agonisingly past 60 minutes.

This wouldn't be repeated today as I moved up an extra gear on the long run in for home, passing below the gantry in 59 minutes and 33 seconds. I was understandably elated, ecstatic and euphoric for want of better words, enjoyed my post race pint and the rest of the day so much the better. I enjoyed the congratulations from colleagues, some who could run under an hour standing on their heads and from others who were unlikely to ever break this target. I enjoyed my cuddle from Ann, making me wish I could run as well as this every week.

Many people have run ten miles in under an hour and a select band have even done a half marathon in that time so even though this was no great performance in the wider scheme of things, it was a personal target achieved and one that I will look back upon with satisfaction.

Still on a high, I decided to run home from work the following evening, felt my ankle twinge along the canal towpath but continued running, not really giving it a second thought. The following morning my ankle had swollen like a balloon and I could hardly put any pressure on my foot. I was sidelined for a week and a half but somewhat foolishly, did make it to the start line for the Sheffield Marathon.

I have never managed to break an hour since so when I close the 'Big Book of Events Completed' for the final time, this performance will stand up there with the best.

CHAPTER 7

Running Scared

ACH TIME he looked around, I was closing the gap. This must have been slightly worrying for a fifteen year old boy being chased by a fifty year old man. I chased him down back streets, along main roads and through ginnels. I swear at one time, in fact I am absolutely certain that someone shouted, "Go on Andy". I was enjoying the chase so much that I even slowed at one stage, so as not to catch him too quickly. The little bastard gave me the slip in a dark passage when he climbed over a fence into an adjacent garden.

I don't do fences as my friends in the Wednesday evening 'Splinter Group' at Pontefract will tell you. I don't do walls, I don't do gates and I don't do stiles. At least not very well. I don't do ditches, I don't do streams and I don't do steep bankings. I am pretty good on long, straight, flat stretches where you can wind me up and I can plod along effortlessly and endlessly.

Returning home dejected, I happened to stumble across the lad's three mates, close to parade of shops. I had started to chase the four of them after they were spotted on top of my garden shed but three had gone one way leaving one on his own. I decided to chase the single lad on two fronts. Firstly I believed he had done damage to both my garage and hut on previous evenings and secondly, I could beat him to a pulp and it would be only his word against mine.

I had asked two boys to climb down from my hut roof the previous evening but they had given me the slip by jumping through the privet hedge and into my neighbours garden. On looking out of my bedroom window a couple of nights later, I was horrified to see that four youths were sitting on the hut roof with one trying to rip the facia from around the rim. The hut rocked when I stood on top to cut the hedge so with four people on the roof, it was a minor miracle it hadn't collapsed. This time I surprised them by approaching from outside the hedge along the back street. Again they escaped through my neighbours garden, but when they came out of his gate I was right behind them.

I crept up on the other three near a parade of shops before they realised I was there, but that's what happens if you are blasé and return to the scene of the crime before the dust settles. The two smaller ones dashed across the road but I collared the big one by the scruff of the neck.

"Put me down you bastard, get off me you poof" he said along with a load of other crap. "A young lady coming out of one of the shops told him not to talk to me like that and to behave. She called the police and waited with me until they arrived. In theory I had made a citizens arrest and was handing the culprit to them on a plate. I presumed they would be elated and would support me by saying things like. "Keep hold of the little shit and whatever you do, don't let him go"..

But obviously my expectations were misplaced as they appeared to be asking the young lady over the phone how I was holding the boy, where I was holding the boy, if I was hurting the boy and if I was exerting any pressure on the boy. Everything seemed so blatantly stacked in favour of the boy.

All the time this was happening he was telling me what his brother would do to me, what his father would do to me and kept reiterating the fact that I was a poof.

After skulking around the street corner but fooling nobody, his two mates eventually returned, but the boy I had chased wouldn't be seen again that evening. Like idiots they talked in front of me using their Christian names and referring to the fourth boy as Scott. I would remember these names for future reference.

As the blue light of the Rapid Response Panda Car appeared after only twenty minutes or so, I'm glad I wasn't holding burglar

Bill, my detainee frantically flagged it down as if he had been the victim rather than the culprit. When the officers got out of the car, he started to give them a load of bullshit, but I found an ally in the young lady who quickly gave them a correct version of events. I thanked her for this, for calling the police and for staying with me.

The first officer had a shaven head and reminded me of Des Taviner of the Bill, one time of Brookside. If the coppers start shaving their heads, you won't be able to tell them apart from the criminals, from the bouncers, from the white van men and from the footballers. The first thing he would probably do on finishing shift would be to put his obligatory earring back in.

I visited Holbeck Police Station around the same time as this to make a statement. In what had become a spate of anti social behaviour and vandalism in the neighbourhood, I had been a witness to an assault. As I sat in the reception at the nick, there were lots of comings and goings at what appeared to be shift changeover time. All those entering would grind out a cigarette butt in the strategically placed ash bin while those leaving the building would immediately light up.

Des made the three youths sit in the Panda Car while the second officer took my statement. I walked him along the street and into my garden showing him the damage that had been inflicted both to my garage and to my hut. He then returned to his colleague in the car where I presumed they would deal with the youths.

But it wasn't to be and according to a neighbour looking out of her window, they were just allowed back out onto the street, ready to re offend again. As I looked out of my bedroom window, I could see them climbing on neighbouring garage roofs and sheds. They scaled fences and raced through gardens but left mine alone. I made all the neighbours aware of what was happening. One was in hospital and another family were on holiday so I pushed notes through their respective letter boxes.

The next morning which was Saturday, I saw two of the youths who sniggered when they saw me approaching. This was like a red rag to a bull and I soon found myself in pursuit of them again. In daylight I picked out the slower of the two, easily overhauling him and grabbing him by the shirt collar.

I dragged him back home and told him to get into my car. My intention was to take him to his parents, but he shouted and screamed at first refusing to tell me where he lived.

When he realised that I was deadly serious, he gave me his address, got into my car and I explained to his mother the reason I had brought him home. Throughout all of this, he denied the accusations crying, screaming and generally throwing a tantrum. His mother apologised for what I had been through, assuring me it wouldn't happen again and telling her son that he was grounded.

Ten minutes later I saw the youth and his mate out on the street again. I warned both of them as to their conduct but this time there was no smirking or piss taking. I hadn't known the mother but I did know her name. I telephoned her and asked what the hell was going on. "Well I had to let him go and tell Scott what had happened" she said. "Thanks for nothing, just forget it" I replied.

If that wasn't enough, a copper quickly arrived at my house saying a call had been made to the effect that I had forced a boy into my car. Either his mate or some do-gooder had reported my car number to the police. He asked to look inside my boot for ropes, chains or any other bondage tackle.

Some weeks later as I was returning home from an early evening run, I saw the same four youths smashing the panes of glass in a nearby telephone box. This was commonplace for the box and for other boxes and bus shelters in the area. As soon as the glass was replaced it would be smashed again.

In the days that followed I acted as a one man vigilante. I knocked on doors, visited shops and generally asked around to find out as much as I could about these boys. I notified my neighbours, the police, their parents and their schools as to what they had been doing.

A police officer visited home but what he had to say filled me with little confidence. "Can't you nip it in the bud before they start stealing cars or breaking into homes" I asked, "If we do that, there'll only be others coming along to take their place" he said. When I next saw this officer, he admitted that he hadn't had the opportunity to deal with these youths but asked if would I give consideration to becoming a Special Constable.

The school headmaster contradicted himself when he told me they didn't tolerate such behaviour but strictly there was nothing they could do about it.

One of my neighbours, a rather big uncompromising guy who you wouldn't have wanted as an enemy dealt with the problem in an unconventional manner. He told two of the boys that if he saw them on the street again, they were dead meat.

A black Afro Caribbean youth was a newcomer to the area and quickly became top dog in a local crime wave. One day I had never seen him before and the next day he was everywhere. He was forever on the streets, hanging around or sitting on walls and he would always be passing as I looked out of the window. His party piece was to walk up close behind people as if to take the piss but as more and more information emerged about him, he was clearly a nasty piece of work.

He had been in and out of young offenders institutions and was apparently due in front of the beak with a view to serving a prison term. This seemed little deterrent as he and his assembled gang continued to plunder, steal and vandalise wherever possible. A police officer described him as a petty criminal but try telling that to the man he head butted. Apparently when these acts were carried out he was usually high on drugs. His family had been unable to get to grips with his behaviour so had continually moved him from brother to sister to uncle and so on. Despite this he appeared to be a magnet for the local teenage girls, probably because of his baseball cap with his hood pulled up over the top.

I had a couple of affrays with him but the one I will describe is when I was out running on a dark Autumn evening. I became aware of two youths laughing and pointing at me as I ran past. They started to run alongside me with the bad lad running backwards, forwards and sideways while still laughing and taking the Mick. The second youth, obviously not as fit as his mate dropped back, not to be seen again.

Deciding to teach the tearaway a lesson, I got as close to him as I dare, clipping his heels and causing him fall down. I then trampled all over him before continuing on yet another eventful run.

At the start of an early Sunday morning run, two Panda Cars with blue lights flashing, came by at a ferocious speed. Five minutes later and looking for some action I ran along the pedestrian precinct in Rothwell Town Centre. I could see the two Panda Cars at the far end, still with their lights flashing. One copper appeared to have arrested a kid but another guy was tearing towards me with the second officer in pursuit.

With shops tightly packed on each side and the man bearing down on me, I did what any good rugby full back would have done. Moving to my left, I showed him the outside and as he came by, I fly kicked him. He hit the ground and remained motionless enabling the policeman to apprehend him. The copper shouted thanks as I continued running, but I didn't look back until I was well out of the way.

My first instincts had been to rugby tackle the man but never having made a good one in my life, I decided the purpose would be best served with a good kick at the last minute. I could have hurt myself but came away unscathed. I don't know what these two had done but I read in the local paper that our library had been broken into the same morning only for the thieves to drop in on a local group meeting. I don't believe the guy would have recognised me. I was well wrapped up in woolly hat and gloves to combat the cold and there have been no recriminations since. I do hope he wasn't hurt, well not too badly anyway.

My speed or lack of it was put to the test when I chased a youth who had stolen crisps, snickers, mars bars and the likes from a local garage. The attendant had left his position to take pursuit but stood no chance. He was a big or rather fat guy, similar to the restaurant proprietor in 'Pie in the sky'. He seemed to run with his belly with no pumping of the arms and after ten feet or so, gave it up as a bad job. I closed in on the lad but he jumped over a wall and clambered down the railway banking. I certainly wasn't going to start dodging the trains.

My running friend Gary Buck made local headlines and became hero of the hour when he chased and rugby tackled a youth who was attempting to get away with a ladies hand bag. The youth actually had the audacity to turn around during the pursuit and shout, "You won't catch me you fat bastard".

CHAPTER 8

Follow The Dream

IN CONTRAST to the Washington flight, the one to Pittsburgh passed off without a hitch. Whenever I catch a flight I seem to become sandwiched in between the guy who likes to sit horizontal and the child with lone parent who throws himself against the back of my seat. The flight to Washington was no exception.

A burly businessman sat down in the seat in front after placing his brief case and lap top in the overhead locker. He removed his jacket, rolled up his sleeves and immediately adjusted the tilt of his seat several notches until his head was virtually resting on my lap. I could have combed his hair and given his considerable neck a massage.

Enter the unruly child with single mother. After coaxing, cajoling and then ordering him to remain still, he perpetually crashed into the back of my seat, causing me to grunt or jolt forward on impact. I brought about a improvement in the short term when I knelt on the seat and looked menacingly over the back to find out what was happening. Between the two of them, they were squeezing every last inch of available space for which I had paid.

I pulled out the fold away table from the back of the seat in front in readiness for when the stewardess brought my meal. After placing everything where I wanted it and just about to tuck in, the wanker in front decided he should sit bolt upright. The cutlery flew onto the floor and the tea ended up on my lap. Have you ever tried looking for a knife or a fork on the floor of an aeroplane. They never stay where they land either shooting under your seat or the one in front.

On the bus from the airport into Pittsburgh, the guy sitting in front leaned around to ask if I minded if he tilted his seat back. "Yes I do mind, can't you sit upright for 20 minutes" I replied, and in doing so made my first enemy on American soil.

Of course the way to counter this phenomenon is to tilt your seat back accordingly. If everyone did this, the rows of passengers would end up looking like a pack of dominos that have been toppled over. The only time I have had cause to sit like this is in the dentist's chair.

I stayed at The Omni-William Penn Hotel, located downtown and fairly central for all the activities. After unpacking I afforded myself a wander around to familiarise myself with the immediate vicinity. The city seemed to be spotlessly clean and not in the least intimidating.

On Saturday morning I caught the Gateway Clipper Sightseeing Boat from Station Square Dock to gain an insight into the great river city. I could recollect Bruce Willis regularly pulling bodies from these waters in the film 'Striking Distance' where he played a river patrol cop alongside a young Sarah Jessica Parker.

Pittsburgh is situated at the confluence of the Monongahela, Allegheny and Ohio Rivers, is the largest inland port in the U.S. and was voted among the countries top five liveable cities. Most of the smokestacks have now disappeared to be replaced by futuristic buildings and glistening skyscrapers. This area between the rivers is known as The Golden Triangle.

The first blast furnace was erected in 1792 and Pittsburgh became known as the Iron City. By the 20th century it was well and truly established as the largest Iron, steel and aluminium producing city in the world. It had the world's largest cork manufacturing plant and also produced 20% of the countries glass.

Foreign competition caused most of the iron and steel plants to close in the 1970's and 80's and the city has now reinvented itself as a centre for high-tech industries such as computer software, industrial automation and biochemical technology.

So with New York, Boston, Chicago and a whole host of other

U.S. marathons beckoning, why Pittsburgh. I saw the 1983 film 'Flashdance' set in the city in which leading lady Alex is played by the stunning Jennifer Beals. In the opening footage, she cycles to work through the warehouse district, up and down the city's hills and across the bridges, all to the haunting background music of 'What a feeling' sung by Irene Cara.

Alex works as a welder by day but at night, she is an exotic dancer or 'Flashdancer'. She harbours an ambition to move away from the seedy bars where she dances for blue collar workers to become a classical dancer and this is the main story line. Alex follows her dream and with a little help on the way turns it into reality.

Despite the film been described as naff, I have never missed an opportunity to watch a rerun or a recording. Occasionally if I have felt down and in need of a pick me up, I have watched 'Flashdance' or another favourite, 'Groundhog Day'. Her performance lead to girls across America donning leg warmers and sweatshirts with the neck cut out. Alex's party piece was to remove her bra with her shirt still on.

The Pittsburgh Marathon would cross some of the cities bridges and no doubt run past some of the other places featured in the film. The day after the race, providing of course I was still moving, I would be free to explore the city and some of the other film locations.

The race expo was small compared to others with perhaps only twenty-five booths and I noticed that it came in for some criticism afterwards on the web site. The machine that dealt with the championship chips wasn't working correctly so they were unable to set mine, register it or do whatever is required.

I enjoyed a steak at Hoss's Steak and Sea House, one of a chain situated in and around the city, and then I retired to my hotel room early.

On Sunday morning, Shuttle buses transported runners from the cities hotels to the race start at Heinz Field on the north bank of the Allegheny River. The Stadium opened in 2001 and is the new home to the Pittsburgh Steelers having replaced The Three Rivers

Stadium. Another state of the art stadium next door is home to the Pittsburgh Pirates basketball team. Heinz Field could be reached by bus, car, riverboat or shuttle and there was ample parking available. The new start and finish had replaced the previous downtown start and the Point State Park finish and again this had sparked some criticism in certain quarters.

There would be approximately 3,000 runners in the Marathon with many more in the four man Marathon Relay and the children's mini-marathon. The Race sponsors were U.P.M.C. Health System and the purse for the winners was $59,250. There were special incentives for American citizens and Pittsburgh and Pennsylvania residents, no doubt in an attempt to prevent the Africans walking away with all the cash.

The route would pass through many of Pittsburgh's diverse neighbourhoods, there would be forty musical acts around the course and many districts held their own gala or festival in conjunction with the race. The traffic free course was described as rolling and the changes to the course meant two extra bridge crossings.

There were the usual announcements and rendition of The Star Spangled Banner which was well received before we were eventually underway. The field quickly sorted itself out and the early miles were enjoyable, completed at a comfortable pace. The weather at 7-30 was pretty cool but would turn out to be hot for the later stages.

We quickly entered The Strip District, which constitutes a narrow strip of land sandwiched between Grants Hill to the south and the Allegheny River. Penn Avenue, Liberty Avenue and Smallman run parallel and were formerly the home to iron mills, foundries and glassworks. Rail yards once ran down Liberty Avenue and in the 1950's there were over seventy wholesale dealers.

The area is now better known for fresh fruit shops, restaurants, bars, food stores and coffee shops. From time to time the tell tale harp would indicate an Irish Bar along with advertisements for the local Iron City and I.C. Light beers. The area is home to immigrants and their descendents from all around the world with large communities from both the Emerald Isle and from Poland.

We cross the 16th St Bridge at mile five and re-enter the North Side, past the Heinz Factory and the Mexican War Streets. These are named after battles in the 1846 war such as Buena Vista, Monterey and Palo Alto. The area at one time was pretty upmarket but has recently undergone restoration.

Andy from South Carolina and formerly a resident of Bristol, introduced himself after spotting my Union Flag singlet. It is his 37th Marathon and apart from the high profile events, he tells me of some of the lesser known marathons he has done. He describes South Carolina as the marsh country and say's that his local marathon, The Kiawah Island has alligators as spectators. I told him that perhaps I'd give that one a miss.

We cross the Ohio River by way of the West End Bridge which provides stunning views of Point State Park, The Golden Triangle and the mountain backdrop. A slight downhill brings us onto Carson Street and the South Side. Boisterous spectators line the pavements through Station Square past antique shops, bookstores and bars. The bands make for a lively atmosphere and provide a pleasant distraction from the arduous task in hand.

Birmingham Bridge crosses the Monongahela River after which there is a significant climb for almost a mile on Forbes Avenue to Oakland. Still running with Andy, I reach the summit fairly comfortably, but some of the runners really making heavy weather of it judging from some of the comments I hear. The next stage beyond twelve miles past the University of Pittsburgh Medical Centre is flat to rolling depending on what shape you are in and how you tackle it.

We ran through two university campuses where spectator support was pretty sparse. Mile markers were displayed on huge boards along with clocks so you could regularly check your progress. Drinks stations were situated every mile and with the temperature soaring, it was now imperative to take liquids on board. Bananas, strawberries and chocolate were being handed out at the many drinks stations where enthusiastic volunteers treated every runner as a champion. Entertainment was provided every mile including a bagpiper who was playing a lament at one of the mileposts in the later stages.

Entering Shadyside along Fifth Avenue provides a pleasant running environment along tree- lined streets and past Victorian mansions, art galleries and upmarket restaurants. The course is relatively flat along Penn Avenue and through Point Breeze, Homewood and East Liberty becoming more rolling again near Highland Park. There are fine views of the skyline from some of the more elevated sections. The predominantly Italian Community gives huge support through Bloomfield where more bands and music are provided to spur on those tired legs.

The other Andy feels stronger than this Andy, so wishes me well and presses ahead. Almost immediately my shoelace comes undone, a cardinal sin among runners. As I stop to refasten, it seems as if hundreds of runners pass me by. Several of these are with an official group pacer holding a 3-45 sign aloft. He calls out instructions and words of encouragement, making sure that none of his flock drop back off the pace. I couldn't be bothered with this, finding it hard enough to run my own race without having to keep up with a group. I did run near to a paced group several years ago in The Robin Hood Marathon. One guy appeared to question the leaders every instruction, there was friendly banter and they seemed to be having a great time.

I take some time to regain my rhythm after the set back with the lace but some useful descents in the final miles enable me to regain some momentum and I keep pressing along nicely. I feel pretty comfortable at this stage and with the end in sight feel pleased with my efforts so far.

We cross the Allegheny River for a final time before entering Heinz Field where we run through the parking lot. But with the finish almost within touching distance, there is a sting in the tail as we are required to run around most of the perimeter before we can enter the stadium. Runners were able to look up and see their likeness go through the finish on a giant screen. I am pretty chuffed to complete in three and three quarter hours which was a little better than anticipated.

There was a convivial atmosphere inside the stadium to greet the many weary runners who were able to have a bath, a shower or a free massage. Runners who I spoke to appeared to prefer the finish of previous years in Point State Park, at the Three Rivers Nexus, apparently a symbol of the city. I had believed the course to be challenging but not unduly tough, but many criticised it's severity saying the elevation profile and information provided had been misleading. I wondered what these people would have made of some of the races back home in West Yorkshire.

Before leaving Heinz Field, I took the opportunity to browse around the Coca Cola Great Hall. Here, giant trophy cabinets, banners and murals depict the history of the Pittsburgh Steelers and the grid-iron game in general. There were videos, movies and banners providing a real bonanza for the enthusiast.

Washed, changed and recuperated, I potter about on Sunday afternoon catching the bus or metro wherever possible to rest my weary legs, with most of the transport in Pittsburgh free. On Sunday evening I hit The Strip where trade is fairly brisk. I quench my thirst in Mullaney's Harp and Fiddle, The Foundry Ale Works and Joyce's to name but a few. With a big day of sightseeing ahead, I hit the sack and sleep like a baby.

On Monday I ventured here, there and everywhere to 'Follow the Dream' on bus, trolley, boat and even an incline ride. Jennifer alias Alex rode the Duquese Incline on visiting her friend and mentor, Hannah in 'Flashdance'. There were panoramic views of the city from Grand View Avenue and a museum depicting rail car travel from all over the world. I saw Hannah's house on 21st Street returning to the waterfront by the Monongahela Incline Ride.

I saw Alex's house at 2100 Sidney St on the South Side, saw where she auditioned for the ballet school at the Carnegie Institute and saw where she ran through the Hall of Sculpture at 4400 Forbes Avenue. I even saw where she was taken for an exotic meal at The Grand Concourse on Station Square. On a budget I opted for a bite to eat at Prinanti's Sandwich Shop, one of many across the city

Up and running again in search of more 'Flashdance' locations. What a bore! No wonder I can't get anyone to come away with me. However I did draw the line at visiting the underpass where Alex told her date to pull over before getting from car, removing her stilettos and storming off into the night, following a tiff.

On Monday afternoon I strolled the streets, walked the waterfront and crossed the bridges. I visited galleries, shops and The John Heinz Regional History Centre, calling for a coffee or beer whenever it took my fancy. Who needs a friend? Everyone seemed so friendly and the atmosphere a touch laid back. A guy in a bar asked me if I had the time. "Quarter past" I replied. "Quarter past what" he said. How wonderful not to be governed by the clock I thought. I decided that I would work towards this as my desired future state.

Mawby's, the bar where Alex danced for the steel workers was filmed in Los Angeles, but when I ventured onto East Carson Street on Monday evening, there were those that could have easily taken it's place. I visited Philthy McNasties, Pipers and several more before turning in to contemplate my long journey home the following day.

The Pittsburgh Marathon wasn't held in 2004 due to the lack of funding and to date hasn't reappeared on the calendar, so I'm glad I took the opportunity to run when I did. Apparently prize and appearance money was a huge drain on resources and a new sponsor has yet to emerge. The high profile 10K run in the city has also apparently hit snags for pretty much the same reason, but there has been talk of arranging lower key races with fewer elite runners but to date this hasn't happened.

The only disappointment was the fact I didn't receive an official finishing time and could only guess at my position, no doubt due to the malfunction on the software that programmed the chips. I'm sure this was also the case for many others too. So where to next?

While browsing on the Marathonguide.com website, a pop up hit my screen for The Fargo Marathon in North Dakota. Who can forget those long straight roads in the frozen wastelands, in the film of the same name.

CHAPTER 9

The Golden Mile

I WAS FORCED out of Marathon retirement yet again, this time by Roy who was spending a few days at Blackpool in his caravan with better half Marion. The plan would be to pick him up at the caravan site and return there after the race where I would have lunch.

I had premonitions of not being able to find the caravan imagining row upon row of look-alikes. I could remember 'The Likely Lads' returning to their caravan site after a boozy night out and eventually giving up the ghost when their navigational skills met with little success.

Roy saved me the embarrassment by agreeing to meet me on the main road but reported that his van was one of only two on the site. This didn't appear to bode too well for the proprietor of the site particularly in the middle of June.

The next task would be to locate the race start at the Hilton Hotel on the North Promenade. Apart from running in a couple of shorter races, the last time I had visited Blackpool was back in the eighties on a players day out with the White Swan football team. We had made a beeline straight from the coach park into the huge Foxhall Pub and were almost kicked out at 1-00 clock lunchtime for singing.

The next pub refused our group admission but not to be outdone, we managed to bluff our way past the doormen. We retreated around the corner and entered at strategic intervals, two by two like the animals entering Noah's Ark. Once inside, we assembled together again before the bouncers came over acknowledging we had pulled the wool over their eyes and asking us to behave. As if we wouldn't?

On the coach home, for reasons that must have made sense at the time, a group of reprobates brought on board a couple of deck chairs and half a dozen milk churns. My friends father, Richard glanced out of his bedroom window the next morning to see these arranged in a druids circle on his front lawn.

Worse still, I must have dozed off on the coach, and someone had the audacity to cut off, half of my then fashionable Zapata moustache. Even worse was that I didn't notice it until my squash partner called later in the day and fell about laughing. That was nothing compared to what I had to put up with when I next visited the White Swan. What was I doing playing football with these morons?

The Blackpool Fylde Coast International Marathon started at the Hilton Hotel which doubled as race headquarters, Fylde meaning an area of marshland and forests dating back to Roman times. The hotel also doubled as main race sponsor and staged a small exhibition of running kit and memorabilia. We toured the surrounding streets in search of a suitable parking space and found one adjacent to Kwik Fit. I had visited one and the same only the day before in Leeds to have my exhaust secured so I was handily placed should it suddenly decide to come loose again.

We changed in the car, made our way to the Hilton and joined a group of runners, huddled inside the foyer to avoid the stiff breeze and the drizzle. Word spread of a twenty minute delay due to several marshals not being in place and this did little to steady the nerves. We chatted to our Club Chairman Cyril who was taking in the race on a family weekend. This was a nice gesture as Roy and myself, Mick Walsh and Cathy Berry would be the only Ackworth representatives. One thing for sure was that he wouldn't require his clip board to record the times today. We sounded out 100 Marathon Club runner and Sports Tours representative, Wally Oakes about any possible vacancies on New York trip.

Eventually, all the runners were called forward onto the North Promenade to face the elements. As usual I was under prepared so would take my time, take in the sights and try to enjoy the day. I would run as far as I could before resorting to a struggle and inevitably to a walk. My marathon target these days was four hours. 3-59-59 would constitute a good mornings work but 4-00-01 would be disappointing.

I had previously run the Fleetwood Half Marathon in the days when I was a bit faster. The familiar Norwester had blown sand over the sea wall onto the promenade making the going even tougher. I had run in the Windmill Half Marathon and the Blackpool 10K. This race would constitute parts of all three rolled into one.

The Blackpool 10K of 1992 still remains my personal best for the distance when I came close to the magical forty minute mark. And all of this after getting off to a slow start, running a mile or so while chatting to a friend and forgetting to start my watch. After the race, we called for a pint, played a few slot machines and strolled the promenade. A small crowd had gathered around a guy with a giant snake around his neck and I can remember crossing the road to give him or rather the snake a wide berth. I would be useless on ' I'm a Celebrity, Get me out of here'.

We started cautiously chatting away to each other with the breeze nicely at our backs. The sea front is dominated by the tower and at 518 ft comprises 2,493 tons of steel and 93 tons of cast iron. The tower opened in 1894 after taking two and a half years to build. Today it houses a ballroom with ornate ceiling and Wurlitzer organ, the Tower Circus and Aquarium.

Steady away past Harry Ramsden's where work colleague took sanctuary, while competing in a Brass Band competition on a cold November weekend. He complained about the tariff and the less than generous portion of haddock and chips.

Next up was Yates Wine Lodge followed by Louis Tussauds waxworks. "Why is this called Louis Tussauds and the one in London, Madam Tussauds " I asked Roy. "Don't know " was the reply. I later found on investigation that Madame Tussaud was born Marie Grosholtz in Strasbourg, France in 1761. She became art tutor to the sister of King Louis XV1 and later became imprisoned in Paris. She made death masks including those of King Louis XV1 and Marie Antoinette who were both guillotined in 1793. Marie wed Francois Tussaud in 1795.

We passed the Manchester pub followed by the Foxhall where I had almost been booted out all those years ago. We systematically ticked off the three piers, the North, the Central with big wheel and the South, the last to be built in 1894. This was far better than our average Sunday run with so much to see and but for the runners, hardly a soul about on a bright and breezy morning.

Trams rattled past on their dedicated track and with assorted shapes, sizes and colours, just like a working museum. This was the first Electric Tramway in Britain and possibly in Europe when it arrived with ten trams in 1885. There were many problems with the track been laid to the wrong gauge, sea water soaking the rails and sand blowing across the track. The current was picked up from a slot between the rails but converted to overhead lines in 1899. One of the original trams is in the Tramway Museum at Crich in Derbyshire.

The Promenade was widened in 1902 reclaiming land from the sea and this provided for trams to have their own dedicated track in 1905. The Toast racks named because of the rows of wooden seats were open topped and open sided. They were replaced by Boats, Dreadnoughts, and eventually Balloons. Some trams are customised as rockets or boats for the illuminations in Autumn and travel the twelve mile track from Starr Gate to Fleetwood, much of where we would run today.

Roy and I chatted about the possibility of a race along the sea front on an Autumn evening to coincide with the illuminations. No doubt this idea will have been tossed around as races have been organised just about anywhere it is remotely possible to run. An unopened stretch of carriageway on a new by– pass immediately springs to mind and a race up the flights of stairs in a tower block office building.

The Golden Mile with novelty shops, amusement arcades and fortune tellers, passed quickly and was replaced by the Pleasure Beach. Here the Pepsi Max Big One, at one time Europe's tallest and fastest roller-coaster, rubs shoulders with the Grand National, the Log Flume and other rides. I was soaked to the skin on the Log Flume on that unfortunate White Swan day trip, when I was told that if I wanted to remain dry, I should sit in the rear of the carriage.

Beyond Starr Gate, the amusements and rides were replaced by small hotels, guest houses and B & B's. The Viking Hotel was the best on the coast according to a huge bill board outside and who was I to argue. Who needs the London Marathon when there was so much to see here.

The course moved slightly away from the seafront past the huge Pontins complex and Roy moved onto the pavement to give Marion a peck on the cheek at a pre arranged place. He stopped again moments later, disappearing to have a pee in the sand dunes and caught me up effortlessly within a few hundred yards. The rolls were reversed from a couple of years ago with Roy comfortably staying with me and being able to pick up the pace at anytime. I had beaten him only once in something like thirty races over the last year and did I keep reminding him about it.

The guest houses became fewer, changing to fine residential properties. The marshals at each street end were marvellous in their encouragement of runners and the twenty minute delay had probably been worth the wait, while they took to their places.

With Roy now forging ahead, I started to notice the colours and clubs of other runners around with good representations from Red Rose, Preston and Clayton – le- Moors along with one runner from the splendidly named Trawden Celtic. There were good contingents too from the North Wales clubs such as Abergele and Prestatyn.

At St Anne's Pier, the half marathoners turn right for their return journey into the teeth of the wind, however the die-hards carry straight on towards Lytham. I recognise some of the roads and greenery as part of the Windmill Half Marathon course which I ran some years ago. I now see the distinctive white windmill where we turn at ten miles, completed in 77 minutes.

The going becomes tougher as we transfer onto the footpath where the Ribble Estuary meets the sea and presumably the buildings across the water belong to Southport. I immediately start to struggle as runners begin to drift by, among them a group of a dozen or so who share the workload between them. I try to attach myself to the back of this group but meet with little success and soon drop off the pace.

A giant of a man tries to take shelter behind me which I find hard to believe. I put this theory to the test by moving to the right and he follows. I move to the left and so does he and when I quicken the pace, he also picks up speed. I teach him a lesson when I slow to grab a drink at the first of several tables, forcing him to pass me to collect his cup. He then gradually disappears into the distance which make his tactics a little pointless.

I fare better as we turn inland and gain immediate shelter from the wind. The course circles Fairhaven Lake and I slow to give a wheelie a push up the steep slope out of the park. A pocket of spectators lend their support but no one came across to help the wheelie who had lost momentum and had started to go backwards. The last time I did this while out running was to help some Indians, not the North American variety, to push a van. On that occasion my knees locked but fortunately there was no harm done today.

At Squires Gate the runners would turn away from the main road to the rear of Sandcastle Leisure Centre and onto the new sea wall. The paving stones formed a zig zag pattern and it was tempting to follow this rather than to maintain a straight line.

In the race literature, the next section between the three piers was described as narrow in places and would accommodate pedestrians, but marshals would be on hand to assist. This was perhaps an understatement as with almost 18 miles completed, and two and a

half hours running under my belt, the holidaymakers and day trip-
pers were now out in force. Marshals were strategically placed, no
doubt doing their best and the route was coned off, but this made
no difference.

Some people were supportive of runners and gave way, some
were oblivious to what was going on while others crossed in
front of runners or just stood around on the course. Others were
dammed awkward like a group of lager louts, one who shouted as
I approached, " You're not last this year ". I can remember thinking at the time how brave he had been to shout at me. He certainly
wouldn't have murmured a word had he been on his own and
probably wouldn't have said anything had he been only one of two
or three. He was lucky that I hadn't dragged him to the floor and
trampled all over him. I was nicely warmed up at this stage and
ready for anything. What a pity this small section had spoiled what
otherwise would have been an excellent event.

The nineteen mile marker came shortly after the North Pier where
we were directed onto the lower sea wall. By now the field was well
strung out and though sparse, the spectator support was still pretty
supportive. Still moving forward, a short gradient brought us onto
the Middle Walk where the half marathoners would have turned
off for their finish. The die-hards still had a further 2 ½ miles on the
Lower Sea Wall, to Little Bispham where we would turn for home. I
looked up in envy to see the runners ahead returning along the cliff
top path but still the turnaround point failed to materialise. This
was becoming a long hard slog and I began to regularly glance at
my watch in desperation to make sure I was on target to break four
hours.

Eventually a sharp turn and stiff climb brought us onto the cliff
top. Now the rolls were reversed as I looked down upon the runners on the Lower Sea Wall who had yet to reach the turnaround
point. I had no idea that North Blackpool was so hilly and that
cliffs in fact existed here. I had left myself 33 minutes to complete
the final three miles and while not a tall order at the start of a race,

can be pretty tough with 23 already completed. Even though I remained focused and resisted the temptation of a badly needed walk, I needed every one of those minutes to complete the course. Our Chairman, Cyril reckoned I had run 3-59 exactly, almost twenty minutes behind Roy. How had he put so much time in-between us, particularly running into the wind? Mick split the two of us with Cathy coming home some way further back.

My car was parked exactly where I had left it with the exhaust pipe still intact. With another marathon under our belts, we discussed the why's, the where fore's and the but ifs back at the caravan over lunch.

I said cheerio to Marion and Roy as they prepared to hit the road north. Roy would run in the Isle of Arran Half Marathon the following weekend and I promised to meet up with them again in two weeks time at the Kilburn Feast Seven. What a life!

CHAPTER 10

Wet, Wet, Wet!

ELAYING THE inevitable until as late as possible before leaving the changing marquee and making my way to the start, a clap of thunder enhanced the already torrential downpour which if anything was becoming heavier. As the pipe band lead us forward into Saltmarket where the race would start, a rapturous cheer or groan rang out as the seemingly impossible happened and the ferocity of the rain appeared to move up another gear.

The heavens had opened half an hour before the start, with the tented village turning into a quagmire and everyone would be soaked to the skin before even a stride was taken in anger. I had been caught in the rain on Friday evening watching an Under 21 International at Paisley. Not content with just one football match over the weekend, I had travelled to Kirkcaldy on Saturday to see my adopted team Ross County take on Raith Rovers.

The rain had started to fall while I was on the Edinburgh train so my anticipated stroll around the historic city was curtailed. Instead I dodged in and out of arcades and shopping malls with no real intention of buying anything but decided it would be advisable to purchase a roll up brolly.

My next train meandered around the Firth of Forth coastline and as it slowed on the approach to Kirkcaldy, I could see the floodlights of the Starks Park ground, which would only be a short walk from the station or so I thought. Twenty-five minutes later with newly acquired umbrella angled in an attempt to remain dry, I arrived at the ground to find pockets of spectators milling around, presumably awaiting for the turnstiles to open. I walked towards the considerable sea front returning twenty minutes later to find the place deserted. A couple of guys were hurriedly walking away from the ground and I asked, "Is the match off". "Yes, waterlogged pitch", one replied. "What at the beginning of September", I said. Fancy coming all this way, only to find the game postponed. I would have to be very selective in who I told about this!

My journey had been to no avail and I was soon on the train, heading back to Edinburgh, changing at Haymarket for the express to Glasgow. The weather fared up on the journey but the sky turned black on approaching Glasgow and the rain started bucketing it down. I took sanctuary inside the station bar only to find that Scotland were 2-0 down against the un-fancied Faroe Islands in a World Cup Qualifier.

A group of men wearing Scotland replica shirts, dashed along the pavement, heads bowed and shoulders hunched in a hopeless attempt to dodge the raindrops. They presumably thought a change of bar may bring about a change of fortune in the outcome of the match. I afforded myself a wry smile as I sat warm and snug in the sanctuary of the bus. The rain continued into the evening but had stopped by next morning.

As I waited for The Great Scottish Run to start, water cascaded from the brim of my peaked cap and I could feel my tee shirt clinging to my back and to my chest. Without doubt, these would be the wettest conditions and the heaviest rain I had run in and thinking about the next couple of hours, didn't exactly fill me with anticipation.

I had arrived early and put out hundreds of flyers for my first book, 'Middle of the Packer', placing them meticulously behind car windscreen wipers. Despite the glossy paper, all of these would now be soggy with the ink having run and the paper saturated.

"Why did they have to change the date", I heard somebody say,"It never rained like this in August. If it isn't broken, don't mend it". I tended to agree in part but can remember a couple of years previously on the one occasion when the race start was changed to an afternoon. A group of us sat in the mini bus, soaked to the skin and freezing cold, with windows steamed up and the heater on full belt as we waited for the remainder of our group to finish.

Conditions had usually been fine in the years in which I have run the Great Scottish, generally warm and sometimes hot. The half marathon course through the city and suburbs, shows Glasgow at it's finest, taking in three parks and crossing The River Clyde. Attracting in excess of ten thousand runners, the event enjoys a big race atmosphere but is more manageable and less congested than some of it's larger contemporaries.

Glasgow has a rich and diverse architectural heritage, world-class museums and galleries and is an ideal city for a weekend break. There are over seventy parks and gardens, fine bars and restaurants and the largest retail centre in the U.K. outside London.

A buzz of expectancy presided as the stewards pulled away the tape inviting those at the front of our section to break rank and squeeze up to the block of runners in front. Faces could be seen peering from behind closed windows of tenement buildings and rooms above shops, in contrast to other years when they would have been leaning out of them, shouting and cheering.

Despite jogging slowly at first, water was still been splashed around my ankles and feet, with my toes feeling like blocks of ice. High Street was all but a river while in George Street the grates resembling mini whirlpools, struggled to cope with the deluge and the drainage covers were like water fountains. But despite the weather, those around me appeared to be rising to the challenge and everyone appeared to be in good spirits.

Slightly downhill through the Merchant City into the wide expanse of George Square, the symbolic heart of the city, the outlook was of the Victorian skyline dominated by towers and spires. The pavements would have normally been lined with spectators, but today, only a few braved the elements. Builders and tradesmen working on the cities many new developments generally use the race as an excuse to down tools and take five, but today they weren't in evidence, more than likely busying away to keep dry.

Passing 'The Counting House' on the corner of George Square where I have spent the occasional happy hour and would most likely do so again later today, put a spring into my step. The Wetherspoons hostelry converted from a former bank building is a popular meeting place and watering hole in the heart of the city.

Turning left into Jamaica Street, I approached and eased past a group of Sikhs, resplendent in brightly coloured turbans. One had stopped and with the help of his colleague was adjusting his head-gear and I really felt for these guys as their turbans would inevitably become saturated. I made a mental note to add the recently established Mumbai Marathon to my list of must do events.

On Bridge Street a guy came striding through the puddles kicking up water and giving my feet and ankles a real soaking. "Hey watch who your splashing", I said. "I'm going to have to clean these now". He pressed on regardless but a young lady runner smirked, obviously seeing the funny side of the situation. Another clap of thunder and almost immediately the ferocity of the rain increased to yet another level.

People huddled in doorways and against walls on the long, straight Paisley Road section where the roadside would have normally been lined with spectators, vociferous and generous in their appreciation of the runners. A police motorcycle outrider came down the outside, throwing up more spray and a group of people with brollies aloft, shuffled hastily to the centre of the road at one of the organised crossing points. Away from the buildings and out into the open, hailstones the size of marbles began to pepper the sides of my cheeks. I continued to tread water and splash through puddles.

Large pools covered the pathways as we zigzagged through Bellahouston Park. Some ran on the waterlogged grass to little advantage only succeeding in throwing up mud and spray. I noticed the ankles and calves of runners ahead and most looked as if they were taking part in a cross country or fell race rather than one on the roads.

Turning into Mosspark Boulevard, I passed the five-mile post in 38 minutes, not bad under circumstances. There was some respite from the rain, through the woods in Pollok Park but the road was awash with the speed bumps resembling rapids. A lone piper playing a lament at one of the mile-posts was looking wet and bedraggled but still played on heroically.

And still the rain fails to relent through Pollokshaws and Shawlands as we head back towards the city. In Pollokshields, members of the cities Asian community try to lift flagging spirits with words of encouragement as they hand out drinks. On Ballater Road where I took a tumble some years ago, I start to think about finishing the race and imagine changing back into warm clothing. I didn't relish this and would really prefer to carry on running. My tee shirt has become part of me, my shorts are clinging to my legs which in turn have severely chaffed and my nipples feel as if they are on fire. Why don't I grab my bag and carry on running back to the hotel?

Not far to go now as we enter Glasgow Green, running on the sheltered pathway alongside the River Clyde. I go through twelve miles, still in with a chance of breaking 100 minutes. Those around me sense this too and start to pick up their stride and quicken their pace for one last effort, only enhancing the amount of mud and spray which is been flung into the air. Spotting the Nelson Memorial, I realise the end is in sight and put in one last effort around the great sweep and up the home straight. I reach the finishing line at The People Palace in around 100 minutes but may have dipped below, fingers crossed when I receive the official time.

I queued for a tea, which continued to top itself up with rainwater as I headed to the changing marquee. The floor of the tent was like a mud bath as I tiptoed precariously to retrieve my baggage, Finding a vacant chair and hardly daring to pull off my wet clothes, I reflected for a few moments on the morning's events. I had been soaked to the skin before the race, during the race and now after the race.

The marquee was starting to fill as more bedraggled runners entered through the door flap. Seating was now at a premium with runners standing on plastic bags, towels and any other available garment in order to keep their feet dry. Perhaps it was time to make a move and pull off my wet clothing, which I reluctantly started to do. My legs began to smart as I peeled the shorts from the top of my legs, before turning attention to my socks. Is it worthwhile washing these or do I just chuck them away?

Dressed and ready to step out once again into the rain, I hand out more flyers to anybody who will gladly accept one or anyone who is remotely interested. I trudged dejectedly across Glasgow Green and stopped for another tea before wending my way back to the hotel. My plan would be to have a warm shower followed by a swim in the hotel pool making sure I hit the hotel bar before 2-00 'O'clock for steak, chips and all the trimmings.

But there was no water in the pool, which appeared to be undergoing cleansing and there were no steak and chips either. "But the board outside says steak and chips", I pleaded. "Well I don't know who put it there", retorted the chef, "We haven't any food available". It was probably a decoy, strategically placed to lure unsuspecting punters into the bar. So there was no alternative but to hit the damp and miserable streets once again in search of a bite to eat, preferably inside a pub.

CHAPTER 11

Which Way Did They Go?

Y WORST fears were realised as I resorted to walking up another nasty little hill. We had barely been going ten minutes and this was already my third walk. I wasn't up for the race and was now paying the price as a string of competitors drifted by effortlessly.

Throughout the day at work I was unable to raise any enthusiasm for the race, but the idea of a pleasant sociable run followed by a couple of pints and a bite to eat, seemed like a good idea at the time. The day had been a scorcher and conditions were sure to be hot and humid.

Speaking to a neighbour before leaving home, I told him I was running at Denby Dale. "That's sure to be hilly" he said, "unless they stick to the main road in the valley bottom". I had seen a map of the course, had run here several times in the half marathon and he wasn't wrong. I needed this information like a kick in the teeth, but thanked him for his contribution.

I had further regrets on the journey to the race, as I had pre registered, paid my money and would take my chance. If I had waited to register on the evening as others do, I would have had a suitable excuse to chicken out. This is really unfair on the organisers who have little idea on the numbers to expect or how many people to cater for, not that I begrudged paying the modest entry fee which would go towards a trust fund for young athletes.

The race in question was the Martin Holroyd 10K, commemorating a local man who was tragically killed in January 2001 while running home from work. Denby Dale Travellers were the organising club and were responsible for putting me through this ordeal.

Passing through Clayton West, drinkers were sitting outside The Woodman, taking advantage of the warm summer evening. Once the race was out of the way, I would be free to join them. When I parked up, I could hear the majestic sound of ball hitting willow. Cricket would be a more sensible option and an altogether steadier pursuit on an evening like this. I wondered if they may be short and if I could perhaps get a game.

Starting from close to The Denby Dale Pie Hall, the course would constitute six hilly miles to High Hoyland and back, and as one of the officials described, a fell race on the roads.

A small loop to make up the distance was tackled at breakneck speed with the Oriental delights of the Tandoori Palace wafting across the pavement. By the time we reached the first testing hill, I was already puffing and blowing and unable to catch my breath. A troublesome knee added to my woes as a stream of runners began to overtake at their leisure. Paul Smith tapped me on the shoulder providing words of encouragement before he too disappeared out of sight.

I soon resorted to my first walk, quickly followed by a second and then a third. I appeared to be the only one struggling with those ahead of me bobbing along quite nicely and others chatting away in pairs, without an apparent care in the world. The course followed twisting country lanes flanked by wooded slopes and rolling fields. The narrow roads were badly potholed and in desperate need of repair. From time to time the surface would be covered with slurry, slush ,straw and all those other things spewed out by tractors and farming machinery.

I received little encouragement when a spectator who I recognised as a former club colleague gave me a load of lip and told me to get my finger out. The same guy would say to me at the end of local races, "What time did you do". I would always skirt around the issue by saying, "I had a bad un" or "I beat you". I believe he was secretly revelling in my apparent misfortune and discomfort.

A signpost to Clayton West and High Hoyland marked the start of some further climbs with splendid houses of local stone contrasting with derelict farm buildings. In places the road was flanked by intermittent dry stone walls topped with barbed wire and thick hedgerows. The views across the valley from the higher ground would have been magnificent if I'd have felt in better shape to enjoy them.

A young lady straddled an impressive chestnut charger, outside the superbly named Toppitt Cottage. Her much needed support must have fallen upon deaf ears and still didn't spark me into life. Instead my mind wandered back to younger days when I would pedal furiously to finish my paper round in time to watch 'Follifoot'. Dora was my heart throb and my dream girl and thinking about those days provided a welcome distraction from the struggle I was having at the moment. What I would have given for that bike right now!

With two further walks before I broke out into a jog again, I spotted a couple of marshals ahead at a road junction. "You're looking good" encouraged one, but I knew this must have been said very much with tongue in cheek as I certainly didn't feel good. In a race that I would have normally expected to complete in under 50 minutes standing on my head, I would be lucky to break an hour this evening.

A much better road surface now presided and a signpost said 'Welcome to Barnsley'. I gained some momentum on the downhill to Clayton West where two elderly gentlemen viewed the proceedings from a seat placed strategically on a triangle of grass. My dad always drummed it into me that it was much better to participate than to spectate, but right now I would have gladly swapped places with these two.

Upper Common Lane brought about another tough hill before a furious descent enabled me to home in on a couple of other strugglers. They exchanged pleasantries but caught up again on the next painful climb to Wheatley Hill Lane, although I did pass a couple of cyclists who had dismounted to walk.

As I approached the junction at Hollin House Lane, I was surprised to see half a dozen back markers still approaching from the opposite direction. At least I wouldn't be last or would I? With the field now well strung out, I approached a junction with no marshal there to direct me. Confronted with the decision as to carry straight on or to turn left, I chose the former. After a couple of hundred yards, the road petered out into a track and then appeared to stop. On retracing my steps I could spot the tell tale floating heads of runners above a hedgerow several fields away.

Desperate times call for desperate measures and I called out to a man walking his dog, "Which way did they go"? He put me back on track but why hadn't he stopped me from coming this way in the first place. This was rapidly developing into a low point of my running career at least for the time being. Soldiering on and regaining some sort of rhythm, I caught up with the man and woman still jogging together, passing them for a second time. My navigational error had enabled several runners to steal a march and I would really need to get a move on now to dip inside an hour.

At least I would have my pie to look forward to at the finish. Well I presumed there would be a piece of pie as Denby Dale is after all The Pie Village and the race would finish at The Pie Hall. As a small boy, Denby Dale was my dream location to live, when I grew up.

The village of Denby Dale has been making giant pies for over 200 years. The first recorded pie was baked in 1788 to celebrate the recovery of King George from mental illness. Since then nine further pies have been baked to coincide with a special event or to raise money for a local cause.

The earlier pies contained game but in 1887, poor hygiene control amounted to a pie that was unfit for human consumption. The remains of the pie were paraded through the streets in funeral style and buried in quick lime.

Each pie has become bigger and better and the year 2000 saw the making of the tenth record breaking pie. The Millennium Pie weighed in at 12 tonnes and measured 40' long. The pie not only celebrated the millennium but also marked the 150th anniversary of the Penistone Railway Line which gave Denby Dale it's most famous landmark, the viaduct.

With my dander up and my nostrils on fire, I could almost smell the pie at the finish. Some useful downhill's enabled me to pick up the pace, making up for lost time. A late bid saw me finish outside The Pie Hall in a shade over 53 minutes, which at one time looked like being far worse. What was far worse however was the fact that I was rewarded with only a Mars Bar for my efforts instead of my rightful piece of pie.

There was no food at the inn either, so we had to make do with Walkers Potato Crisps. With wasps forming a queue to drink my lager, and an overdue chill descending, we decided to move indoors. My final recollections of the evening were of the openly gay barman, telling anybody and everybody how he had almost pulled in Wakefield at the weekend.

CHAPTER 12

I've Got Your Number

A REASONABLE WEATHER forecast had been predicted for the big day so I looked forward in anticipation as I made the short walk to pick up the coach. People were already starting to board as I approached but there was no need to panic as we had to wait for stragglers. An overnight frost had provided one of those brilliant mornings where mist sits in valleys and hovers over dips in fields and along streams.

The 2003 version of the BUPA Great North Run marked my nineteenth appearance at the event. Good fortune and few injuries have always seen me make the start line but each year I pledge will be my last. With the dust settled a few months down the line, next years application form duly arrives in the post. I complete it and return along with my cheque and mark the date on the calendar. This ensures that I keep running and motivated for another year.

Once underway I wrote a postcard to my workmates in the form of a poem comprising song titles with a Great North theme. The songs I came up with included The Fog on the Tyne, The Jarrow Song and Lindisfarne's Run for Home while the postcard was one I had picked up the previous year. It featured the Marsden Rattler, one of the sea front hostelries where we would probably spend a happy hour later in the day. When such postcards tended to arrive at the workplace, the comments would be something along the lines of "Where the hell has he gone this time"!

Feeling chuffed with my efforts, I passed it around a small selection of people for approval and would post it on arrival in Newcastle. I have always had the knack of being able to write neatly be it on a bus, train or plane no matter how rough or bumpy the ride. This knack must have stemmed from the days of doing my homework upstairs on the school bus.

The coach pulled in at Washington services where runners desperately alighted to pay a call. The queue for the cubicles stretched out of the toilet block and into the corridor. How anyone can sit there and concentrate, mindful of the long line of people standing at the door waiting to get in, I will never know. Those just wanting to stand were in and out in no time.

Back on the coach I changed, vaselined, secured my number and completed my preparations by pulling on a carefully prepared bin liner with suitable holes for my head and arms. Back on the road again, we passed the Angel of the North Statue and the Metro Centre before crossing the Tyne and hitting slow moving traffic close to the race start.

When the coach could go no further, we were deposited by the roadside with spectators, family and friends staying onboard for what looked like being an arduous journey to South Shields. I had grabbed a pile of flyers advertising my first book 'Middle of the Packer' and would place these beneath windscreen wipers of cars parked on the roadside or abandoned on grass verges. I would keep back half a dozen in case of emergency or if I spoke to anyone who was remotely interested. I had left a huge wad of flyers with June and Cyril Jones who had kindly volunteered to make inroads into the hundreds of cars that were sure to be parked at South Shields.

I walked with colleagues along the Central dual carriageway somewhat against the flow, similar to salmon battling to swim upstream against the current. Hundreds of competitors were approaching from the opposite direction in a last ditch attempt to deposit their kit on one of the baggage buses. I've known people who have missed the buses to either run the race carrying their bag or alternatively to dump it in a nearby garden and return to collect it later in the day.

To eliminate any such problems and accommodate late comers this year, two tail end baggage buses would leave well after the others. Due to road closures they would take the scenic route arriving in South Shields at 3-30, some three hours after I would have hopefully finished.

We walked alongside the enclosures where runners were already assembling an hour before the start. Those to the rear were for runners with standard white numbers and towards the front they were packed like sardines. Ahead of these were runners with orange numbers who were likely to break 100 minutes. This section was pretty solid too.

There was plenty of room in the green section where several of us would line up. Green numbers are awarded to competitors who have completed ten or more Great North Runs. It is the equivalent of the First Class section on the train or Business Class on the plane. It rewards those who have regularly supported the race and provides for a relatively trouble free start.

Upfront were competitors with red numbers who had completed all 22 GNR's. Ahead of these were the yellow numbers for elite male runners and the blue for elite ladies. Our team mate Karen Ball would line up rubbing shoulders alongside world marathon record holder, Paula Radcliffe. I had voted for Paula in the BBC Sports personality of the year ballot. As winner of both London and Chicago Marathons plus European and Commonwealth titles on the track, Paula was a worthy winner. Wait until we next win the next World Cup before voting for 'Golden-balls' Beckham or the likes.

Many people were making use of the woods at the top of the embankment in order to relieve themselves before the start. When I first came here all those years ago, these trees were merely saplings but had obviously benefited from their annual soaking. Over the fence is the large expanse of Town Moor and beyond Exhibition Park.

I returned to sit on the embankment overlooking the proceedings with John Heap, Ken Denham and Malcolm Marshall. These three are GNR veterans with probably 50 starts between them. We

observed the steady stream of competitors making their way to enclosures further back. Many were running in the colours of mainstream charities, others had donned fancy dress while by far the
most popular outfit was that depicting the two look-alikes in the
adverts for new 118 telephone numbers. Complete with long black
wigs and Zapata moustaches resplendent of David Bedford in his
heyday, people would shout"I've got your number".

B.T. had been under fire because some operators for the 118 500
enquiry number were on a bonus scheme and would either cut
people short or fob them off with any number in order to meet their
quota of calls. B.T. also came under fire from Bedford who hadn't
been approached to copy his likeness. The downside of this however were the constant jibes and abuse that runners would suffer
on the streets. Children and youths would shout, "I've got you're
number" with some adults even getting in on the act too. One runner who stood out from the rest wore a smart suit with his face
painted in an insipid green colour like the 'Incredible Hulk'.. He
featured in one of the BBC highlight programmes the following
day.

Two familiar faces in Paul Sanderson and Peter Mullery came
over and there were handshakes all round. This seemed strange as
I had only seen Paul two days previously but it is one of those nice
touches we runners like to undertake at races. I next saw Paul four
miles into the race when I was walking with a bottle of water and
he had turned as if waiting for a colleague to catch up.

Announcements were being conveyed, records being played and
interviews taking place over the loud speakers as we made our way
into our enclosure. Our numbers were checked on entering the gate
to ensure we were in our rightful place.

The wheel chair competitors were first away to terrific applause
followed by the elite ladies. Regular time checks were given as the
atmosphere and anticipation started to build. The barriers and tape
were removed as we moved forward packing tightly together. Bin
bags were ripped off and tee shirts were jettisoned to the side of the

road as we edged forward. The Dire Straits instrumental number 'Local Hero' blasted out over the loud speakers, while standing on a podium between carriageways, that grand old man of marathon running, Sir Jimmy Saville sent the runners on their long journey.

The alleged 47,000 field included celebrities from stage, screen and the sports world. Football commentators John Motson and Ray Stubbs are regulars here but pundit, Mark Lawrenson was going for the first time. Jockey Richard Dunwoody, reputedly a flyer, rower Matthew Pinsent and Emmerdale actors, Chris Chittell and Tony Audenshaw would be among the many running for charities. Race chairman and founder, Brendan Foster would be going for only the fourth time.

Jane Tomlinson, the remarkable mum fighting terminal cancer would again be running only weeks after completing the tough Half Iron Man triathlon in Dorset. Earlier in 2003 she had cycled from John 'O' Groats to Lands End on a tandem with her brother Luke. May she have a safe journey today.

Despite starting towards the front, early progress was still slow, fraught with runners pushing through from behind or suddenly swerving as they hit an impenetrable wall upfront. Hundreds waved as they passed below the first television gantry, no doubt desperate to get their faces on the box. Through the first underpass, the rapturous chant of Oggy, Oggy, Oggy in years gone by was today only a murmur. I ran to the left hand side of the road over the Tyne Bridge in order to have a glimpse of the river and quayside below. My tactics today would be to take it steadily and then ease back.

Coming off the bridge and turning towards Gateshead, 'The Dinosaurs from Hell' one of several groups that lined the route, belted out a number. They appeared to have far more energy about them than I had today. I started to struggle very early on a warm day and was desperate to reach the first drinks station. I had been climbing the hills well in training but the first stiff test to the Black Bull roundabout really sorted me out today.

That first drink hit the spot but I was ready for the next one beyond six miles at Felling. I stopped to walk with my drink but a friendly tap on the shoulder from a familiar face prompted me to break out into a plod. A welcome downhill and a flat stretch ensued before the big right turn into John Reid Road. On the corner, the superbly named 'Bagdaddies' were playing middle eastern jazz.

This is where the hard work really starts with a long drag to beyond eleven miles. I received welcome encouragement here from Helen, Diane and Michelle who were manning the New Marske drink tables and trying to quench the thirst of the avalanche of competitors now streaming through. Graham Hall, the man with the loud haler called out my name in between the instructions of 'Keep Moving' and 'Drinks on both sides'.

A colleague from Selby Striders drifted effortlessly by enquiring about my state of disrepair and commenting that he had seen me the previous Sunday at Nottingham. "I struggled there and I'm struggling today" was my reply. The day was warm, I had been up for hours, it felt like mid afternoon but it was barely midday. My projected 100 minute finish time was rapidly plummeting towards two hours.

At the King George roundabout, runners cut the corner, not a bad idea under the circumstances. A guy in batman costume glided by effortlessly, milking the applause from the crowd. Small children on the roadside held out their hands in anticipation of a slap but I stayed towards the centre, resolving simply to keep moving forward.

One last pull and the sea beckoned ahead but after all the climbing, the downhill comes in one demoralising section down Coast Road Bank. Enthusiastic spectators spill onto the road as the twelve mile marker emerges around the corner. As badly as I have struggled today I run reasonably well along the final straight mile.

The route profile in the race programme shows this section to be slightly downhill but it doesn't seem that way. The aroma of hot dogs and onions and the sight of the elevated television gantry signify the end is in sight. As I turn onto the short stretch of grass, a sprint is required as I try to break 1 hour and 50 minutes.

The check out funnels are an area of mixed emotions with people either delighted or disappointed in their performance. The relief and the feeling begins to return to weary bodies for a job well done. Last year I spoke to a girl who was set to run in the New York Marathon. Today the man finishing one place ahead of me had completed the Comrades Marathon in South Africa, earlier in the year. I told him of my book 'Middle of the Packer' and gave him a flyer from my shorts pocket.

Clutching my medal, goody bag and space cape, I walked with club mate Dave Bancroft in the direction of the baggage buses. The view as we headed slightly downhill from The Leas is of The Bents with hundreds of cars, buses and caravanettes depicting the enormity of the event. To the right is the sand and the sea with Tynemouth Priory on the headland in the distance.

Dave too was disappointed with his performance but we both optimistically pledged to do better at Bridlington in a couple of weeks time. On reaching the baggage buses, Dave's bus wasn't there but all the bags had been otherwise removed and lined up on the grass. He now had to search through the hundreds of bags to try find his own.

At the serious end of the race, Hendrik Ramaala had won for South Africa in 1 hour and 1 second to stretch the dominance of the race for the African continent to thirteen years. Surely a British man would emerge triumphant before too long. The redoubtable Paula Radcliffe was victorious in the ladies race with a new world best time of 65 minutes and 40 seconds providing the superb crowds with cause for celebration.

Back on the coach there was the usual comparing of times and inquest into the race. Terry and I strolled along the sea front and through the amusements. We purchased a fish at £2-60 eating it out of the paper, always tastier by the seaside. There was no mention as to whether it was haddock or cod but it went down a treat. We called at the Sundial pub for a pint which hardly touched the sides. We had another and with the coach departure still two hours away, yet another.

As more and more runners came in, each with their own individual story to tell, we avoided the temptation to become involved in a session. Instead we meandered between the Sea Road and the sand dunes where hundreds of runners were still making their way from the finish. Mini coaches parked near the Waters Edge pub were waiting to fill up or move into the traffic stream. We made our way back to the coach calling for a coffee and a cake and arriving well in time for the 5-00 'O'clock departure.

But despite all the free time, we inevitably had to wait for a few stragglers who boarded as the coach taxied forward with the driver chomping at the bit. Terry phoned home for the rugby results but there was little luck here with Castleford Tigers and Wakefield Wildcats both soundly beaten.

We left South Shields to join the A19 with unusually very little delay. Organiser Tracey handed out the anticipated quiz papers which held our attention for most of the journey home. Terry and I failed dismally on the antiques questions, clearly no budding David Dickinsons. We fared little better in the next category being unable to decipher which combination of Arthur Askey, Tommy Trinder and Charlie Drake had said "Hello my darlings", "Hello playmates" or "Wakey Wakey".

The coach driver played a blinder in order to avoid a potential traffic jam near Wetherby and we arrived home safely in time for 'Heartbeat'.

A month or so after the race I received my certificate, photographs and glossy magazine. I came 5047 from the 35,307 finishers but failed to dip below 1 hour and 50 minutes. A far cry from the days when I was looking break 90 minutes and with it a place in the first 1,000.

Also enclosed was a priority application form and a firm date for the 2004 race. What the hell, in for a penny, in for a pound, or in this case £27. If I didn't enter now, I would regret it closer to the time and wouldn't be able to bring myself to watch the event on T.V. Twenty on the trot is a nice round number and sounds much better than nineteen. Most impressive!!

CHAPTER 13

Mad About The Guy

APPROACHING THE final couple of miles in the Selby Half Marathon on an unusually hot October day, I had begun to struggle badly. Setting off far too quickly in the warm conditions, I had been unable to sustain my reckless early pace and was now paying the inevitable price. With an outside chance of breaking 1 hour 30 minutes at the half way mark, I would now have all on to beat 1-40.

Mick Mattinson of Kippax Harriers had remarked at the start, that a drop of sun on my back would do me the world of good but I begged to differ. The open, monotonous and straight roads were really starting to take their toll with only the brief interlude of Bishop Wood providing welcome respite and shade from the sun. But there were many around me who were also struggling and despite losing plenty of places, I was still picking up my fare share too.

I spotted one guy who I knew from some distance away and quickly caught up to him. He was one of those irritating runners who although a club member, never bothered to wear his club vest but no doubt still took advantage of the discount offered to such people at most events. I told him to stick at it as I passed by and he returned words of encouragement to me.

Whilst unwinding with a drink at the finish and about to start the usual inquest into the race, the same guy wandered over and asked what time I had finished with. "I just broke 1-40 but had to sprint, how about you" I said. "Oh I didn't finish" he replied"."You didn't finish" I asked surprisingly. "You were in the final mile when I passed you". "Well my heart wasn't in it", he said. "I'd run badly, lost interest and hadn't really wanted a finishing time or position, so I just peeled off before the funnel".

This seemed a strange thing to do but on recollection, I had heard of other people doing this. If they'd had a disappointing run by their own standards and been beaten by no hopers like me, they preferred not to figure in the official list of race results rather than have a poor performance to their name. If I had been so inclined, I could have gladly dropped out of many of the races I'd entered but I still preferred to finish officially, whether I'd run well or not too well.

Some time later, I bumped into the same guy at the Kilburn Seven race in North Yorkshire. His story today was that he had arrived too late to register after having problems with his car. He would nevertheless run the course and use it as a training run. This appeared to be a reasonable excuse and I gave him the benefit of the doubt.

I didn't have too long to wait before I saw him again, in fact the following Wednesday at a local 10K event. As usual he didn't sport club colours but what really stood out was the fact that he wasn't wearing a number. "Haven't you registered yet" I asked, "It's a five minute walk and were pushed for time now". "In all honesty", he replied, "I wasn't going to bother entering, I just intended to jog round. Do you have a problem with that".

"As a matter of fact I do have a problem" I said, "I've paid to enter, so has he, she has and they have too. What would happen if nobody bothered to enter but still ran". Struggling to hold his corner, he replied. "Well they're only awarding tee shirts to the first hundred and I didn't really want one anyway, I've drawers full at home".

But this really only further incensed me and although I am usually fairly placid and try to avoid an argument rather than stand my corner, I wasn't prepared to let this one go. "These guys go to the trouble of organising a race, they mark out a course and people give up their free time to marshal", I snarled, "Yet you can't be bothered to hand over a few quid. You should be ashamed of yourself." I believe I then went on to call him a tight something or other which wasn't a person and on recollection, not particularly nice.

The call to starters orders spared him from more of my wrath and any further insults. So this had been his game all along and he had been rumbled which hadn't really been too difficult to detect. I wondered in how many more races he had wangled a freebie, how many times he had peeled off just short of the finish and why hadn't he been spotted. He may well have been previously spotted and asked to retire or better still, unceremoniously pulled from the course by a steward and deposited in a hedgerow.

As we headed out on the footpath at the start of the two lap course, I was still seething at what he had told me, not the ideal preparation for a race. As we tore around the first lap neck and neck, never more than few yards separating us. I was determined not to let this rogue runner beat me and was running on angry. I pulled away on a long incline but he drew level again on the flat. Then to my astonishment at the beginning of the second lap, he looked across and said. "I'm not going round again, I've had enough, I'll see you later". Whether he'd had enough of the race or enough of me was another matter but I wasn't about to find out.

I settled down on the second lap still running strongly but started to really enjoy the race. The bogus runner had probably done me a favour at least in this race. He may not have wanted a tee shirt but I wasn't going to pass on the opportunity, so running hard on the first circuit had probably elevated me those few places I needed to sneak into the first hundred finishers. The rogue runner could have probably made the top hundred too and won a tee shirt for himself had he been prepared to enter the race legitimately and perhaps more importantly, hadn't lost a friend.

The rogue runner didn't in fact see me later as he had promised. When I arrived back at the car park he had vanished, never to be seen again. Lost to the sport but no loss to the sport!

CHAPTER 14

A Stewards Enquiry

*W*HERE WERE you when England won the World Cup. No, not the great day all those years ago at Wembley Stadium, the Rugby Union equivalent down under in the Autumn of 2003.

I was standing in position along with Roy Young at a godforsaken spot in Pontefract Park, West Yorkshire. We were acting as marshals in the Ackworth & District Schools Cross Country Championships, with only the tea from Roy's flask to keep us warm on a bitterly cold morning.

The early frost had given way to a damp, miserable and murky day with the usual roar of traffic on the busy M62, only a distant hum. The recently opened Xscape Ski Centre which dominates the skyline in the vicinity was barely visible against the grey backdrop.

I had volunteered for duty, believing that England would be on an early plane home after some stuttering performances in earlier rounds. When I left home, the game had just started but after calling for some petrol and listening to the game on the radio, it was half time as I parked up at Pontefract.

England had just scored a try to extend their lead to 14-5 and surely there was no way back now for the Aussies. I discussed the success with Trevor who had parked next to me. "Don't tell me the score" cried Dave Bancroft, "I've recorded the game and don't want to know". Shades of the likely lads who took sanctuary inside a church all those years ago, so as not to hear the outcome of an England football international. "I'd recorded the game too but unlike Dave, I badly needed to know the result.

After discussing pleasantries with various people and exchanging quiz questions with Roger, I walked the half mile or so with Roy to our marshalling positions. An eternity seemed to pass before the first runners were upon us in the Girls U13 race. Flying machine, Jessica Clarke had a hefty lead but further down the field they appeared to be a struggling with some girls alternating between walking and jogging.

Dave may well have had no desire to find out the score but I had. A man of stocky build shrouded in steam with an equally stocky dog at his heel came jogging by. I could see he had earphones and was clutching a small device which could have been a transistor radio. "What's the score" I shouted. "14-8 to England" he replied and so the Aussie fight back had begun.

Next past were the U13 Boys followed by the U15 girls. "The game must be over now" said Roy, "I wonder if they've held on". We'd encountered the same difficulty the previous week while running at Leicester, when England beat France in the semi final. I'd kept asking stewards around the course for the score, but had to wait until 10 miles into the race. A fellow competitor at a drinks station finally confirmed that England had made it into the final.

Our misery was compounded when a boy passing by, told us the score was 14-14 and they were into extra time. The U15 Boys race was more like it with three runners battling it out for first spot. We tried to encourage those further down the field but our efforts were met with mixed responses. "How far is there to go now?" or " We don't have to run all the way around there, do we?".

With the exception of a guy in the distance searching for golf balls, the only people to pass were women walking dogs. One of them was amicable enough but another couple wouldn't make way for the runners despite my polite request. The guy in the undergrowth appeared to find a golf ball which poses the question, why can't the golfers find them. Do they not look or do they just give up too easily. I've found one or two myself while jogging around the perimeter of the Oulton Hall Golf Course. A friend of a relation turned this into a cottage industry by taking them home, washing them and flogging them to the local priest.. Two poachers were reputed to have dredged the lake for golf balls at nightfall.

We tried to cajole a couple of U17 girls to break out into a jog. "Will you run if I run with you" I offered. "Yes" was the reply, so I found myself jogging 400 yards or so alongside them. With four layers of clothing rubbing together, I sounded like Clint Eastwood walking into the shanty town in the opening footage of 'High Plains Drifter'. Once I stopped, they stopped too.

Roy commented on how he had witnessed the demise in fitness or lack of fitness among our youngsters in his role as a Scout Leader. But at least these people had turned up and were having a go.

I asked a man walking two dogs if he new the rugby score. The larger dog, a Labrador bounded across almost bowling me over. "He only wants to play" was the familiar response. "Isn't he grand for two" said the man. "I wouldn't like to see him when he's five", was my reply. He said that he had just come through the car park and thought he probably might have heard somebody say that England had won. What was all that about then, what the hell was going on!

Last up were the U17 Boys who were again well spread out. I told the third runner he was well clear of the next man but alas, there was no next man as he turned out to be the last in a field of only three.

"There's more marshals than runners" claimed another dog walker. "Yes, I thought they were desperate, I could have been at home watching the rugby" I said. "They've won anyway", he replied. "Did you know? It was exciting, a drop goal in the last minute of extra time". I thanked him and immediately life and warmth started to return to my cold and limp frame.

What a great day, a pity our Rugby League counterparts couldn't followed suit later on. Leeds United were stuffed again but at least Ross County held their end up.

The first time I wore the marshals bib was at a Sports Direct Cross Country League fixture hosted by my club Ackworth. For some years I had competed in these fixtures always struggling and usually finishing towards the back of the field. The skipper at the time always emphasised that by just turning up and beating a few runners, I was depriving other clubs of potential points. I suppose that it made sense in the wider scheme of things.

In these type of races, there were people who couldn't hold a light to me on the roads, effortlessly gliding over the surface as I ploughed my way through the mud. Everyone seemed to be able to run down bankings, through streams and up slippery slopes except me.

The final straw came one miserable February morning at a cross country fixture held at Temple Newsam to the east of Leeds. I had already stopped to retrieve a running shoe when it had stuck in the mud and a further water crossing necessitated clambering up a steep banking. I managed to get part of the way up but slipped back down with my feet ending up in the water once again.

I repeated this act several times but to no avail with my knees, chest and chin creating furrows as I started to slide back down. A dozen or so competitors came past before I eventually pulled myself clear re-entering the race covered from head to toe in mud. I hated those narrow spikes worn for cross country and I hated getting my socks dirty.

And so next time I vowed to be the man in the yellow bib, shouting the encouragement rather than making a fool of myself. I was positioned at the foot of a steep slope known locally as Constitution Hill. As the runners approached the bottom, I would send them over a stile and into an adjacent field. I began to wonder why I had arrived so early and made a mental note to bring a book next time.

The time passed quickly enough talking to horse riders, dog walkers or people merely out for a stroll. They were keen to know why the man in yellow was standing in the middle of nowhere. One splendid chap even afforded me a cup of soup from his bottomless flask. I even pulled a lad clear of his quad bike after he

98

managed to overturn it and become trapped underneath. With no bones broken or damage to the bike, he carried on merrily.

The moment I had been waiting for arrived as the race leaders came tearing down the hill towards my position. But as they closed in, a family with a dog were approaching the stile from the other direction. I'd asked them to stay put at least for a couple of minutes until a gap emerged in the runners but the head of the family wouldn't cooperate and chose to cross the stile as the race leader came the other way.

The momentum of the runner sent the man crashing backwards onto the floor and he could only sit on his backside and look up as the next three or four runners narrowly avoided trampling all over him. While this was happening, the family dog appeared to run amok, darting back and forth over the stile and generally impeding runners.

Back on his feet with only his pride hurt, the man didn't appear too impressed as he dusted himself down. In trying to smooth things over, I emphasised that I had warned him and had asked him politely. And so not only was I a useless cross country runner but a bloody awful marshal as well.

Undeterred by this set back, I was posted at the next race on what would be described as a metalled farm road. Runners would join the road from the adjacent field and run along it for fifty yards or so before re-entering another field..

My job would be to direct the runners onto a track while at the same time making the public aware what was happening and stopping any traffic. The first time around, all the runners were past me within ten minutes but on the second circuit, the field become strung out so the road needed to be closed for a longer period.

All appeared to be going well with only the occasional farm vehicle approaching, but each time waiting for a suitable gap in the runners before progressing. So far so good until a souped up Ford Fiesta approached at break neck speed, screeching to a halt as I held my hand up.

The occupants were four baseball cappers listening to the continual boom, boom, boom, emerging from the speakers to no apparent tune." Can you wait here for a few minutes until they start to thin out" I asked. "The driver neither said"You cannot be serious" or "No problem guvnor" instead choosing to look at me vacantly. His jaws chewed hard on gum to the incessant pounding from the speakers. The rear passengers were sprawled over the back of the front seats, wearing smirks as if to say, "What's this wally all about then?"

They waited patiently for all of a minute before the driver nicely negotiated the car in front which had opted to wait, and proceeded to scatter the runners. One or two appeared a little upset judging by the comments and gestures. Not only was I a useless cross country runner but a bloody awful marshal as well.

As a result of this incident and others, the committee decided to display signs on the road for the next event stating 'Race in Progress'. This would surely do the trick.

A year later I found myself at the same spot on a wet, grey, miserable morning. No trouble with cars today, just women on horseback. Asking two riders to wait with the usual story, the more forceful of the two said to my colleague, "Put that umbrella down, it's frightening my horse". "I won't, it's raining" she replied. "Put that umbrella down" said the rider once again. It reminded me of the air raid warden, Hodges, in Dads Army who would repeatedly say, "Get that light out".

Fortunately her colleague saw sense and the two waited patiently, that is until the clever one had had enough and proceeded to plough through the tide of oncoming runners. Not only was I a useless cross country runner but a bloody awful marshal as well.

I was roped into doing a marshalling stint in an evening 10K race organised by my club in the Ackworth and Hemsworth area. The bombshell was dropped upon me at the last minute that I would be responsible for closing and reopening a road. "Am I allowed to do that" I asked as my heart sank into my boots. I was given the written authority from the West Yorkshire Police Traffic Division in the form of a letter in a plastic transparent sleeve. This was in case anyone questioned my authority, doubted my word or was about to lift me up by the lapels and sort me out.

I watched the race start and then I headed along with my sign, my tape and my cones to the designated spot. Another poor sod had been suckered into doing the same thing at the opposite end of the road, Catchpenny Lane, a narrow country lane but a busy thoroughfare and a short cut.

I parked my car on a strategic patch of grass at the crossroads and observed the steady steam of traffic in all directions. I would do well to have a gap sizeable enough to be able to close the road. I attached the Road Closed sign to a sturdy cone and when the time came to close the road, I waited for a suitable lull in the traffic and then planted the cone to stop the traffic entering the lane.

Immediately a guy leaned out of the window of a pick up truck and shouted, "How longs this closed for then?" "Twenty minutes, tops" I replied. I continued to place the other cones across the entrance to the lane but continually had to table the same questions from other drivers. The evening was windy so I had to keep securing the tape and wedge the cones with bricks to stop them moving about.

"I only need to go 100 yards down the lane" said a van driver. "You should be OK, they won't be coming yet" I said. But after letting him through the cordon, he mysteriously completed a U turn and came back out again. I think he was just trying to test my resolve

And at last the runners started to show with our boys, Andrew Jackson and Martin Sanders among the leaders. I encouraged those I knew and others I didn't while still having to justify my actions to impatient motorists. I wouldn't have cared but I was only adding a detour of perhaps two miles and five minutes to their journey times.

As the bulk of the runners had passed and the field started to spread out, a ladies voice from behind me shouted. "How the hell am I expected to get to Featherstone then". I turned around to see an irate looking young woman in a clapped out Escort. "Straight on and turn right, I should think" and with a screech of the tyres and steering wheel and fag both in her right hand, she sped away into the dusk.

Was I glad to see the last of the runners and the rear vehicle pass through so I could at last collect the cones, the tape and the sign and reopen the road again. Not only was I a useless cross country runner but a bloody awful marshal as well.

I've manned drinks stations which can be quite enjoyable, I've marshalled in a car parks and at the thin end of the wedge, I've even been deployed to walk up and down a road to ensure nobody parked illegally to impede the start and finish of the race. I kept popping into a garden where a sale of work was taking place to have a look at the books on offer.

On one of the better days, I was required to stand close to where the model aircraft club were doing their stuff and a nice lady afforded me a drink from her thermos.

Every year at work I would have to take stick from a guy who lived near the sixteen mile point on the Leeds Marathon course. Apparently on race- day morning each year, for several hours he would have difficulty driving his car out of his street and back in again. On this particular year he had desperately needed to use his car but had been prevented from leaving the street for some considerable time by my friends in yellow. He made a point of telling me this several times throughout the day so I suggested that he buy a house away from the course. Obviously unimpressed by this, he had another moan at me in the canteen, to which I replied.. "Oh!, by the way, have you brought my sponsorship money"?

CHAPTER 15

A Year To Forget

STEADY FLOW of patients came in and out of the room but throughout all of this, I remained seated in the passage. Eventually the Cardiologist walked me along a series of corridors and into a lift. "I wouldn't be doing my job if I ignored this" she said, "But it's probably nothing to worry about".

My doctor had sent me for an E.C.G. or heart tracer after I had reported pains to my chest, shoulder and left arm. He hadn't been able to diagnose anything wrong but thought I had better be sure. Several weeks earlier, he had authorised and signed a medical certificate giving me the all clear to run the Medoc Marathon which is apparently a requirement for races in France. How things had turned around for me in such a short space of time.

Once inside the lift, the Cardiologist explained she was taking me to Casualty but couldn't foresee a problem. On arrival I was told to sit on a bed and they would wheel me to wherever they intended me to go."I'm alright, I can walk", I said. "You'll sit on here and do as you're told" was the response.

They wired me up, stuck needles in me and took blood samples. The lady doctor asked if I'd had a heart attack. "Not to my knowledge" I replied, but starting to panic I asked, "Do you mean recently or in the past" The answer wasn't forthcoming and instead she chose to confer with a young male doctor. This had come like a bolt out of the blue and in an attempt to stand my corner, I said. "They're can't be too much wrong with me, I ran in the Wakefield 10K yesterday". At this, the male doctor turned to me. "How long did it take you", he asked. "Forty-five minutes" I replied. At this he turned to the lady doctor and the two nurses present and said. "If he can do

103

1111111111111

10K in forty-five minutes, there's nothing wrong with his heart.

Apparently the E.C.G. scan had shown a slight defect and also my blood sample hadn't come up to expectations in certain criteria. I would have another blood sample taken but would stay in a bed, on a ward until 6-00pm. I spent the afternoon laid in bed and wired up. I was given several drinks and a sandwich. I phoned work to say I wouldn't be in today and would keep them informed of any developments.

The upside of this was that I was able to read numerous copies of 'National Geographical Magazine' and familiarise myself with the Inca Trail in Peru, the Cajun people in the Bayous of Louisiana and a whole host of other interesting topics. The nurse said that she had brought these magazines onto the ward and was glad that somebody had had so much enjoyment out of them.

Throughout this time in the ward, my mind would wander to the words of the lady doctor and her reference to a heart attack. After all, people had been known to suffer heart attacks, not realise at the time and come through relatively unscathed, but surely this couldn't have happened to me. I tried to rack my brains as to when I had felt under the weather or suffered pains in races but nothing stood out.

Six 'O' Clock came and passed with still no word. I was told to allow for a shift changeover and it could be some time before I was spoken to. Other patients were sitting around on beds and in chairs also hoping to be discharged. When at last the Doctor spoke to me, the news wasn't particularly good. The blood sample still didn't conform so I would be kept in the infirmary over the Easter weekend. They would carry out further tests on Tuesday and I would need to do some exercises on a treadmill or a cycling machine.

I challenged this decision by saying I felt well enough to go home and could see no advantage in keeping me in over the weekend. The Doctor reluctantly agreed asking me to take things easily. He said they would call me on Tuesday morning when a bed would be ready and waiting for me in the same ward.

Taking things easy obviously meant I was unable to run so instead I took in a couple of steady walks over the weekend. On the first of these I called for a pint at the Golf Clubhouse and bought an Ice Cream from a vendor in the park. If I couldn't run, this would have to be the next best thing but it would take some getting used to.

Tuesday morning came and there was no phone call. There was still no phone call on Wednesday or Thursday, so on Friday morning I called the infirmary. They had no record of what I was trying to tell them but returned my call to say my records had gone on walkabout. I was asked to return the next Monday for exercises on a treadmill.

These exercises were like food and drink to a man of my calibre. A rather attractive Indian Nurse wired me to a monitor, and as the treadmill stuttered into action, I was asked to walk for three minutes. This was then followed by a slightly brisker walk, again for three minutes, a steady jog and then a slightly faster jog. The line on the graph remained pretty steadfast throughout, with no alarm bells ringing or lights flashing.

While all of this was happening, I was comfortable talking to the doctor and nurse explaining that I had entered the Leeds Half Marathon which started adjacent to the infirmary, in Millennium Square."Well don't build up you're hopes" said the doctor, "You're going to have to wait for the results to be sent to you're G.P." "Can't you tell me anything, I asked". " Afraid not" was the reply.

I changed back into my normal clothes and left the infirmary, but as I was walking back to the car, they were just opening the doors at O'Neil's hostelry. I decided to go in so as to be their first punter of the day. Over a pint, I sat and pondered what the future would hold for me.

I had entered my local race at the weekend, the Rothwell 10K, but would clearly have to give this one a miss. Although not feeling unwell, it would be folly to run after what I had been told. I considered starting at the back of the field and plodding around the course but decided against this. Instead I would walk from home, watch the runners at the five- mile point and from there would make my way back to the finish.

The leaders started to come through followed by people I knew. Some didn't look to be running too quickly and my thoughts were that I would have beaten many of these even though I was well below par. I stood with two other people, we applauded and cheered those we knew and others we didn't and I shouted myself hoarse.

At the finish people asked why I hadn't run and I explained that I hadn't been too well. I had done enough walking for one day and took the opportunity of a lift home. Kevin talked about his team Brentford and I talked about Ross County.

A further couple of weeks elapsed with still no results from the infirmary or phone call from my Doctor. I felt reasonably well so took it upon myself to start jogging again, only very steadily to begin with. A couple of well-wishers phoned to ask about my well being with one of them remarking. "So if you aren't running, there'll be a number going spare for Leeds then? Apart from the fact that race numbers are allegedly non transferable and there is no such thing as a spare number, I wasn't giving mine up for anybody. This comment just stiffened my resolve and made me all the more determined to run the Leeds Half Marathon come what may.

With still no word of my tests on the tread mill, wishing to speed up matters, I phoned the infirmary but once again it appeared that my records were not readily to hand. I was put through to the consultant's secretary and an appointment was made for me to see him in two weeks time. I was only too glad to make the start line at Leeds. Since I started running in 1983, I had only missed out on this fixture once and wasn't about to start now. I deliberately arrived late, fortunately finding a good parking space. The day was warm, I wasn't particularly up for the challenge and at the back of my mind couldn't help thinking I was being foolish. I jogged to the start, joining the race towards the back a minute or so before start time.

The worst scenario was that this race could be my last so I was determined to take it easy, enjoy the day and finish comfortably. With this in mind, I ran well below eight minutes apiece for the first couple of miles. The arduous drag up Stonegate Road tested my resolve and once beyond the brow of the hill, took me some time to recover. The conditions became hotter with the occasional shower but not too uncomfortable and fortunately I finished with no discomfort. Starting at the rear had enabled me to pass people throughout the race and this had added to my enjoyment and feel good factor. Although unspectacular, my finishing time of 1 hour 47 minutes had provided a finishing position of 711 from 1994. I could only hope that my infirmary results were as favourable.

Leeds in fact wouldn't be my last race as the Sunday after, I ran the Sandal Castle 10K on a bright and breezy morning and the following Wednesday, the Askern 10K. This race was in our club Grand Prix fixture list but rather than run for points, I ran mainly to keep in touch with club colleagues and friends. The heavens opened with rain belting down for most of the race, leaving large pools of standing water on the course. The evening ended with a bar meal along with the usual pleasant banter.

My interview with Mr Williams, the consultant was both positive and successful. He had been unable to diagnose anything wrong with my condition but would like to monitor my situation. To do this, he would need to send me for an X ray, Heart Scan and Angiogram. He thought the pains to my chest, arm and shoulder must be down to stress.

For the last two years my Mum had needed regular visits to the doctor, infirmary and optician with her conditions not particularly improving. A stroke had left one eye blind and had obviously reduced her mobility. Other complaints such as Asthma and Arthritis, left her needing a fair amount of support. I was left having to call in favours at work in order to take time off to run her about. While this may have brought about a fair amount of worry, I looked towards the actual job which was in itself becoming pretty stressful.

My department at work had recently been required to report directly to Head Office, some 200 miles away in Chelmsford, rather than to the Senior Managers on site where I worked. While this operated well at first, an us and them mentality soon developed which in itself posed problems. Factory team leaders soon shifted the blame onto my department in justifying poor output or line performance. The production plan was in the wrong sequence, time hadn't been built in for a changeover, no time allowed to washout the machinery, the materials weren't available, the cartons hadn't been brought to the line. A whole load of excuses surfaced that could deflect the blame away from the Factory, towards my department and inevitably towards me.

My new boss from Chelmsford would spend a couple of days a week at Leeds with his part piece being to call us on his mobile to advise of his impending arrival, just as he was walking down the car park. This would inevitably lead to cries of 'He's here', as we rushed around in those final minutes to get everything shipshape.

Our bosses at Chelmsford changed on several occasions without any real benefit being seen or achieved, the backing we received appeared to be structured so as to appease all parties and at times I felt out on a limb. It got to the stage when driving into work, I would be wondering what problems and issues would be awaiting me. Would there be any messages at the security box, would anyone stop me before I reached the office, would there be a deputation waiting at my desk, how many E. Mails would I need to answer. It all seemed rather funny at first but later I became paranoid about the situation.

I welcomed the news that my boss at Leeds had been promoted internally but with other changes afoot and positions up for grabs, I was given little encouragement to apply for them. The thirty-three years of loyalty I had built appeared to count for nothing so I decided to apply for early retirement from when I reached my fiftieth birthday and find a less stressful job or some part time employment.

I had really been looking forward to the Sheffield Half Marathon especially after the favourable response from the infirmary. But I overindulged at a wedding on the Friday, a short run on Saturday morning was disastrous and I carried this form over into the race on Sunday. In the past, the Sheffield races have usually been blessed with glorious weather and today was no exception. The conditions were hot and humid, I never felt comfortable and struggled all of the way but still enjoyed the finish on the track inside the Don Valley Stadium.

The course through former steelworks, industrial units and parts of the city has niggling climbs rather than tough hills. I was well up in the large field but my time of 1 hour 51 minutes was nevertheless disappointing. I decided there and then that a Marathon was beyond my capabilities at least for the time being.

I returned my acceptance slip to the Medoc Marathon with an explanatory letter to say why I couldn't compete but two letters later and in fact to this day I have still received no recompense. More importantly I had entered the Edinburgh Marathon in mid June and I clearly would be in no shape to run this one either. The officials there were more understanding and allowed me to carry my entry over into 2004, needless to say, I still didn't use it then.

With accommodation booked for Edinburgh, I looked for an alternative shorter race during the same weekend. I travelled to Edinburgh, visited Leith on the water-front and walked back into Edinburgh following the pleasant path alongside the Water of Leith. I enjoyed a couple of pints and fish and chips on Saturday evening at North Queensferry, overlooking the Firth of Forth.

Leaving my hotel on Sunday morning for Waverley Station, I observed a trickle of lycra-clad and track suited runners heading for the start of the Edinburgh Marathon at Meadowbank Stadium. I should have been going along with them but instead had chosen to head across the water to Fife for the Raytheon Glenrothes 10K. I had searched bus and rail timetables to find a way of reaching the venue in time for the race.

I caught the Aberdeen train from Waverley crossing the Forth Bridge, worth the price of the ticket alone and then hugging the Fife coastline to Kirkaldy. A half hour bus journey followed by a two mile dash in a taxi saw me arrive safely at the Fife Sports Institute in time to register for the race. Registration and baggage storage was in one of the large sports halls with the race starting and finishing on the outdoor track.

Glenrothes is a New Town or 'Dormitory Town' of which there are many in Scotland with Cumbernauld and East Kilbride being prime examples. The houses were much of a much ness, set out on tree lined new roads with grass verges and communal lawns. The course followed these roads with some sections negotiated twice and others being out and back. There were some gentle gradients but nothing too savage.

With little pressure on me to do well and with conditions rather stifling, I would have looked to complete in around the 50 minute mark. Starting cautiously and building up a head of steam as I progressed, I was delighted to come away with 46 minutes. The race and accompanying 5K finished on the outdoor track to the applause of a sizeable contingent. Despite the course being unspectacular, the officials and marshals were an enthusiastic bunch and there was a feel good factor about the race.

Whilst changing back inside the sports hall, I put my foot in my mouth when saying to the guy next to me, "How did you do, you look like a sub 40 minute man" to which he replied. "I ran 32 minutes, I was the race winner" After handshakes all round, I went from where I came, arriving back in Edinburgh for a well earned bar meal and a pint. Runners were walking the streets carrying goody bags from the marathon, some even wearing their race tee shirts and medals. Why hadn't I done this I thought, but on reflection had probably made the correct decision.

I attended Mass on Sunday evening, always nice to visit a service in a different city away from home and see how they conduct their business. There was a large congregation and rather than the traditional hymns, the choir sang to the musical accompaniment of guitars and woodwind instruments. The priest made a reference in his opening address to the Edinburgh Marathon and I noticed a couple of people go down to communion in race tee shirts.

I met a friend John, for a pint or two in Grass-Market. Here six pubs with diverse names such as Biddy Mulligans and the Last Drop sit comfortably alongside restaurants and delicatessens. We compared notes of our respective days, John having run the marathon and saying it was bloody hot!

The day before my Angiogram in July, I ran the Kilburn 7 in North Yorkshire in customarily hot conditions. The first two miles went well but things would go rapidly downhill from there and I would struggle for most of the way. The course through Coxwold and Bylands Abbey is one of the more scenic, as it twists and turns through the Hambleton Hills close to the famous 'White Horse' on the hillside.

The shandy and pork roast sandwich outside the Forresters Arms seemed to be like the last supper as I had become somewhat paranoid about my Angiogram. I had received literature from the infirmary about the procedure but had even found it something of ordeal to shave around my groin.

At the end of the day there had been nothing to unduly worry about apart from my nether regions being a bit sore. I was first man on from the three who were waiting which suited me fine. The other two were much older and had their wives to provide support. The medical team were excellent and I was told there and then that nothing was wrong having no blocked or narrowed arteries. There was no pain as such with the procedure, just minor irritation. At one time, the dye that was pumped around my arteries caused me to hot flush which is apparently normal.

I lay on a bed until the bleeding to the incision had stopped and I read a magazine. The other two patients were wheeled in and out and as I left the ward, I wished them both the best of luck. No pint in O'Neil's today, just a taxi straight home and a lazy couple of days.

The following week I attended a heart scan followed by an X ray on my shoulder and arm. The results of these weren't as conclusive and once again I ended up ringing around and chasing up the results.

I was soon up and running again, entering the Yorkshire Heartbeat Run from South Leeds Stadium through Middleton Woods. Predominantly a shorter race for business teams, the course is a killer. I was pleased to complete the four mile course in around half an hour but felt awful for the rest of the evening.

However my running would hit an all time low over the next few weeks when I felt to be running on empty and had little to offer. On another stifling evening, I ran the Millennium Bridge 5K at York in a shade under 24 minutes finishing last of twelve runners from my club. Two weeks later I ran the Multi-Terrain race organised by my club Ackworth Road Runners and finished 32nd from 43. In my diary I wrote, 'From the first mile, a procession of runners who I would normally hope to beat drifted by effortlessly. I gave my all but there was nothing in the tank. I worked hard up Constitution Hill but ended up walking. I felt drained, unwell and ashamed. With so many races to do and places to go, I must strive for a significant improvement'. I would use these two races, the Millennium Bridge and the Ackworth Multi-Terrain as benchmarks and see how significantly I could improve on them in future years.

I was eventually discharged from hospital, which was a huge relief, but not before having to track down my results and follow the paper trail. Chasing around the different departments and trying to speak to various people shouldn't have been my job and in itself proved to be pretty stressful. Anyone sitting in the waiting area or along a corridor of any hospital can't fail to notice staff on the move carrying files or paperwork, people crisscrossing with files in their hand, people exchanging files and even porters pushing trolleys full of files. Almost everyone is carrying a file. Is there little wonder that documents and files go missing.

I took early retirement slipping away almost unnoticed under the shadow of darkness without too much hype and razzmatazz. My intention was to have some time out and then look for one or two small part time jobs. With Mum's continued illness, these plans failed to materialise, however I was on hand for any doctors visits or hospital appointments she required.

Initially, I could have become quite used to daytime television. I watched Cash in the Attic, Bargain Hunt, Car Bootie and Flog It, becoming something of an expert on antiques and junk. I watched Egg Heads, Beat the Nation and Fifteen to One. I could have been or rather I was hooked on Countdown. I don't know how I found time to work for all those years.

My running at first didn't improve although I was able to get out more during the day using routes that were normally reserved for lighter nights or weekends. I ran a shocker at the Great North Run and performed little better at the Guy Fawkes Ten from Ripley Castle. The day was remembered more for the bar meal at the Union Inn on the journey home.

I did manage to make the start line at the Leicester Marathon in November to maintain my record of at least a marathon a year since 1983. The day was cold with the start delayed due to cars unable to get into the Mallory Park venue. We put out flyers for my first book 'Middle of the Packer' and unable to get a tea, listened to the first half of France v England in the Rugby World Cup Semi Final. Although England were losing at half time it was a formality they would win with an apparent gale force wind at their backs in the second half.

The race went nowhere near Leicester instead concentrating on hilly and undulating country lanes near the Mallory Park circuit. This disappointed me as I had quite fancied running along Leicester's Golden Mile. I seemed to spend most of the first half of the race trying to find out the final score in the rugby match. Roy and I ran together for fifteen miles but when he left me, I struggled all the way finishing rather disappointingly in a shade over four hours.

My belated improvement eventually came in December with a promising run at the Guy's Ten near Preston on a bright and crisp morning, my best performance for several years. I carried this form into the next couple of races gaining in confidence all the time. I got myself a shorter more meaningful haircut and was ready for anything that 2004 could throw at me.

CHAPTER 16

A Christmas Cracker

As we awaited the arrival of the coach at the usual pick up point outside Pontefract Bus Station, a taxi pulled up and two middle aged couples emerged along with suit cases and considerable hand luggage. "We're going to Benidorm" said one of the men, "Where are you going". "Loftus" replied Les. Would we have swapped places with these people?, Of course we wouldn't.

This would be my ninth Loftus Poultry Run and likewise for some of my colleagues. It had become something of a must do event on the club calendar as well as an excuse for a Christmas fuddle. There would be those among us who would be running here for the first time and could look forward to becoming hooked on this unique event, just as many of us had done over the years.

We were warm and cosy inside the coach but weren't kidding ourselves. The heavy rain of the previous days had given way to a biting northerly wind which would no doubt impact upon the race. If we had taken notice of the weather forecast for gales and snow showers, we wouldn't have even left Pontefract. Looking out of the coach window as we left the A19, I didn't relish the challenge ahead.

The River Leven roared below the quaint bridges alongside the main street in Great Ayton. The imposing peak, Roseberry Topping overlooks the village and dominates the countryside with it's distinctive profile. A young James Cook moved here from nearby Marton when his father secured the position as a farmhand.

The Cleveland Hills were rife with folk lore in those days and every village supposedly had a witch like Nanny Howe of Kildale. These people were held in great fear by the many law abiding citizens and peaceful folk.

The sea came into view beyond Brotton and looked non too inviting. The road followed the railway line that closed in the Beeching era but reopened more recently to service the Boulby Potash Mine. Negotiating the sharp hairpin bends near the former Skinningrove Iron Works, the coach stuttered up the steep bank to Loftus.

It hardly seemed a year ago that we had to send out a search party for two of our members, who not too impressed with the catering arrangements had set out in search of their own Sunday lunch.

The Poultry Run would be the first race of a Christmas treble in which I had somehow been cajoled into taking part. On Boxing Day I would run the Chevin Chase at Guisley with the Hot Toddy Race at Todmorden, a few days later.

There was a Christmas feel about the event with some runners taking to fancy dress and many wearing Santa hats. One guy dressed as a clown was continually blowing a hooter while at the same time collecting money in a bucket for charity. If he were to run with the bucket, there would be few donations around this isolated course.

After a steady warm up around the muddy field, adjacent to the Leisure Centre, I felt the brunt of the bitterly cold northerly and decided to go back inside for a woolly hat and gloves. Les, wearing four layers of clothing himself, immediately chastised me for being soft and started to take the micky. As usual, I opted to run in shorts to give my knees some fresh air and to let the girls see my gorgeous legs.

Two guys in our party who were running here for the first time asked about the severity of the course. I told them to take it steady to begin with, as much from the point of view of me being able to keep up, rather than for them to conserve energy.

A sizeable field of around 400 assembled on Deepdale Road and barely ten minutes later, we were being pushed nicely by the stiff breeze up the many niggling inclines onto the moorland road.

After 20 minutes, we turned onto the first off road section beyond a row of remote stone cottages and along a muddy track. These cottages appeared to have been recently renovated with two of them displaying 'For Sale' signs. What an idyllic moorland re-treat, I thought, with just a hint of a sea view. They would need to be well insulated in this exposed spot as the image of Ted Moult sprung to mind, holding up a feather in the old double glazing ad-vert. Probably a little out of the way though with a long walk back from the pub and all uphill.

There was a raised section at each side of the track created by a tractor and trailer and this is where most people ran. Others took the lower, muddier route while some ran in the adjacent field.

The track runs away from the coast and is predominantly down-hill with views towards the North York Moors. The only views I had were of the ground as I slipped on the muddy surface and staggered for what seemed a lifetime but somehow correcting my-self and remaining on my feet. I ended up running in the field with many more and this is where I stayed until we joined the main road at Easington when my shoes felt like lead weights. Scraping the soles as I ran to loosen the considerable amount of mud, I began to run more comfortably once again.

I noticed a signpost to Grinkle which I hadn't seen on my pre-vious forays here. I recently read in the Business Pages of a Daily that the under fire directors of a FTSE 100 company had used The Grinkle Park Hotel for their own pleasure, whatever that had been. Consequently they had received a rough ride at the company AGM for their misdemeanours.

The coast road brought welcome respite from the muddy tracks and for once, I found myself pressing along quite nicely overtak-ing several runners in the bargain. The Middlesborough bus which usually passes at this point didn't disappoint today, being bang on time once again.

The land falls away steeply towards Boulby Potash Mine and be-yond, nestling between huge craggy cliffs, the sea washed cottages of Staithes. Towering white pillars of foam raced towards the shore bringing back fond memories of school camp in Staithes when I was ten or eleven years old.

Suddenly there seemed to be fewer runners ahead with clear road beyond. This was because we were being directed up a banking and through a gap in the hedge. This lead to what can only be described as a muddy gully with running water as nuisance value. If you didn't feel the need to walk at first, you soon would due to slower competitors ahead blocking the path.

A gateway brought a wider field with runners now choosing their own particular line, either up the muddy track or in the adjacent field to secure the firmer footing. I chose to run wide in the field but I was conscious of the perpetual chatter of the man dressed as the clown behind me, punctuated with regular blasts on his hooter. He must have been a useful runner to talk his way around this arduous course while acting the clown at the same time although he seemed to have dispensed with his bucket. It appeared to be all too easy for him.

A couple of gates through a farmyard saw everyone squeeze together once again before a left turn onto the road at the highest point on the course. Looking forward to some well overdue downhill, I was immediately faced with a testing little climb to the communications mast. The icy headwind was strong and my decision to wear hat and gloves proved to be fully justified. Loftus recorded the highest wind speed of 71 mph on one of those gusty winter days which was not surprising.

The rugged coastline came into view on elevated sections of the course with the industrial skyline of Teeside in the distance. The going was tough but for once I was up for the challenge and appeared to have all the answers in my armoury. I dipped my head to combat the ferocious wind and pumped hard to gain momentum up the many niggling climbs.

A girl making light of the conditions and seemingly without a care in the world asked me how far to go. For some inexplicable reason I said twenty minutes rather than stating the distance in miles. Shear hard work and determination kept me slightly ahead of her and the clown, but she eventually drew level and glancing across said, "Not far now".

She wasn't wrong of course and a furious descent down Hummersea Lane and further downhill sections provided the opportunity to pick up the pace through the urban streets. I agonisingly missed an hour but was three minutes quicker than 2003, not bad for an old un!

Ready and changed in the sanctuary of the Leisure Centre, the faster runners in our midst awaited the prize giving. Some not content with running 8 miles made use of the indoor pool while others took refuge in adjacent hostelry ,'The Mars Inn'. I chose none of these options, instead joining the driver back on the coach where he afforded me a generous measure of coffee from his flask.

This just hit the spot before the formidable helping of Shepherds Pie, courtesy of Cheryl at The Britannia, where our fortunes were discussed over a few pints. We bid a hasty retreat when a blanket of snow threatened to engulf the pub and our coach, but promised to return again next year. Who would bet against it?

I opened the bedroom curtains on Boxing Day morning to a grey forbidding sky, unlike last year when torrential rain gave me an easy excuse not to run in The Chevin Chase. I pretended to leave it until the last minute should the rain show any sign of abating, but in truth, I hadn't really fancied ploughing through forest trails over my ankles in mud.

But today would be different as I was looking forward to 'The Chase' with some enthusiasm. I was in a rich seam of form at least for a 'Middle of the Packer' and was raring to go.

I parked in the vast William Morrison car park and completed final preparations, secured my number and vaselined in the car. Trying to cross the busy A65 to Aireborough Leisure Centre proved problematical no doubt bolstered by race traffic. When a suitable gap emerged and I stepped off the pavement, I was almost ploughed down by a car coming the wrong way off the nearby roundabout. The near miss got the adrenalin flowing and my heart pumping before the start of the race.

I had run here half a dozen times previously but had entered and chickened out on a further couple occasions. When posting application forms in early December, it seems like a great idea to run a race on Boxing Day morning. Unfortunately it doesn't always capture the imagination nor is met with the same enthusiasm come the day.

The distance from the Leisure Centre to the start provides the opportunity for a gentle jog to make sure all parts are functioning after the previous days indulgences. On these such warm ups, one can usually tell if they feel good or feel sluggish and if they are going to go well or struggle. Today was no exception but fortunately I was running easily and should have no problems.

Runners had assembled tightly on Moorland Avenue and banter was light hearted with compliments of the season and well wishes being exchanged. People were already making their customary excuses with no one apparently up for the task ahead. Much of this would be subterfuge of course and once underway they would forget about what had been said and probably be well up for it. Once again, there were many fancy dressers, fairies and Santa's with the usual array of good club athletes. I was mindful not to stand too far forward but not too far back either as there would surely be the usual influx of late arrivals pushing towards the front.

Early progress was slow up Carlton Lane with patience being the virtue. One runner finding himself too far back was having none of this as he systematically worked his way through the field using his elbows and forearms to remove anyone in his path. The offending runner unusually had socks pulled up, wore khaki shorts and had the look of a squaddie. He clearly had no race etiquette or regard for his fellow competitors. One man none too impressed with these tactics protested but was just met with a cold stare.

My reaction was that I wouldn't let this fellow beat me, but after keeping him in my sight for some time, he proved even too good and too strong for a man of my calibre. My wish was that he would push his way through once too often and on reaching the moorland tracks, a couple of heavies would unceremoniously despatch him into the undergrowth. I hadn't seen this guy previously on the local race circuit and fortunately haven't seen him since.

Despite being unable to stay with the squaddie I was nevertheless moving quite nicely and took the first hill in my stride. After the first of approximately seven miles, a left turn signifies the first off road section in the shape of a muddy track. It may have started the day as a firm track but by the time three hundred pairs of feet had run along here, it was certainly muddy. I moved from one side of the track to the other in order to secure the firmer footing and definitely wouldn't keep my socks clean today.

We ran adjacent to the grounds of The Chevin Lodge Hotel where a bunch of hapless work colleagues played hide and seek on a team building day. On a separate occasion, I had attended a firms presentation evening there and a row had erupted as to who would take home our award. My boss instructed me to look after the trophy but I let another guy have it when the beer started talking and he threw a tantrum saying he had done more than I had in helping us achieve it. Another workmate who had been nominated to make a speech had one drink too many in order to summon Dutch courage and was found slumped in the little boys room tightly clutching onto the piece of paper on which his speech was written.

The road crossing on Yorkgate was completed to the applause of a sizeable and supportive crowd before we embarked upon the rocky descent onto the first of the Chevin's trails.

Still running well, I completed the testing climb beyond two miles onto the Danefield Estate where more spectators made themselves heard. The undulating tracks were pretty firm underfoot, unlike a couple of years ago when I lost my footing on the icy ground and was dumped on my backside. The path twisted and turned around huge rocks and over wooden bridges spanning deep gorges. From time to time between the closely planted trees, there were stunning views over Otley and Lower Wharfedale. I hadn't time to take in the views today but promised myself a walk or a slow training run on this part of the course in the summer.

Two men in black and white spotted jump suits eased past with tongues hanging out as part of a team of 101 Dalmatians. We passed remote foresters cabins and farm buildings before another nasty climb, first onto the main road and then onto The Dales Way footpath.

The narrow path here clings to the hillside with more fine views over the valley, when I could afford to look up rather than constantly watch my footing.

A sharp left turn up a steep wooded path increases the pressure and increases the pain in my knees. Almost everyone resorts to a walk but a man and a dog at his heel both manage to somehow keep moving forward.

A wall of noise hits us as we dig in for the final pull, leaving the woodland behind and entering daylight. Spectators stand shoulder to shoulder on each side of a paved pathway for 200 yards or more. I work hard to keep going but feel like 'Dead Man Jogging'. I pick out no one in particular in the crowd as I struggle to see for the bright glare with all the faces merging into one.

There are cries of encouragement for the runners in general but amidst all of the noise, I pick out a "Go on Ackworth" and a "Well done Andy" so somebody obviously loves me. We negotiate cones and tape in the car park where spectators are still solid." Is this the finish" asks a girl alongside. "Sorry, still two miles to go but mostly downhill".

For many of the spectators, like many of the runners, this race has become an annual ritual. A brisk walk on the moors is just the ticket to blow away the cobwebs and to make room for more Christmas fayre on returning home.

A hole in the wall near The Royalty pub on Yorkgate leads into a tufty field which quickly churns into a muddy field where cows graze at an uncomfortable distance. The guy behind me appears to be grunting and groaning but then I realise he is doing this in tandem with nearby gunfire, appearing as if shot with each round. A sense of humour is always an advantage in these races.

The panoramic views from the next field are across Airedale towards Shipley with Bradford beyond. A queue has formed to negotiate steps over the wall at the bottom of the field and marshals warn us to be careful on the far side. I lose valuable time here but at least have a few seconds to catch my breath.

As the next stony track eventually turns downhill I summon more effort, pick up the pace nicely through Moor Farm and into Moor Lane. I really go for it on the final road section but there is a sting in the tail in the form of a nasty little incline but my efforts are rewarded as I just manage to break the hour mark.

The Chevin Chase takes my vote as race of the year in West Yorkshire. A good course with panoramic views, good quality tee shirt with a nice design and the best spectator support around.

I had never visited Todmorden but as a teenager had cause to pass through the town on the slow train from Manchester to Leeds. At the time I was taking 'O' Level Examinations but on a free day had gone to Old Trafford with my mum to see England take on the West Indies. We stayed until almost close of play in anticipation of seeing Geoffrey Boycott reach another century.

Missing the express, we caught the slow train home stopping at every station and as we entered the steep valley towards Todmorden, the shadows were lengthening.

Large as life in a field at the side of the track stood a large silver dome shaped cylindrical object which glistened in the evening sun. A glimpse was all we were afforded before the object disappeared out of view behind trees as the train headed into a cutting. As the years have passed, certain events have made me wonder if what we saw that day was actually a flying saucer.

Policeman, Alan Godfrey was on early morning patrol in Autumn 1980, and came across what he believed to be an overturned bus blocking the road. On driving closer he saw a diamond shaped object perhaps 20' wide and 14' high, hovering above the ground. There were banks of windows in which he could see the reflection of the panda car's blue light and the lower section of the object was rotating. All around, he could see the bushes and trees blowing.

With his radio failing, he suddenly found himself 100 yards further along the road and the craft had vanished. On returning to the scene with a colleague, they noticed this area of the road to be dry in contrast to being wet elsewhere. He was obviously very frightened and realised he had suffered a peculiar time lapse.

After this incident, he was apparently asked to sign official documents, keep quiet and disassociate himself from any person interested in UFO's.

Another incident involved the disappearance of a man who had gone out to a local shop near Morley on Saturday tea time. He never returned home but was discovered several days later in a builders yard in Todmorden, with scorch or burn marks to his body that couldn't be identified. To the knowledge of anyone in his family, he had never been to Todmorden, had no business in the area and knew nobody there.

This corner of West Yorkshire has remained a hotbed for UFO sightings with a wave of reports alone in the winter of 1980. A herd of cows were mysteriously relocated to another field with no hoof marks to indicate passage. A truck driver reported being abducted by aliens while a night fisherman witnessed a space craft emerge from a reservoir before taking off. Rumour has it however, that he was worse the wear for drink.

Another bitterly cold day beckoned as we headed along the M62 before taking the main road through the mill towns of Sowerby Bridge and Hebden Bridge in the Calder Valley. The railway track, river and canal all follow the tight valley floor with weavers cottages of local stone perched precariously on the steep hillsides.

Roy must have been bored stiff as I pointed out places of interest such as the ground where we were stuffed at football by Luddendenfoot when I was in my prime and the field at Hebden

Bridge where I scored a blinder. I played so well that day that for the one and only time in my football days, an official from the home town club tried to poach me. I remember telling him that I didn't play as well as this every week.

We parked at the railway station just as the express train belted past. I once again dressed to combat the cold before handing out flyers for the Ackworth Half Marathon and securing others behind windscreen wipers of parked cars. I wondered how many people would take up the challenge and how many forms would end up in the bin.

We made our way down the steep flight of steps to The White Hart, the headquarters for the 'Hot Toddy Race'. On the forecourt outside the pub, they appeared to be doing a roaring trade selling sportswear from baskets. Upstairs was a hive of activity with runners registering for the race, collecting numbers, or clustering in small groups to drink tea.

The fun run appeared to be a low key affair as the youngsters set off along the station car park and down the ramp. The main race started alongside the Rochdale Canal, only 8' wide here and used by narrowboats and pleasure craft.

Competitors were limbering up and doing their own particular routines or simply waiting for the race to start. Roy and I jogged along the tow path mainly to kill the time and to stay warm. Once again I had chosen to wear a woolly hat and gloves but unlike the previous two festive races, I felt heavy legged and not up for the challenge ahead.

Stuart Anderson, a regular on the West Yorkshire race scene turned up late with his ready made excuse of having forgotten his running shoes. Quite by chance he happened to have an old pair in the boot of his car. These must have been go faster shoes as Stuart forged ahead of us and remained there throughout the race.

Apart from Stuart, I didn't see many familiar faces here. I spoke to Sue Nuttall of Halifax Ladies while three girls from Royton Runners kept distracting me as they completed their impressive warm up routines.

As usual, the race started at breakneck speed, heading along Rochdale Road towards Walsden. The road stayed close to the canal on the left hand side with the railway viaduct to the right. The outlook was of shops, small businesses and mills with Todmorden at one time being the centre of the countries cotton manufacturing industry.

John Fielden, a former woollen clothier converted three cottages in 1782 and his sons built the business into the biggest cotton manufactures in the world. They were at the forefront of workers rights introducing factory legislation and the ten hour day.

For a relatively small town on the West Yorkshire and Lancashire border, Todmorden boasts two Nobel prize winners. Sir John Douglas Cockcroft won the prize for Physics in 1951 and Sir Geoffrey Wilkinson picked up the Chemistry award in 1973. More recently, Todmorden hit the national headlines as a former practice of serial killer, Doctor Harold Shipman.

I chatted to Roy as we ran along but with little spring in my step clearly wouldn't repeat the exploits of my last two races. A left turn at Walsden signified the start of the climbing on Hollins Lane and immediately one of the Royton girls, clearly struggling resorted to a brisk walk.

The lane climbed between mill cottages until it eventually became a moorland road flanked by dry stone walls. Although not severe, the climb was long and arduous with the brow of each rise bringing with it a further pull. A fellow competitor alternated between walking and running and when I provided words of encouragement, his ready made excuse was that he had only decided to enter on the morning of the race.

The Shepherds Rest pub signified the end of the climbing and the start of some useful down-hills. When I chose to look up, there were excellent views of Stoodley Pike Peace Memorial erected in 1814 to commemorate the surrender of Paris to the allies. Rebuilt in 1854 following it's collapse, the memorial dominates the valley and the surrounding countryside.

On one of the narrow steep descents, I had to squeeze in to the side of the road to let a car pass by. I shouted to the runner ahead 'Big Steve', well that's what it said on the back of his vest, to move in and let the car pass. As I drew level with Steve he insisted that cars had no right to come down here while the race was in progress and this one would have to wait.

With all the down hills completed, the final half mile followed the main road along the valley bottom back into town. I managed to pick up a few places on this section but 'Big Steve' thundered past me in the final run in and was waiting to shake my hand at the finish.

Upstairs at The White Hart, the promised Hot Toddy hit the mark bringing a warm glow to all parts. A fitting end to my racing for 2003 in a nice corner of West Yorkshire. We trudged wearily back to the car, declining the offer to take part in The Auld Lang Syne Race at Haworth on New Years Eve. Well maybe next year.

CHAPTER 17

Trains And Trucks And Tugs

"THERE'S ANOTHER one ahead" was the cry as the bodies manoeuvred and the heads leaned forward in order to gain the best possible view. As the mini bus drew level with the giant tractor and trailer and eventually pulled ahead, all the heads turned in unison. "Catherine Anne" said Kevin, proud as punch, reciting the name emblazoned above the grill and below the windscreen on the truck.

This was one way of breaking the monotony on long journeys to and from races, usually in the North of England, and was known as 'Eddie Spotting'. In the early nineties, my firm decided to dispense with the services of a number of small but reliable haulage firms in favour of a couple of national firms, one of these being Eddie Stobart originally based in Carlisle.

Their vehicles became commonplace in our yard, and the girls names they sported were something of a novelty. Eventually I began to remember these and even started making a list. My visits to the yard office and walks around the site perimeter increased as my list started to build. Names ranged from the basic to the exotic to the hyphenated. From Sally to Genevieve to Donna- Marie. From the older to the modern, from Jane to Jade.

At that time, the Stobart fleet numbered three hundred or thereabouts with each vehicle displaying a girls name on the cab. Drivers had to be smart in uniform and were required to wear a tie at all times. They were expected to be polite both on the roads and at the point of collection or delivery.

There was even a Stobart's fan club and members were supplied with lists containing vehicle names, updates and the opportunity to choose names for new vehicles. Stickers, model vehicles and other memorabilia was and still is available.

This all started on a trip to the Great North Run when I happened to glance around as the coach overtook an Eddie Stobart vehicle. I said to Kevin, seated next to me, "Mary Elizabeth". "Do they have names" he asked. He was quickly on the lookout for names and as the word spread, others also got in on the act.

Whenever we ventured to races by car or by coach, a buzz of anticipation presided whenever the cream, green and red livery of a Stobart vehicle was spotted. We wouldn't always spot the names of vehicles travelling on the opposite carriageway but more often than not we did.

The same vehicles worked similar routes, some became well known, so it was even possible to take a guess at their names. My list numbered ninety and was still growing. In the pursuit for more names I would plan evening runs around Industrial Estates where Stobart's would possibly be queuing to enter premises or be parked up overnight.

I would run past Goods Yards and Trailer Parks, through the Freightliner Terminal and by Haulage Firms. I have run through Motorway Service Areas, clambered up walls and even had a leg up to look over a fence when the tell tale headboard of 'Barbara Ann' was spotted. On early morning runs I would hesitate on footbridges spanning by-passes and motorways and as the traffic approaching Leeds regularly ground to a halt, I would scan the carriageway below for any sign of approaching Stobart's. When the haulage companies organised a drive slow on the M1 close to home in protest against the escalating fuel prices, I was there on the lookout and was apparently seen on the local Look North coverage as I jogged past a camera crew. I had become an anorak, not a train spotter but a Stobart spotter.

Imagine Anne Robinson interrogating me about my hobbies. "I'm a long distance runner". "Oh how boring, isn't there anything interesting about you?". "Well I'm an Eddie Stobart spotter". "Get off, you are the Weakest Link!.

In a previous life I had a job as a transport supervisor or rather as a stand in when either of the regular two incumbents were on holiday. Whilst I am sure that many haulage drivers are really nice people particularly away from the workplace, this lot were the most miserable, childish and whinging bunch imaginable.

On a fairly substantial bonus scheme, they moaned if they had been to the same location twice recently and moaned if they hadn't. I couldn't win as there were particular journeys that some drivers would gladly do every day while other drops, that nobody wanted to do at all. They would also moan if certain colleagues completed a job too quickly as this would be seen as spoiling it for the others.

They moaned if Fred had more overnights than they did or if they had more overnights than Fred. One guy gave me strict instructions that if anyone should phone asking for him on a Thursday, I had to tell them he was doing an overnight job whether he actually was or not. I wonder what was going on there!

Another driver would keep a record as to how many times each driver had completed certain routes and from time to time would take me to task if the numbers didn't stack up. With the best will in the world, it was impossible to spread the work load evenly as some jobs came in late with others being cancelled at short notice.

Drivers would moan if they had a flat trailer rather than a curtain side or if they couldn't find any ropes, couldn't find any sheets, couldn't find their taco card or couldn't find their cab. The night men would even moan if a day man left their shared cab untidy, which was a little ironical as in those days, nine out of every ten drivers smoked. Consequently the ash trays would be invariably bulging and the floor strewn with ash, sweet papers and other debris.

During holiday periods or at times when the workload deemed necessary, we would supplement our regular crew with agency drivers. Rather than making allowances and showing these guys the ropes, our regulars preferred to put any number of obstacles in their way. While I needed to spend a fair bit of time with the agency drivers going over the paperwork, one of our regulars would watch them from a distance and come running to me with the least gripe.

They couldn't rope properly, they couldn't sheet, they couldn't reverse, they jerked the cab, they had gone home and not refuelled and many, many more. I always seemed to get more complaints and hassle on the days I had brought my kit intending to run home, and never seemed to get off to time on those evenings.

I can remember one driver throwing his bag against the office wall in a huff and breaking his flask in the process when he didn't appear too happy with his lot. My favourite incident involved one particular driver who was sitting in his cab at the security barrier ready to leave the premises and start his journey. At that point the fire alarm sounded so he reversed his vehicle back into the yard, climbed out of the cab and lined up with all the other staff outside the building.

These drivers were so far removed from stereotypical image of the hunky trucker with girl on arm and Yorkie Bar in hand.

Whilst out running I have been stopped on numerous occasions by lorry and van drivers to ask for directions. The pick of these has to be the driver of a car transporter asking the way to the motor auctions and the driver of an oil tanker asking the way to the refinery. One evening while out on a run, a vehicle stopped and the driver asked me the way to British Twins. I hadn't a clue but on looking at his delivery note I realised that he wanted British Twines. Surely he must have known the type of cargo he was carrying! However the one that takes the biscuit has to be the guy in full British Rail uniform who asked me the way to the railway station. "You must be joking", I said.

In the mid eighties, a dozen or so runners caused a stir and created some negative publicity for our sport when they climbed or vaulted over a railway level crossing barrier as the warning lights began to flash and the gates started to close, only a few hundred yards into a race. The runners further back were left standing at the closed barrier, waiting for the train to pass by so they could continue the race. The popular Rowntree Ten, a well established race, had always used the same route but on this occasion the train was apparently running either late or early.

The authorities were non too impressed and the police threatened to prosecute the guilty runners including one from my club, Ackworth Road Runners. This resulted in legislation being implemented preventing any road race from using a railway level crossing for future events.

With three railway stations alone in Pontefract, this obviously created a myriad of lines, track and bridges and no shortage of level crossings. Often on our Wednesday evening training runs, we would be stopped short by flashing lights, closing gates or a barrier lowering. Sometimes we would all get through while on other occasions, we tended to be well strung out with some of our group getting through and others not quite making it. On one such run I was struggling badly, had dropped off the back of the group and was left standing alone as the gates closed with all my club mates safely across.

One of the team could name the type of locomotive as we watched a train approaching, accurately predict the number of trucks it would be pulling which was usually nineteen, and state whether it was on time or running late.

On one particular training run, we took in the then recently opened railway station at the Freeport complex near Castleford, the first new station to be opened for several years in West Yorkshire. We stood on the windswept platform freezing to death, studying the mounted timetable to check if a certain member could make it back by train from Leeds after a night out.

One of our favourite Wednesday evening runs would be along the canal towpath between Ferrybridge and Knottingley, below the bridges. Sometimes we would gain access through factory gates, past the canteen and alongside the loading bay. This was apparently a historical right of way. We would pick the darkest, murkiest, misty evenings for this route, never dreaming of coming this way on lighter summer evenings. Street lamps would glimmer upon the surface of the water while youths shouted abuse at us from somewhere in the darkness.

On one such run we were scared out of our wits as the fog lights of a tug suddenly emerged out of the gloom, pulling coal from Kellingley Colliery to nearby Ferrybridge Power Station.

I loved nothing better than the runs on the towpath of the Aire and Calder Canal, becoming a familiar figure along with cyclists, bird watchers, fishermen, dog walkers and mothers pushing prams. The sight of swans, ducks and other wild birds along with the majestic roar of wild geese in flight was so far removed from the noise of the traffic on urban roads.

I began to recognise the more familiar narrow boats moored at locks and in the marina along with their names, colours, owners and places of origin. Vita Nova, Destiny, Nettle, Anna Livia, Ballinger, Coventina and the superbly named Narok. Who thought up these names and what did they mean? Many displayed names of the owners such as Jessop and Long, along with far off place names such as Stourbridge, Market Drayton and Chepstow. How long had it taken these boats to reach this point and what were they doing so far away from home? Oh for a life in the slow lane!

On stopping to let half a dozen cyclists cross the footbridge spanning the canal in Hunslet on the outskirts of Leeds, the last one dropped off the pace and we struck up a conversation. Over the three miles or so that we ran and cycled together, we talked about numerous topics including our jobs and places of work.

He asked if I knew Mick Jones whom I didn't. He elaborated on Mick Jones saying that at one time they had played badminton together. All of a sudden the penny dropped and I said, "You must mean Michael Jones". He had transferred to our factory in the mid eighties from a site that had suffered closure. He had a penchant for insisting the place be kept spotless and tidy which was no bad thing. I told the cyclist that my lasting memory of Michael Jones was when I had applied for a position for which I had already been covering for eleven weeks.

It became apparent that everyone on site apart from I, was aware the job had been offered to another person and that Jones was apparently just stalling for time while the finer details of his contract could be ironed out. On finding this out, I approached our Personnel Manager who told me I would have to see Jones. The same afternoon when I approached Jones, he opened his desk draw, removed a letter and said. " You know who the candidates were. Who would you have given the job to?" "Don't be so stupid" I replied. "Everyone knows who's got the job". At this he picked up the envelope presumably with my rejection letter in and threw it across the desk."We were going to send this to your home address he retorted but you can have it now". "Thanks a bundle", I replied.

I told the cyclist that at least what Mick Jones had done was to force me off my backside, to prompt me into applying for other jobs and eventually securing a better position for myself. "It's a small world", he said and I agreed.

But almost twenty years on, am I still bitter? You bet I am!

CHAPTER 18

Taking The Biscuit

"*T*HEY NEED all three to register with our running order and team name" said Roy as I closed the car door." What is our running order?" I asked. "Dunno" he replied. Barry soon arrived having persuaded his better half, Anne that it surely made sense to run the race before going out for an anniversary meal.

"Who's going first then?, I'm not bothered, I'm easy, I'll go anywhere, I'll go first or last". What a shambles! Out of the blue, Roy suddenly said, "I'll go second". "Do you mind going first Andy?" and so our running order was complete. 'Middle of the Packers' as our team name was much easier to decipher.

The organisation for the recent Athens Olympics was put to shame when the start was created by marking a line across the dirt track with a stick. "The runner must cross the line before handing over to the next man who must stay behind the line. Any team who doesn't adhere to this will be disqualified" said the race director, putting the frighteners up us before a stride was even taken in anger.

For the third time, he tried to count the number of first leg competitors who should have numbered sixteen. He was reliably informed however that Harry was having a pee further up the track while Tom, Dick and Mick were still making their way from the pub.

This was the Reindeer Romp Relay, the grand finale to The Reindeer series of races, which take place on Thursday evenings throughout the summer. The three legs are each of an indeterminable distance, approximately two and a half to three miles over hilly terrain, on tracks and paths around Overton, near Wakefield.

"For anyone who hasn't run the course before" said the race director holding a frying pan aloft, "It's down the handle, around the pan, and back up the handle. Now have you all got that?".

I looked around to see who would definitely beat me and whom I may possibly beat if anyone. The second category numbered one for sure in the shape of a rather rotund young lady. A guy later referred to her as a 'Big Bird', was overheard and immediately torn a strip by one of her team- mates.

"You're running well" said a fellow first leg man. "You easily beat me at Methley last week". And so I shall stuff you again tonight sir!, I thought to myself but diplomatically replied. "I'm a bit hit and miss at the moment". As a tractor and trailer rattled down the lane and turned into the track where we would run, one wag broke the tension by announcing, "That's the lead vehicle".

With Tom, Dick and everybody present, and the tractor well out of the way, we were off at break neck speed down the steep and stony track. My race tactic would be to go with the flow and hang on for dear life for as long as I could. This was easier said than done as the small field hit the knee jarring descent at breakneck speed. The Deep Heat must have been doing it's job as my dodgy knees never twinged once.

"There's a dog at the bottom" shouted a marshal at the first junction which struck me as being rather odd. It made a change however from the usual cries of, "Keep it going" or "You're looking good". On the final descent through the cornfield, I realised what he had meant. An out of control spaniel was darting backwards and forwards across the track with the owner seemingly helpless to intervene. A felled tree and piles of new mown hay provided further obstacles as we ran into a strong headwind around the perimeter of Stony Cliffe Wood.

I made up a place along this section but on glancing around as I negotiated a stile, the runners were backing up nicely behind me and were nicely poised to attack. One or two, if not all of these would surely catch me on the many nasty inclines in the second part of the course. But for whatever reason, this never happened and as I negotiated the final steep pull, back up the panhandle, the first of the second leg runners came belting back towards me. The heads of the runners and officials at the change over point were a welcoming site as I reached the brow of the hill and I afforded myself a token sprint, making sure I handed over to Roy behind the line drawn in the dirt.

It seemed no time at all before Roy returned back up the incline, collapsing in a heap on the ground. With his head swaying from side to side and his face pink as a salmon, Barry brought us home in 58 minutes making a mental note for his diary, 'Must try harder'.

We had finished neither first nor last but somewhere in the middle of the pack. Our other team on the night were the superbly named 'Oh no not again'. Super Veteran, Kenny Bingley had probably covered the distance of all three legs with his warm up routine, warm down and from the pub and back. Christine finished her stint covered in sticky buds but swears she neither fell down or got lost, but this team got their tactics spot on, sending Alan, the man with the glasses on the final leg into the fading light.

At the presentation in The Reindeer Pub, most participants received prizes in keeping with the friendly nature of the events, and we each received each a packet of Melters Biscuits, for our efforts.

CHAPTER 19

What Do You Think Of Sven

SEVERAL YEARS ago, I had a holiday romance or as much of a romance as a fifty, well then 47 year old could expect. Maria was a Swedish National from Stockholm and was on a long weekend with friends while I was in Budapest to run the half marathon.

I had called at Beckett's, a large Irish bar, in anticipation that the Germany – England World Cup qualifier from Munich would be showing on the giant screen. The bar was packed inside and I had to strain in order to see any of the action. I decided to sit outside at a table, getting into pleasant banter with a Belgian couple and two Italian men from Palermo.

Each time a loud cheer erupted, I would pop inside the door to find out what was happening. There were plenty of cheers that evening as England ran out 5-1 winners. As the game finished, three women joined us with Maria immediately sitting next to me.

"Vot do you think of Sven" she asked as an opener. "He seems to be doing well" I replied, but thinking to myself, I much prefer you! "Vot do you think of David Beckham" she enquired". "Pretty overrated" I said. "I'm 47 years old so I have seen much better players in my time for England". "I'm 42" she said which was nice and then proceeded to ask who I thought had been the better England players. "Bobby Charlton, Kevin Keegan, Trevor Brooking, Paul Gascoigne". Before I could think of any others she chipped in, "Vot did you think of Glenn Hoddle". "He probably should have had more caps I said but they seemed to prefer Butch Wilkins at the time".

The questions came thick and fast, the conversation ebbed and flowed and the drinks too with her friends joining in from time to time. A woman with her football knowledge would have been the dream date for most men. When her friends moved on, Maria stayed put and we continued to talk, smile and laugh our way through the evening. We seemed like old friends rather than new acquaintances.

When the goodbyes were said later in the weekend, we failed to exchange addresses, phone numbers or contact details. Five minutes on I bitterly regretted this. What the hell, Stockholm is only two hours flying time from Manchester and probably five hours door to door, not the other side of the world.

But I have always gone through life like this, reluctant to throw caution to the wind or to chance my arm. I have always been happier in a comfort zone where I wouldn't be stretched or put under any undue pressure.

As with my running, I have never been prepared to suffer the unnecessary pain or go that extra mile. If I had done so, I may possibly have surprised myself but I had no desire to put myself through the mill in order to make things happen..

I first ran the Stockholm Half Marathon ten years ago so that was a good enough reason to run here again. I was ten years older, ten years balder but not necessary ten years wiser. I regularly thought about Maria and thought I may even catch a glimpse of her. I could imagine myself hurdling barriers, chasing across busy streets or running after trams whenever I had a potential sighting. What was good for Dr Zhivago in the film of the same name as he pursued Lara around the streets of Moscow would be good enough for me.

The journey was pretty uneventful with the SAS flight pretty empty. I wish I'd made my booking later and perhaps saved some money. I read seventy or so pages of McCarthy's Bar by Pete McCarthy laughing out aloud at times. I caught the Arlanda Express high speed train into Stockholm and was soon in my hotel, The Terminus, changed and ready for an assault on the city.

The day was hot and I was able to wear tee shirt and shorts. I walked the narrow streets of Gamla Stan, the Old Town and more or less found the race registration in Kungstradgarden without a problem. I must have been pretty early as they were still assembling the trestle tables and marquees, however I was able to register and was given an envelope containing race information, number and chip along with two small packets of Nestle Fitness Flakes. I spotted one of those postcard racks that swivels around, containing flyers for other Swedish events. I placed flyers in one of the compartments to advertise my book 'Middle of the Packer'. Swedes could read and understand English so surely there would be a big demand for 'Packer' here.

The St Eriksloppet, Stockholm's Half Marathon would take place on Saturday evening at five o clock and conditions were likely to be hot. Erik Jedvardsson was a 12th century Swedish king who later was chosen to become Sweden's patron saint for the crusade he undertook to christianise Finland. Sweden's first icebreaker ship was named the St Erik and throughout Stockholm there are numerous references to him in street names and squares.

I walked the waterfront, far busier than on my previous visits with passenger liners, ferries and cargo vessels all moored comfortably within a stones throw of the city centre. I was fascinated as I watched the boats passing through the huge lock gates at Slussen when I suddenly received a call on my mobile. Mum couldn't get a good picture on TV so I talked her through what I believed to be wrong which apparently solved the problem. My good deed for the day but no rest for the wicked.

I retired to Patrick's Bar in Sodermalm, ordered a Carlsberg Hof and read up on the guide book I had received as part of the hotel package. Also provided was a Stockholm Card which entitled free travel on buses, boats, trains and the Tunnelbana for the duration of my stay. When venturing out later in the evening, I had difficulty swiping my ticket at the automatic barrier and only later realised that I should have shown it to the attendant in the kiosk.

The intention had been to have a steady and relaxing evening but my plans would be soon in turmoil as the night progressed and the mood changed. I started in the Limerick Pub, a good old Swedish name and then walked through Gamla Stan to Gotgatan, a street with a large conglomeration of cafes and bars. My plans for an early night were shattered when I fell into conversation with two ladies.

I bought them both a drink which must have been a quadruple of the most expensive short on the tariff. I even provided them with change for the cigarette machine. One of the ladies, a large Jamaican said she smoked menthol. I must have been mental to fork out for her fags. Her friend was more of a Latina and very nice too. She asked if she could come to my room and I do believe she mentioned something about payment. What was all that about them?

I made a pledge to myself that in future I would always drink wisely, would remain in charge of my faculties and not drop my guard. On a recent visit to Prague I lost, misplaced or had my mobile phone stolen. I had one hell of a job getting through to BT to report the loss and to replace the phone. When I received the next bill, the thief or finder must have made and received calls non stop throughout the night until BT were able to put a hold on the number.

On Saturday morning I overslept missing breakfast and was in clearly no shape to run a half marathon. With lots of time to kill I opted for a boat trip that would at least rest my legs for an hour or so. On my way, I passed race registration and noticed that most of the flyers for 'Middle of the Packer' were still in the rack.

The boat trip was very pleasant along the cities waterways and canals and under bridges by historical buildings and palaces. The boat was packed and I sat next to a Swedish National and his wife. She was Thai or certainly from somewhere in that neck of the woods and their two children were beautiful and impeccably behaved. We talked away throughout the journey which passed all too quickly.

On leaving the boat, I spotted another Swedish-Thai couple and then another. In all I counted eight such couples on my way back to the hotel. It was no good, I would have to become a Swede.

A youth tried to snatch my rucksack but I easily thwarted him. "Don't make it so obvious next time" I shouted as he ran off into the crowd. When I first spotted the youth, it was nailed on that he was planning to do something. The angle at which he stood and the way his eyes met mine. I would have put money on it.

On arriving back at the hotel, I had to quickly vacate my room for the chambermaid. "It isn't too bad is it, I'm sure you've seen a lot worse" I said. The maid was West Indian which made me realise how cosmopolitan Stockholm had become since my previous visit here, ten years ago. To give the maid carte blanche, I retired to the lounge to continue reading Pete McCarthy. A sign caught my attention which said, 'At no time leave you're bag unattended'. Too bloody true!

Race time beckoned so I gathered my bits and pieces, putting them into my rucksack and fastening a tag with my race number to the outside. I needed safety pins, my notebook, some loose change and one bank note for if I needed to purchase anything after the race, most probably a beer. I wrapped up my mobile phone and a credit card in my cagoule pocket and placed it inside the bag. Hopefully the baggage area would be reasonably secure. The afternoon was a scorcher so I meandered along to the start in tee shirt and shorts wearing the shoes and socks I would run in.

I cut through the St Clara churchyard served as a thoroughfare. The entrance doubled as a gathering place for groups of vagrants and down and outs, some with beer cans and smoking roll up's, others with angry looking dogs.

I walked Drottninggatan, a long pedestrianised street with chain stores, souvenir shops and restaurants. Another angry dog, probably a pit bull, growled nastily at a family pooch, despite the mean looking owner holding the leash short and tightly. He had no business to walk this dog along such a crowded street on a busy Saturday afternoon but probably got a buzz out of these situations.

Further along the precinct a crowd of people were tucking into food and drink outside Pickwick's. At least it said Pickwick's on the sign but only Pickwick on the canopy. I wonder if anyone knew or had realised. What a legacy Dickens left with the wonderful names of his characters. Joe Gargery, Daniel Quilp, Ham Pegotty, Barnaby Rudge, Mrs Gummidge to name but a few. When I go into the blood stock business with Alan Tattersall and Ken Barton, our horses will be named after Dickensian characters. Abel Magwich, Herbert Pocket and my own favourite, Wackford Squeers.

As I approached Kungstradgarden, the place had altogether, much more of a race feel than the previous day. Athletes were already changed with still an hour to go, others were talking within their family groups while queues were starting to form outside the urinals.

A pop group belted out numbers from a considerable sized stage. The front man wore a white flat cap and worked the stage like a veteran rocker while the flaxen hair of the lead guitarist swayed in the gentle breeze. The accompanying singers were pleasant and easy on the eye with one sporting a tattoo on her shoulder.

One of the race sponsors was Cloetta Kex Choklad and promotional girls were handing out samples from their marquee. A stand advertised Scandinavian Training Camp and another Axelson's Massage. The name didn't particularly fill me with a great deal of confidence. There was one of those stands where you kick a football through holes in a backcloth to win prizes. I can remember some friends searching for me at Blackpool Pleasure Beach to do just the same on a White Swan Rovers day out. They must have had more confidence in my ability than I had.

The after-effects of the previous nights indulgences were still lingering on, but at least I was beginning to feel more in the mood. I sat on a wall to change whilst trying to take in the atmosphere. I would generally have taken a couple of photos but had left my camera back at the hotel. Passing registration, I noticed my flyers had disappeared so I placed another wad in the rack. Had people really taken from the previous pile or had the organisers seen fit to remove them. I noticed a Thai girl on registration, one at baggage handling and another handing out water. They were everywhere.

I joined the steady stream of people making there way to the start at the Strombron. With still half an hour to go, there was no desperation but people were beginning to assemble in their respective blocks. I would start within the yellow group, the first of three, but decided to follow others in a steady jog along the waterfront. I would do well to run a mile the way I felt today, let alone thirteen.

With each stride, I felt aches, pains and a lethargy that told me not to put myself through this agony. There would always be another day and another race. After 200 yards or so, I turned and walked back looking out across the water at the boats bobbing up and down, the islands and beyond to the far shoreline. This was indeed a beautiful setting to start the race.

I drifted into the cordoned off area that constituted the yellow start and stood listening to more pop music playing over loud speakers. At races back home I would be passing the time chatting to club mates, colleagues or somebody I knew. Today I was among hundreds of other people, feeling all alone but not for too long.

The solid intro to 'Bad Moon Rising' by Creedence Clearwater Revival came belting out over the amplifiers. This is more like it I said to the person next to me who introduced herself as Annekka as in Rice and Sorenstam. She was fair, well toned and looked the part as she limbered up and down on the spot. She eagerly anticipated the action and was looking forward to a good run. As we talked she irritatingly folded each leg in turn behind her back, holding it within both hands and pulling. I have since tried this and can't do it and when I almost did it, I toppled over. Annekka was going for ninety minutes so I wished her luck as the runners were walked forward ready to start.

A single pistol shot marked the start of the race, but thirty seconds or so elapsed before I was able to break into a jog, crossing the carpet to the perpetual whistling of championship chips. Patience was the virtue as it would take the field of four thousand some time to settle down. A stocky guy in bandana and yellow shades was having none of it, perpetually changing the line of his running and using his elbows to work his way through the field. I believe the bandana was concealing a shaven head as the obligatory tell tale earring gave the game away.

The early stages were through Norrmalm, the cities main shopping district. Late afternoon shoppers and workers alike took to the pavements to give their applause and occasionally people would pick out my St Georges vest and provide encouragement. The field was cosmopolitan buoyed by a large proportion of traditional Scandinavian blondes.

There was a guy running in the distinctive green and white stripes of Djurgarden Football Club, one of the cities three main teams. He seemed to receive many plaudits appearing to enjoy every minute but I wondered for how long he could keep this going. I easily slipped by him and switched attention to an older runner on the left hand side of the road. Each time I tried to pass, he would move out and block me, probably not deliberately, but it appeared to be that way. He couldn't possibly keep doing this for nineteen kilometres so I ran wide of him, momentarily picking up the pace until I was well clear. Little moments like this make each race so different.

I passed 5K in 23 minutes, only a minute slower than a dedicated 5K race at York a few evenings ago and I started to settle nicely into my rhythm. A drab industrial section along railway sidings is followed by a more pleasant stretch along a waterfront path in Kungsholmen. People stand on balconies, shout from high windows or lend their support from pavement cafes. I spot a tasty looking croissant as I run close to a table and think that's mine, but decide to hold back at the last minute.

At 8K, a swarthy guy wearing a head band grunts something directed towards me. I don't understand his instruction but having just looked at my watch he must be asking me for the time. 37-50 I shout and he raises his hand in acknowledgement.

10K in 47 minutes and another rock band commemorate the spot beneath a flyover. The next section is along Norr Malarstrand heading towards the old town. The unthinkable happens as I catch a glimpse Annekka walking back along the pavement, drinking from a bottle and obviously in distress. Her race was clearly over and she would be so disappointed. She had been like a coiled spring at the start and was chomping at the bit so had probably gone off too quickly, paying the inevitable price.

The spectator support was solid at Slussen where we negotiated tunnels and bridges between Gamla Stan and Sodermalm. I was going along quite nicely on the long straight stretch between the steep cliffs to the left and the waters edge to the right hand side and begin to wonder what all the fuss had been about. I catch and overtake Bandana man who is still working hard but unable to match my basic speed.

A large bill board advertised a Walkathon which would indeed be the next day. Distances advertised were 15K, 10K & 6K. After running a half marathon, that would be a doddle in comparison and perhaps just what I needed to while away a Sunday morning.

The course moved away from the waterfront at Langholmen through pleasant parks and neighbourhood streets. Punters sitting outside bars and in beer gardens shouted encouragement occasionally picking out a favourite or someone who they recognised.

After slowing for water at 17K, I was unable to pick up the pace again but a useful downhill towards the waterfront at Slussen enabled me to regain some momentum. Here one section was coned off for runners inside a lane of slow moving traffic. Two young blonde girls in the back seat of a convertible had their heads turned and were shouting at the runners. When it was my turn I shook my fist in their direction. They responded by doing the same, while howling with laughter.

I played cat and mouse with the car as the girls continued to shake their fists at me. I'm glad I had been able to make someone happy. I was now inside the final kilometre, crossing a couple of bridges in the Old Town. Beyond the Opera House, I turned towards the finish in Kungstadgarden.

I ran under the clock in 1 hour & 43 minutes, as good as I could have hoped for and an impressive looking medal was placed around my neck. The baggage handler had spotted my number as I approached so my bag was ready for immediate collection.

I sat on a bench feeling no better than before I had started. I changed slowly and deliberately as darkness presided over the park, before heading wearily back to the hotel.

As I passed the St Clara Church, two men obviously down at heel were being arrested and bundled into the back of a police van. The women with them appeared to be hurling abuse at the officers, which was nothing new.

I showered and rested for an hour but was reluctant to go out, although I needed to find out the football results. Struggling to walk normally, I headed for O'Leary's where there would be live football on several large screens. I wasn't in the mood for drinking so I ordered a diet cola which came in a large glass, with ice appearing to make up most of the content. I wasn't hungry so would perhaps grab a bite later on.

One of the smaller screens quickly told me Leeds United had beaten Coventry 3-0 but I was unable to find out the Ross County score. Italian Football was showing on one of the large screens and a guy told me this was very popular in Sweden. His team A.C. Milan were playing newly promoted Livorno.

"Have you ever been to see A.C. Milan play" I said,"No"."Have you ever seen them play in Sweden" I asked."Swedish clubs don't get into the Champions League" he replied."Well Rosenberg seem to qualify each year" I said referring to their Norwegian neighbours."Well they always seem to have an easy draw" he retorted.

He asked me vot I thought of Sven. It seemed as if every Swede who I would come across valued my opinion on England's Head Coach."He's had some good results but I believe we've under-achieved in the tournaments" I said."No, I meant vot do you think of Sven as a person" he asked. "He's pretty small, bespectacled and wears stacked heels", I replied. "No" he asked again, vot do you think of his private life". "He seems to be a hit with the ladies" I said.

The man lived every moment of the game, standing up from his stool when Milan came close and throwing a tantrum when they gave away a sloppy goal. He thumped the table from time to time, threw his arms aloft in despair while occasionally covering his eyes if something went wrong. I found the whole scenario a little over the top and at half time said my cheerio's.

I walked a couple of doors to Tiffany's where trade was fairly slow for ten 'o' clock. On the screen here, Tim Henman was bat-tling to stem the tide against Roger Federrer in the semi final of the US Open, but unfortunately to no avail. The barmaid cum waitress was Latina and tugged on a Marlboro at the end of the bar between serving punters. She appeared to be hard faced but when I caught her eye as she came past, she smiled and was indeed very beautiful. So much so that called here again the following evening.

I moved up the street to Patrick's and ordered a Holsten Pils. Barcelona were playing Seville on television and each time there was a close up of Swedish darling Henrik Larsson, four girls at a table appeared to go hysterical.

Barcelona took the lead and a peculiar thing happened. The camera focused on the directors box and presumably the president of the club. A man in the row behind ruffled his well groomed hair, he was fortunate in having some to ruffle, and then shook his hand. The man was distinguished and flanked by two smart women. People on either side shook his hand, some leaned over to pat him on the shoulder while others came down the gangway to lend their congratulations. People were queuing up and bending over backwards to congratulate him. It was as if the president had scored the goal himself.

The other strange occurrence happened towards the end of the game with Barcelona two goals to the good. A spectator ran onto the field and placed a silly hat on the head of a African player by the name of Etto'o who I hadn't heard of at the time but has since become famous..

I caught the underground and called for a last Orange Juice in the hotel bar. I became embroiled in a conversation at the bar with Tomas, a Swede and John an American from Georgia. The name John made a refreshing change from Gus, Chuck or C.J. He said that for the first time, Hispanic voters would outnumber white Caucasian's at the next presidential elections.

Tomas visited Scotland regularly on holiday and had been as far north as Inverness. I told him I could better that, having been to Wick and John 'O' Groats. I asked him if he had visited Dingwall, home to Ross County. Tomas said he had been on holiday to Greece once, but his face ended up looking like a Tomato. He much preferred a cooler climate.

I felt little better on Sunday morning but was second man down for breakfast. First man in was grey haired, perhaps sixty-five in a grey jacket. He reminded me of Jim Trot, the yes, yes, yes, yes, no man on the parish council in the Vicar of Dibley. He irritatingly got up out of his chair an unreasonable amount of times to replenish his supplies or to look for cutlery.

I let a Japanese girl into the breakfast room who had either forgotten her swipe card or hadn't realised the entry procedure. She wore a rucksack and neither took it off to get her breakfast or when she sat down to eat it, which must have been pretty uncomfortable.

The coffee looked like sludge and tasted little better while the croissant shrunk out of all proportion when I put the knife into it. Surely the orange juice would revive me but unfortunately it appeared to be the powdered type watered down. I finished my breakfast and stood on the pavement outside the hotel sucking on a mint. The weather had changed from Summer to Autumn overnight and had brought with it a chilly breeze.

I wrapped up accordingly and with my trusty rucksack headed through the Old Town towards the waterfront. The pleasure boats didn't start until 10-30 and I wasn't particularly in museum mode so I was in for a morning of walking and generally pottering around.

I crossed the bailey bridge into Skeppsholmen with the wind really biting, but once in the shade, the warmth from the sun was glorious. I passed the three masted schooner A f Chapman which houses a youth hostel and many smaller vessels all proudly flying the blue flag with the yellow cross. Apparently in the late 1800's, the unbelievable figure of 300,000 ships, boats and craft harboured in Stockholm and it's environs.

Back at Kungstradgarden, competitors for the walkathon were browsing around the Exhibitors marquees, some still there from yesterday with one or two additions. I looked around some stalls selling sports goods but didn't make a purchase, instead retiring to an adjacent pavement café for the first of several cappuccinos today.

From here I could observe the activities and decide if the walkathon would be for me. Some competitors wore lycra or track suits while others had walking gear and boots. They each had a tag fastened around their necks and a cord with some sporting Walkathon stickers on their rucksacks or bags,

Deciding to give this one a miss I moved on looking into one or two shop windows before visiting Riddarholmen Church. Crossing several bridges and walkways I headed to Sodermalm climbing gradually until I found an idyllic vantage point. High above the cliffs where I had run yesterday, I looked out over Riddarfjorden towards the city, the islands and the archipelago in the distance.

I could trace much of the route taken by the race and quietly congratulated myself on my efforts. There were picnic tables here and a telescope. I peeled a banana and stayed for ten minutes gazing across the water at the myriad of buildings, domes and spires.

A couple asked if I could take a photo to which I asked, "Is it idiot proof". I must have looked the part because a further two men asked if I could also take their photo and then another couple. By rights, I should have been having mine taken with Maria.

With thoughts of what might have been, bouncing around inside my head, I walked the streets of Sodermalm passing Scottish Pub, The Halfway Inn. A board outside indicated Millwall would be playing Ipswich later in the day. I would pass on that one too!

I chose a nice sheltered table at a café in a large square and ordered sausage and chips with all the trimmings washed down with a large glass of orange juice. I wouldn't have a beer just now for fear of what it might do to my delicate system. As I enjoyed my lunch watching the world go by, several people with rucksacks in outdoor gear started to pass by. These were obviously the pacesetters in the walkathon.

I walked back towards the waterfront passing a check point where some of these people were queuing to have their tags punched. It all seemed fairly civilised. Continuing down Gotgaten, more and more walkers came up the hill until one pavement was solid, forcing me to cross onto the other side of the road. Some were pushing youngsters in prams while others walked reasonably behaved dogs. Elderly people were striding out with walking sticks or contraptions similar to ski polls. It seemed like a perfectly pleasant way to while away a few hours on a Sunday.

In Sergels Torg, a huge concrete bowl in the new town linked to subways, a peaceful demonstration was taking place towards General Augusto Pinochet, the former self appointed president and dictator in Chile. There were several banners referring to the missing millions and another claiming him to be a puppet to George Bush Senior. There were dozens of Chilean flags and others in blue and white logo with the white star on the red background representing Cuba.

When Pinochet came to power, thousands of people sympathetic to the socialist government were detained. Throughout his tenure from 1973 to 1990, his government were accused of violations of human rights and mass torture in prison camps. Political activists disappeared without trace, government opposition was subjugated and religious activities restricted.

Chubby cheeked Chilean chappies played drums and panpipes while dusky girls danced exotically to the haunting sounds. A distinguished looking man with a mayoral chain of office took to the stage milking the applause from the crowd. He made a short speech, enjoyed more applause and then joined in a toast with a guy on a podium, dressed like a circus ringmaster, in long tailed tunic and top hat. They raised their glasses to an appreciative crowd but I was standing directly above the proceedings, and no liquor was in fact exchanged from bottle to glass. I spent an enjoyable half hour here but would have liked to understand more about the nature of the speeches.

I had Monday morning to kill before my flight home late afternoon. I was up early and breakfast was only marginally better than yesterday. I scanned the newspapers in reception for the Ross County result but to no avail. There was Spanish, Italian, German, Swedish and English football. There was even the Scottish Premiership but no Scottish Division One. What was wrong with these people?

The St Eriksloppet received good footage with photographs and leading positions. Said Regragui of Hasselby was the winner in 1-05-19 and Lena Gavelin of Trangsvikens was the leading lady in 1-13-45. Where were all the Kenyan's? Sarah Brightman would be appearing at The Globe this week..

The weather was still Autumnal with a blustery breeze as I left the hotel. With the No 47 bus pulling into the stand, I made a snap decision. I boarded, joining smart office workers and a guy with a set of golf clubs before alighting at the Vasa Museum in Djurgarden.

My eyes took time to adjust to the dimly lit rooms, but suddenly out of the gloom appeared the largest preserved ship of it's kind in the world. The Vasa was built in 1620 when Sweden was at war with Poland. There were two gun decks with 64 cannons, making it the mightiest ship in the fleet.

At the time The Vasa was considered heavy and began to lean on it's maiden voyage. It sunk 1300 meters from shore with 39 people losing their lives. The death toll could have been far worse as many more crew had arranged to board the vessel at a pick up point in the Archipelago.

And so the Vasa remained on the harbour floor until 1959 when the first lift was made to re float the warship. Six tunnels were dug beneath the Vasa and each threaded with steel cables, attached to two water filled pontoons. When the water was pumped out, the cables stretched, gradually lifting the Vasa from the sea bed. The lifting took place in sixteen stages over two years. The saline within the Baltic Sea served to perfectly preserve the wood for three hundred years. 95% of the ship is original with most of the 500 sculptures of Swedish symbols, warriors and biblical figures still intact. The reconstructed masts stick out of the sloping roofs of the museum. The dry dock is low lit and temperature controlled and the ship continually sprayed with polyethylene glycol.

Nobody is allowed to board but there is a reconstruction of one of the gun decks and also a theatre charting the history of the Vasa and her discovery. Recently a new problem has emerged where sulphur believed to have been absorbed on the sea bed has reacted with air to form sulphuric acid. This has started to eat away at the wood so plans have started all over again to save the vessel. The Vasa Museum is Stockholm's largest attraction and a must for every visitor to the city.

Artefacts and treasures from the Vasa are displayed in adjacent rooms along with reconstructed skulls depicting some of the crew members. Scientists have even been able to state the approximate height, weight and ages of some of these people, the kind of lives they lead and diet they took. One of the men was even said to have been knocked about in his younger days.

Still enthralled at my visit, I caught the nearby ferry to Slussen being the only passenger onboard. I stood on deck and watched the dramatic Stockholm skyline gradually unfold. A large proportion of buildings are painted in complimentary shades of pink, orange and red with grey or peppermint green roof tiles.

I disembarked and headed through Gamla Stan where I called at Tavelmare, a shop selling traditional Scandinavian paintings, prints, postcards and memorabilia. I could have gladly bought every article in the shop but left clutching a six pack of coasters portraying views of Stockholm.

Next stop was John Chris for a coffee. Two young Latina women were at a window table and were looking at a strip of photographs taken at a booth."Hey can I have one of those" I'm Andy. Next stop was Ahlens City where the beautiful people shopped in stores such as Chanel and Dior.

Returning to the hotel, I packed, vacated my room and left my bags in a room close to the lobby. With time still to run on my Stockholm Card and with the system just about cracked, I caught the underground to Gotgatan. There was no reason why I couldn't have one last beer. Tiffany's was closed and I wouldn't see my Cuban beauty again, so I moved to The Beefeater where I took a window seat.

Stockholm is a cycling city, highlighted by at least twelve bikes padlocked to the railings. A girl walked up the hill pushing a bike only to be overtaken by another girl with a basket full of groceries standing on her pedals to gain momentum. Two guys walked by wearing trilby hats and long black coats with loads of buttons and badges like pearly kings.

Six business men came by the window and into the pub, all of a similar age and all wearing spectacles. That reminded me, I must make an appointment at the opticians. An oriental girl in sharp black suit with killer stilettos caught my attention. Why did I have to go home today, but I'll be back for sure!

My travelling companion on the plane was Swedish and thumbed the sports pages of the newspaper, stopping at the Italian Football. His preference was for Juventus. I wondered why he waited for everyone leave the plane before leaving his seat, until I realised he was lame. The labyrinth of corridors and walkways to Baggage Reclaim at Manchester Airport would have surely done him no favours.

The train from the airport was packed with standing room only. The obligatory stag party had started a card school within seconds of boarding. I asked the young lady next to me if she had been anywhere exciting to which she replied, "I've been in the terminal building all day, meeting and greeting overseas students for Huddersfield University. I'll be there for the rest of the week". "Do you have to hold up a card", I asked. "Yes" she replied, "I feel a proper Nellie". I asked how she filled the considerable amount of time between flights. "I talk to people doing the same job for other universities, there's a crowd of us there", she said.

Some of her students had to stand up in the aisle of the carriage, probably a culture shock and a rude awakening to our transport infrastructure. We talked throughout the journey with her interests of travel and walking being similar to mine.

People alighted at Manchester Piccadilly but the places quickly filled. A family boarded and a small girl with spectacles started crying when her older sister hit her in the face. After more treatment had been handed out, their mother intervened and the girl was laughing just as quickly as she had started crying.

The vendor tried to force his way past the students using his refreshment trolley as a battering ram, but this proved nigh on impossible. He continually requested that people should move but to no avail. With his patience and commission obviously wearing a little thin, he shouted for one last time, "I'm coming through", to which the mother of the two girls replied,"They don't understand you, they're foreigners". Oh happy days!

Walking through the station concourse, a sign above a stand said, "Leeds Universities welcome all overseas students". I couldn't help but be a little envious.

The first job on arriving home was to sort through the post and papers.

My jaw dropped and my heart sank when I read the football scores, Ross County 0 St Johnstone 1.

CHAPTER 20

A Run To Be Reckoned With

I HAD BARELY started my Sunday morning run before I was subjected to a torrent of abuse. As I crossed the first main road, two newspaper boys were just finishing their rounds, the tell tale luminous bags a dead giveaway. Amidst the sniggering, one of them made the snooking noise that one makes when trying to hold back a laugh aloud.

I chose to ignore this at first but stopped and turned around after they had subjected me to taunts and wise cracks. As joggers will know, this follows an all two familiar pattern. Most of these yobs wait until you are well past before they start to hurl the abuse. As I turned around, the two lads had stopped in their tracks and were gawking, as they say in Barnsley. I knew for sure they had shouted something so I jogged back.

"Sorry, what did you say", I said. "Nothing" was the reply. "Don't give me that crap", I said, lifting the taller of the two lads by the lapels of his coat. "Now go tell you're Dad what I've done, tell you're big brother, tell the police, tell Martin Brown (the newsagent), tell who you bloody well like, but in future, don't come knocking on my door for a Christmas box."

This appeared to be the latest money making gimmick, with the newspaper boy knocking on my door to give me a Christmas Card and wishing me compliments of the season. While all very jovial and festive, it was also a polite way of asking if their was any possibility of a tip, and until now I hadn't really minded. When I had delivered newspapers in my youth, I wouldn't have had the audacity or impudence to knock on doors asking for a tip. I tried to be polite, to provide a good service and usually did very well at Christmas. I didn't even know if this was my paper boy but at least I let him know where he stood.

Unfortunately I had let out all of my anger on this boy. I wasn't in a particularly good mood to begin with, and was a reluctant starter this morning. The previous day I had spent ten hours on various trains only to see my team Ross County lose out to a last minute goal against Airdrie.

I had caught a taxi to Leeds City Station only to find the early train to Edinburgh wouldn't be running due to a technical failure. The announcements concerning this were pretty glib and sporadic to say the least and this had put me in a foul mood before the day had really started. I had forked out good money for a taxi which I hadn't really needed as I could have caught the first bus and still been in time for the next train. Add to this the train between Edinburgh and Glasgow suffering a diversion due to maintenance and I was an hour or so late on arrival. This resulted in my usual wander around Glasgow and couple of pints being curtailed.

My next train to Airdrie stopped at twelve stations and the stated ten minute walk to the ground was nearer twenty five. For games in England you just follow the flow of spectators to the ground. In Scotland with the exception of a handful of clubs, there is no crowd to speak of. Instead I chose to follow two purposeful looking young men whom I overheard talking lower Scottish League Football on the train. They didn't let me down and as we walked, other small groups converged and all appeared to be heading in the same direction to form a steady trickle towards New Broomfield Park.

The longer walk had in itself posed a problem as I would now be pushed to reach the station after the game for the 5-15 train back to Glasgow, unless I left the ground early. I overcame this obstacle by jogging the two miles or so in the light drizzle, my back pack bobbing up and down gently all the way. Shades of the Calderdale Way Relay when I needed a back pack to carry map, compass, food and clothing. I jogged across Glasgow to catch the next train and sprinted across the platform at York to catch the Leeds train. The plus side of the day was that all the rail travel had enabled me to read 200 plus pages of the Frank Skinner Autobiography.

Arriving home eventually, I settled down to watch Match of the Day only to see Dutchman Arjen Robben of Chelsea sprint literally thirty yards to stick his face in the referees. I saw the re-run again this morning along with angry man, Roy Keane and trusty side kick Gary Neville barking and snarling at anyone and everyone and shunting the hapless referee up and down the park. I wondered why this was allowed to happen and why they appeared to get away with it?

After putting the two paper boys in their place and, with my Sunday run off to the worst possible start, I hadn't contemplated for Alfie the Dalmatian. He tried to use me as a climbing frame with the lady owner saying he only wanted to play while trying to call him to heel with no apparent success. Little wonder that Cruella Deville tried to wipe out this particular breed.

The next thing to annoy me was a newly burnt out car or should I say a burnt out car that wasn't there the last time I came this way. Who leaves these here, why do they do it and what is anyone doing about it.

As I join the canal tow path, two lady joggers bid me good morning but a twitcher gazing through binoculars hardly say's a word. The fishermen sit motionless and silent in their holes although one does afford me a grunt. I was now pressing along nicely as I often do when I am annoyed and have fire in my belly. I begin to rue the amount of clothing I am wearing as on an unseasonably mild winter morning, I am starting to perspire.

I leave the tow path briefly and cross the road at a set of traffic lights. A smart young man of Caribbean origin dripping with jewellery and wearing a black woolly hat is doing likewise. Watching me approach he says, "You're looking good man" to which I reply "You're too kind". The woolly hat made this guy look cool but I probably looked a proper wally in mine.

I am now in the heart of Leeds and stop for a minute on the foot-bridge spanning the River Aire to wipe the sweat away from my eyes. I look out across the water at the skyline, at the many new developments and at the guests finishing their breakfasts in the restaurant of the newly opened Jury's Hotel.

Things begin to look up when I hear the click, click of heels as a young woman starts her approach onto the bridge. Unlike Alfie, her pooch is much better behaved and only sniffs around my ankles and feet." Have you finished?, she asks"."If only" I reply, "I'm about half way, another five miles to go yet"."Have you really" she says. " Even though our conversation lasted but a couple of minutes, she pointed out her apartment with riverside view and balcony telling me she had paid 189K, eighteen months ago. "So I'll be alright for a coffee next Sunday" was my parting shot. "Look forward to it" she replied. Oh to be young again and know what I know now!

Continuing along the waterfront I pass luxury apartments merely a stones throw from the city centre and more developments alongside Clarence Dock and The Royal Armouries. Narrow boats and small vessels are moored here probably for the winter.

If the first half of my run had been eventful then I have seen nothing yet as I plan to return along the notorious Belle Isle Road. Our Church bulletin displayed a notice asking for volunteers to staff a charity shop located on the very same. No thank you!

I stop on a railway bridge to ask enthusiasts with cameras and binoculars what they are waiting for. The name of the engine means nothing to me and certainly wasn't in the same league as the Flying Scotsman or Mallard. New age Train Spotters or Loco Chasers as I understand they like to be known, look out for Diesels and Deltics these days rather than the traditional steam locomotives.

A car with darkened windows cruises by to the perpetual boom, boom, boom of powerful speakers. I believe the driver wound the window down slightly to shout something but I couldn't make out what.

Belle Isle passes fairly uneventfully. There's only dog walkers about and people calling for their newspapers. It's still early with the hooligans and yobs safely tucked up in bed. On a weekend there's no necessity for these people to get out of bed and out of the house so they can bunk off school.

The rest of the run passes peacefully with the exception of an owner having to sit on his Great Dane to prevent it from tearing me to pieces. As I approach the final downhill 500 yards, I try to pick up the pace, straighten my back, put some spring into my step and pump my arms to impress anyone who knows me. Roll on next Sunday.

Back home I solemnly pledged to myself that I must rise above all the taunts, abuse and crap that is hurled at me, each time I go out for a run and that nothing like what happened earlier today must happen again. Two weeks later I chinned a youth, or rather pushed him in the face or jabbed him, 'Know what I mean Harry?'.

I was out with the Wednesday evening splinter group, running around the mean streets of Pontefract. Every group of youths we saw, gladly hurled insults and abuse. It had reached the stage where we were expecting abuse and would have been disappointed had it not been forthcoming. A gang were sitting on the wall of a petrol station forecourt and started pointing and smirking as we approached. This was quickly followed by taunts, ridicule, insults and much merriment as we drew level. They probably thought it ridiculously sad for a bunch of grown men to be jogging through the dark streets on a bitterly cold evening but cool and acceptable to drink beer and alco pops on a petrol station forecourt.

I thought about knocking the beer can out of the hand of one of these morons but instead chose to jab the last lad in the face when a torrent of abuse came my way.

Three or four of them made a token gesture to run alongside us, but obviously not having the stomach for any exercise, quickly gave up. I spent the next ten minutes rueing the fact that Andy Coope and Paul Herman no longer run with the group as they wouldn't have suffered these fools gladly. There was no retribution for my deed except for the ribbing I suffered from my mates as we continued our run. They told me the police would soon be here and would take the lad's word rather than mine. They reiterated this when we happened to spot a panda car on patrol later into the run, but I could have always said to the coppers, "Get lost filth, scum, pigs" like they do on The Bill.

The blow took on far greater significance when I told someone about it afterwards in the squash club. I could picture the lad's head jolting back with beads of sweat shooting off in every direction just like in the Rocky films. This then evolved to his knees buckling and staggering all over the place in a desperate attempt to remain upright, just like Bradfordian, Richard Dunne at the hands of Muhammad Ali all those years ago. I had struck a blow for our hobby and for running.

My mates did say that if the worst came to the worst, they would visit me in prison and bake me a cake with a file in it.

CHAPTER 21

You've Gotta Be Jowken!

ICKETS FROM Dewsbury" shouted the inspector as the late night Trans Pennine Express train pulled out of the station. "You've gotta be jowken" piped up the scouser, "nobody gets on at Dewsbury".

Well the wag obviously hadn't been in town on February race day morning when tramps, vagrants, junkies and people visiting the Sunday Market are bolstered by over 1000 runners and spectators for the latest edition of the classic road race. No doubt the ticket inspector and other railway staff would be kept busier than normal with the comings and goings at the station.

After a gap of a year due to Transco work along Bradford Road, the race returned as the Yorkshire Mill Mile 10K, run on the usual course along the valley bottom from Dewsbury to beyond Batley and back. The first class organisation of Dewsbury Road Runners has seen the race develop from a five mile fun run in the early days, into a major event with county runners and international athletes taking part in recent years.

Away from the sharp end of the race, many are just content to plod around to raise money for Martin House Hospice Appeal or for their own nominated charity. The field has regularly topped 1,000 and conditions over the years have varied from driving wind and rain to almost perfect.

Activity outside the impressive Victorian Station building was perhaps busier than usual if only by way of runners and their families parking up ahead of the race. With still half an hour go, I made my way down the steep narrow streets taking care to avoid a dumped tin of paint with the contents oozing out across the pavement which did little to raise the ambience of the place. A welcome plan to redevelop the town centre had been recently tabled by way of refurbishing the interiors of some of these grand old buildings, while taking care to meticulously restore the stone frontages.

Runners had started to assemble in the Market Square, each undergoing their own particular ritual or build up. Eventually we are under starters orders as the announcer conveyed last minute instructions and asks us to look out for furniture in the road in the early stages. They obviously hadn't shifted it from the previous race.

We soon edge forward but suddenly break into a shuffle and then into a jog, only to come to an abrupt halt. Already the leaders are a couple of hundred yards ahead and theirs no chance of me winning the race now! We are soon jogging once again and moving along quite nicely.

Under the railway arch and past Safeway's, the procession continues along Bradford Road, sometimes four, five and six abreast across the carriageway. Tall buildings of local stone, some no doubt former textile mills, line the roadside as the first K is reached near O'Donoghues in a shade below five minutes.

Passing Legends with the Elvis Presley figure fixed on the canopy above the door, a sign indicates we are now in Batley. A work colleague recently told me that Batley was on fire at weekends and Dewsbury folk even ventured up the road for a night out. There is no shortage of eateries with Maharaja, Indian Spice and Sizzlers to name but a few, A crowd of young Asian boys are fooling around on the pavement. Do I hear a Dire Straits number coming on!

Marshals spontaneously wave us through the traffic lights and up a slight incline or at least it feels like one. With steep hills on either side and into the distance, it's hats off to the organisers who do well to find such a flat course in the vicinity. There are plenty of places for the Sunday shop with the giant Tesco building quickly followed by Netto and Aldi. Lots to see on the course and much more interesting than those boring runs along country lanes and canal tow paths.

Heckmondwike to the left and Morley to the right but still we press on past more industrial units and Mill Shops advertising furniture, beds and windows. No loop around Wilton Park Lake this year to distract the ducks and the model boat enthusiasts, instead straight on to the turn around point at Brookroyd Lane.

The flashing lights of the lead vehicle come into view with the front-runners battling it out. I quickly see Karen Ball belting down the other side followed by Glyn Jones. Then Roger Ward of Rothwell who I'm sure to catch on the way back if I get a move on.

On this part of the course, runners are solid on both sides of the road. You can spot who's slightly ahead and those who you will have your work cut out to catch. Once the turnaround point is negotiated, you can then see who's behind and those who you need to shake off. Individual races within the main race can start to develop.

I call across to Derek and Milly with words of encouragement, as we pass yet more eateries, namely Kings Restaurant and Posh Nosh. There are more industrial units advertising beds, windows, furniture and yet more beds. With the amount of beds for sale, the good people of Batley are probably all still slumbering tightly rather than in their rightful place on the pavements supporting the race.

Plenty of garages advertising Tyres, Service and M.O.T but at this stage I spare a thought and try to encourage the runners still coming the other way, albeit only a trickle now. Through the speed cameras without registering and around the bend past the ghastly Batley Bats stone arch monument. A sign on the gable end say's Bigfella's at Jessops.

A slight curve in front of the impressive Buttons Mill where a fire destroyed the previous building in 1874, but I'm certainly not on fire today. All the greats appeared at The Frontier when it was Batley Variety Club but no one is billed today.

"Go on Chunky, you should be up near the front", is the cry from the pavement. "Less of the Chunky", I instinctively reply, turning to see three leather jacketed men following the progress of the race. Chunky was a nickname in a former life as I am reminded in some of the most unusual places from time to time, but for the life of me, I couldn't and still can't place who these three reprobates were.

The next flat and straight stretch to Redbrick Mill provides the opportunity to pick up the pace, build momentum, gaining those vital few seconds required to achieve your target, depending upon how you feel. The Redbrick Mill have been the main race sponsors in recent years and a sign below the logo, advertises the Iron Bed Co. Certainly no shortage of places, if you need to lie down in a hurry.

New Cars, used cars, vans & motor bikes to suit any taste or price bracket. You can buy any vehicle along this stretch which must be paradise to the car enthusiast or the browser, but back to the race which is now reaching it's climax.

I pass H.S.L. from where I recently purchased some chairs, mentioning to the salesman Martin, that I would be running today as you do. True to his word, he was looking out for me from the comfort of a sofa in the showroom window so I gave him a friendly wave. Perhaps he would be sitting there for quite some time as customers would be a little thin on the ground this morning, neither being able to get in or out for the premises for the time being.

Another fast stretch beckons if there is anything left in the tank. Welcome to Dewsbury says the sign outside Pillows and Quilts, no doubt to supplement the many beds on offer. The Poacher public house stands back from the road but isn't open for business yet.

Under the viaduct again with a dog leg by the market and I'm almost home. One last effort and I try to look good along the finishing strait towards the Town Hall. Feelings of joy, satisfaction and relief emerge as I make my weary way through the check out funnels.

No time to catch my breath or have a well deserved cough before application forms, freebies and tee shirt are thrust upon me. Well done everyone, see you again next year.

CHAPTER 22

The Trout, The Whole Trout

RUNNERS KNOW all too well that the same events on corresponding weekends each year tend to provide similar weather conditions, and the popular Snake Lane Ten staged in and around Pocklington in East Yorkshire is no exception. On the occasions I have competed here, the weather has often provided snow, sleet, frost and ice, more often than not topped with a bitterly cold Northerly wind.

2005 was no different and as we started out on our hour-long journey, the outlook appeared bleak. The usual guessing game of 'Is the tide in or Is the tide out' took place as we crossed the Ouse Bridge near Goole, but in truth, the grey sky was so full of snow flakes that we could hardly make out where the waters edge met the land.

This was no day for travellers but perhaps one for sitting in-front of a warm fire and reading of travellers tales.

Our aspirations were further dented when a diversion at Howden turned out to be an eight- mile detour through what would normally have been the picturesque villages of Bubwith and Foggathorpe. The fields in the vicinity had a white blanket, snow was beginning to settle on the road and cars coming towards us had headlights on full beam. But all of this didn't deter the metal detector mob who worked in an adjacent field, all well wrapped to combat the elements.

On rejoining the main road, talk turned to having a full breakfast should the race be cancelled as we passed an inviting transport café. I had called at one and the same for a full breakfast, some years ago on the way to the Bridlington Half Marathon. I bitterly regretted this once the race started as the fried bread started to take effect.

The outlook was bleak as we approached Pocklington, with a generous covering of snow on the ground and more starting to fall. I drove through the Market Square where they were cordoning off the finish area and erecting barriers, but having been here, done it and got the souvenir mug on several occasions, I struggled to find the rugby ground.

We must have circumnavigated it as once again we returned through the Market Square where they were now in fact laying out the souvenir mugs on trestle tables for the race finishers. Not blue again surely! "Follow that car" said Roy, spotting two lycra clad figures inside, and in doing so, we swung into one of several narrow side streets and almost immediately spotted the tell tail floodlight pylons at the Rugby Ground. "Will it be on then" asked Terry. "Of course it will, I've run in worse here", I replied".

As we were being directed into the ground, I wound the window down and asked the marshal if the race was definitely on. "Yes" he replied. "We haven't had to call one off yet". There's always a first time I thought, as I put my hand up to thank him, but this news had put a dampener on our 'Full English' well at least for another weekend.

My inability to find the Rugby Ground at the first time of asking had cost us ten minutes and with it, the chance of a good parking space on terra firma. We were waved around the side of one of the ancillary pitches where the ground was already starting to churn up. Sweatshop were selling sports goods from a temporary stand but were channelling most of their efforts into keeping the tarpaulin down on the roof in the gusty wind.

Inside the club house, pockets of people were huddled around radiators with others cupping hands around steaming mugs of tea or coffee. The home made cakes were practically crying out to be bought but I would wait until after the race. They were selling souvenir tee shirts with the name of every participant in the race printed on, albeit very small. Impressive as these were and much as

I would have liked one, I decided to pass on this having draw upon draw of the blasted things at home, with many unopened and still in the cellophane.

A guy at the local squash club had tried to sell me some at £1 apiece with monies apparently going to a worthy cause. I turned him down for the very same reason and told him that I could let him have some tee shirts, but he nevertheless appeared to take umbrage.

I placed a wad of flyers for my book 'Middle of the Packer' among others advertising various races. "I've read that" said one onlooker, "Did you write it?". "For my sins, yes" I replied, "If you enjoyed it, pass the word on".

We decided to brave the biting wind and add the finishing touches to our preparations. Many runners were warming up by lapping the perimeter of the main Rugby Field. I completed one circuit before returning to the warmth of the car. But having recently enjoyed Richard Askwith's book, 'Feet in the Clouds' about a year in the life of a fell runner, I realised we were having it cushy in comparison to these people. With these thoughts in mind I left the sanctuary of the car behind to complete several further warm up laps.

With race time beckoning, we were marshalled together and walked through back streets, passages and alleyways to the start on the fringes of Pocklington. There was little wonder we couldn't find the Rugby Club at the first time of asking. "It doesn't seem like a year ago that we ran into the blizzard", I remarked to John Faulkner as the snow at last stopped and the sun began to break through. "It's cold enough though" he replied.

This was the first race in our club Grand Prix Series in which the best eight scores from ten races count and was in no small part responsible for a good contingent of Ackworth Road Runners. Everyone was starting from a clean slate and had high hopes for the year ahead. 2004 had seen me finish fifth in the first of three divisions, but unlikely to reach those giddy heights again, I would take it as it comes. For others there were aspirations of medal positions or promotion.

The black and gold colours of 'The Square Wasps' were once again well represented. The Wasps or Knavesmire Harriers had recently celebrated twenty five years and had produced an informative, commemorative brochure. There was also a large turn out in the green and black of East Leeds Club, St Theresa's. Super Veteran, John Johnson told me the race was also in their club championship and that this would be his twenty-third year of running. We talked fondly about the early Leeds Marathons when we perhaps didn't take things quite so seriously.

Best of the bunch was a lad of stocky build wearing a tee shirt cum sweat shirt with the pictures of three fish emblazoned across the front. The humorous slogan read :- The trout, the whole trout and nothing but the trout, so help me cod. This tee shirt was more like it! Why can't they award these to race finishers instead of some of the usual bland designs.

Before I realised it we were off, turning into a long straight road with neatly trimmed verges. The early charge soon dropped to a more sensible pace as the field became well strung out. The early miles were into a stiff breeze but nothing like the blizzard conditions of 2004, although the dusting of snow on the Wolds provided a picturesque backdrop. The decision to go ahead had been fully justified with only slush and water on the road as a hindrance.

We turned left passing the first mile post in six and a half minutes, a tad too quickly for a man of my calibre but the balance was somewhat redressed with two miles completed in fourteen minutes. A slight rise between high hedgerows brought us to an elevated spot where I could see the flashing light of the lead vehicle, far away in the distance.

The course is slightly undulating with nothing to worry about, but a longish downhill through Meltonby provides the impetus to kick on. The other race in this area, The Yorkshire Wolds Half Marathon runs in the opposite direction before heading for the hills, and I remember thinking that I was glad not to be doing that one today.

We run directly towards the foothills of the Wolds but turn sharp left and run in the lee of the hills. This lessens the wind although the watery sun is now replaced with further snow showers. Another ridge at four miles provides views of Bishop Wilton and the spire of St Edith's Church. We hardly enter the village before turning left and slightly downhill, with cottages to the right hand side and a beck running at the bottom of a grassy banking on the left. I go through five miles in thirty-six and a half minutes and feel pretty pleased with my efforts so far.

Conditions are much easier now as we turn into the Snake Lane section with the wind at our backs. The road twists and turns across wide-open fields with the wind at times whipping us along but on other occasions blowing across the road. It was on this section where we encountered severe conditions, several years ago by way of a snow storm. Some prospective runners had turned their cars around before reaching Pocklington while others had made it safely, only to battle their way through the elements. Fortunately the conditions had eased to provide a safe journey home.

The Snake Lane section is predominantly flat with only a slight incline to the main road at Bolton. From here to the finish there are several slight rises which is where the race is won and lost and where vital minutes can be gained for those chasing fast times. We pass Smylett Hall to the left and a signpost to Yapham indicates we have almost come full circle.

I appear to have plenty of running left and start to pick up places. I spot the tell tale colours of an Ackworth colleague up front and on closing in, I realise it is Alan Boyd who I wouldn't normally have expected to beat. But each time I get to within striking distance, he puts in a surge and even though he doesn't look around, he appears to know I'm there. With the final climb out of the way and the imposing All Saints Church in the distance, I really go for it. With half a mile remaining, I can surely peg him back, so I lift my knees, grit my teeth, pump my arms and pump anything else that'll pump. Even though I catch plenty of others, I can't catch Alan. As he turns the final corner into the Market Square, I'm sitting on his shoulder but unable to gain those vital extra couple of yards. We breach the line in consecutive places which is probably why Club Chairman Cyril records Alan's time but misses mine.

I finished in a shade over 1 hour 13 minutes for a mornings work well done. After handshakes and the usual banter, we make our way back to the Rugby Club as huge flakes of snow once again start to fall steadily. I spot a regular face on the running circuit, changing back into warm clothing from the boot of his car and pouring himself a welcome warm drink from a flask. "Where's the next one then" I asked. I'm running in a Cross Country next week at York" he replied. There's just no way of stopping some people.

Despite the adverse conditions, times were generally good with several of our members setting personal bests and Christine McCarthy breaking a long standing club record for ladies over thirty five. Meanwhile in the clubhouse, Cyril was trying to persuade race winner, Dave Watson of Holmfirth that it surely made sense to run in our promotion, the Wilkinson Ackworth Half Marathon to be staged in a few weeks time.

We warmed ourselves by way of a cold beer, but with all the best cakes sold out, said our cheerio's before heading home. Showered, changed and unpacked. I squeezed my three Fangfoss Pottery Mugs and one bowl together on the cabinet shelf to make room for the latest edition. I'm sure I must have another one in a draw or a cupboard somewhere.

Some days later when the results appear on the web site, I am pleased to discover that I came 202nd from 557 who finished. More of a surprise however is the other 250 who had entered but didn't compete, either reluctant to brave the elements or probably preferring a Full English Breakfast instead.

CHAPTER 23

Follow The Country Code

ITH PERENNIAL organiser Dave Bancroft no longer in the fold and nobody coming forward to fill the breach, Adrian Byrom and I set about organising the teams to take part in the 2005 Leeds Country Way Relay. The event meticulously organised by Kippax Harriers is usually staged on the first Sunday in September and covers the 64 miles around the Leeds boundaries, mainly on tracks, footpaths, across fields and with short stretches on the roads. There are sections through Golf Courses, alongside rivers and canals, disused railway lines and even a churchyard. The North Leeds stages pass through quiet villages with a stretch through the grounds of the historic Harewood House. There are fine views over Lower Wharfedale on couple of the elevated sections.

The six legs of approximately ten miles each must be run in pairs constituting twelve runners per team. There are cut off times at each changeover point where the couples still waiting to go all set off altogether. By doing this, all teams should finish for 5-00clock enabling results to be compiled and presentations to be made.

Over the years Dave had been dealt a crap hand with people generally messing him about but each year he would return with batteries recharged for more of the same. He must have had a heart like a Lion. Dave also organised the teams for The Calderdale Way Relay in which we took part for several years but this had raised the organisational grief to monstrous proportions.

Runners had regularly dropped out at very short notice resulting in us been unable to field full teams and along with it, disqualification. One year a particular pairing just hadn't shown up, instead apparently opting for a long training run. They neither notified Dave or anyone else for that matter and never mentioned it afterwards. This prompted Dave to pen an article in the clubs 'Footnotes' entitled 'Thanks for letting us know lads'.

This apart, we had regular occurrences of runners being injured on their leg, resulting in the team being disqualified and not receiving an overall placing. There were also instances of runners leaving their mates who were unable to keep up. There were the understandable moans about teams being changed at short notice and those of unequal ability being paired together. But if somebody withdrew at short notice, short of a reshuffle, Dave sometimes would have very little option.

Adrian and I figured that where Dave and others before him had gone wrong was by leaving it too late to organise the teams. We would make a start immediately after the Yorkshire Veterans Relays at the end of June, giving us ample opportunity to raise two, even three and maybe a ladies team. How wrong we were!

The fact that we had struggled to raise three and four man teams for the Veterans Relays should have served as a warning shot across our bows but it didn't and so we enthusiastically set about the task of organising the teams. Some people were keen and signed up immediately but others said they didn't know what they were doing so far ahead and asked to be reminded again closer to the date. Other people agreed to run, only to withdraw later on while some changed their minds several times.

We received comments such as, "It's too long a day", " There's too much messing about" or "It's a waste of time". One guy said he had done it once and there was no way he would do it ever again. I told him that it would be much better organised this year and that he would have none of these problems, but after that he started avoiding me like the plague.

One lad was in training for an Autumn marathon and asked if he could run two legs. We told him he couldn't do this and suggested that on finishing his leg he should run back from whence he came but he didn't seem too keen on the idea saying he might not be able to find his way back. I didn't like this either as I could foresee problems with the placement of cars.

It soon became apparent that we had been handed the poisoned chalice. The logistics of the event determined that a car had to be left at both the start and finish points of each leg. When the leg had been completed, one runner would need to drive the other one back to collect his or her car. Usually there was a wait at the start of each leg for the previous runners to come through which meant the race could be tedious to run in, let alone to organise.

Adrian had agreed to organise the 'A' Team and I would take care of the 'B' Team and a 'C' Team if we had enough bodies. But Adrian was struggling to get people to commit and I couldn't move forward until I knew who was running for him. We kept in regular contact but soon realised that we would have to settle for two teams rather than three.

But we were still short of runners and asked those again who had already turned us down. I scoured the membership list for likely conscripts and was surprised at some of the people I was able to recruit. One or two said they would run if we were desperately short which was really of little use to us at this stage

As the weeks passed by and still not much further forward, it became clear that desperate times would call for desperate measure. Rio Ferdinand style contracts were offered, the odd bung and a brace a pheasants here and there and at last the teams began to take shape. I looked back over five years to see who had run together and on which legs, and finally the pairings started to come together.

Apart from organising the teams, I had paid the entry fees out of my own pocket and the money needed collecting. That was another nightmare. Then there were the routes and race information and numbers to distribute to people. This was a headache too. The fairly comprehensive literature asked us to follow the Country Code at all times, avoid damaging fences, hedges and walls. Fasten all gates, keep to the paths across farmland, protect wildlife, plants and trees and respect the life of the countryside. You would have thought we were about to go on a rampage rather than run in a foot race. It also stated that anyone found deviating from the route would be disqualified. In good faith, this wasn't always done deliberately.

Then there were the routes to reconnoitre for those who hadn't run particular legs before or were new to the event. Adrian, who probably wondered how the hell he had been talked into organising this, spent time with several people on a couple of the legs. A week before the relay, Roy Young asked me if I would have a dummy run over Leg Four with him. He had previously run the leg several years earlier but felt in need of a refresher.

We met at Golden Acre Park where Mel and a friend of the Chapel Striders club were about to reconnoitre Leg Five. "I'm running that leg, I'll look out for you next week" I said. As organiser I could at least choose which leg I preferred to run and Leg Five was my choice, or so I thought at this stage. We travelled in Roy's car to Thornbury and complete with the instructions, set out to explore the leg.

"Where do we start" I asked Roy. "We run along the edge of this cricket field, or it could be that football field or one of those rugby pitches". It soon became apparent that this was going to be a very long morning. Some of the discs and signs that at one time had signified the Country Way were no longer in place while others were damaged or faded. Apart from this there were signs for the Dales Way and Transpennine Cycle route which added to the confusion. Fortunately we stumbled across other runners who were able to help us out, but we spent twenty minutes looking for a gap in a wall leading to some sunken steps. "Don't you remember any of this leg" I asked Roy. "Only vaguely he replied, Richard knew it so I just followed him. The only thing I can definitely remember" he said, "Was running in the field with the landing lights, next to the airport runway". The whole exercise took us three hours and I told Roy that I expected a big improvement from him on the day.

With the event only a week away, we were still one runner short for each team but I quickly filled the void for the second string. Adrian's team was looking particularly strong but he was still awaiting a decision from one guy who apparently had a bad back and a sore shoulder. This runner would undertake a short training run which would serve as a fitness test, check on any reaction and then make a decision. Until then, Adrian was in limbo. Meanwhile I had to reconnoitre parts of Leg One and make some notes for the two runners who had been drafted in at short notice and would lead us off. Later that day, I received a phone call from a runner who was pulling out. I asked a casual acquaintance who I would see running along the canal towpath if he fancied a run and even asked my neighbour if he was up to doing ten miles.

Awaking on Tuesday morning, my first thoughts were of the Leeds Country Relay and the need to recruit somebody quickly. This was turning into a nightmare! I waited until the evening, phoned three people and persuaded the last one of these that it surely made sense to run. We were up to full strength once again and I could look forward with anticipation to the big day.

Then on Wednesday afternoon while phoning one of our lady runners to confirm her transport arrangements, she told me that she was worried about the event, not looking forward to it and would have to withdraw there and then. I believe that for some reason she had been got at by a negative influence. I sat in the chair for ten minutes without moving, contemplating, totally dejected, and mentally drained.

When I eventually stirred, I walked across to the window. On the triangle of grass outside my house, a man of perhaps 60 years was allowing his dog some slack on the lead and I could see it was manoeuvring into position to make a deposit. As I watched, it deposited three huge stools onto the grass. This was exactly the outlet valve I needed. I would take out my anger on this man.

Despite a disc on the lamp post only feet away advising dog walkers to clear up their mess, this had provided of little deterrent to most but I was heartily sick of regularly having to scrape the mess from under my shoes and from car tyres.

Storming out to the gate, the man had moved further along the street with his dog now sniffing the foot of a wall. "I hope you're not going to leave those there" I shouted, repeating myself when he failed to reply. He reluctantly turned around, foraged about in his pocket and produced some tissue. With his head down he grudgingly hunted for the deposits seemingly to no avail. "You should be able to see them, they were big enough", I prompted.

Humiliated enough, the man looked across and retorted, "Well bloody well look for them yourself then, well bloody well look for them yourself". I thought he was about to chin me as he came over to the gate with mouth foaming and chin dribbling. "It's alright for you", he screamed, "I've got Parkinson's Disease". "That's unfortunate I replied, very unfortunate, but I want that shit clearing".

Batteries charged and refreshed, I enthusiastically set about the task of recruiting the twelfth man for my team by phoning around and leaving messages with people but still to no avail. I contacted one of the people who had said he would run if I was desperate and boy, was I desperate. He said that he presumed we now had full teams and had made other arrangements, but offered to change them. "Don't do that I said" not wanting to be in his wife's bad books. I contacted another guy for a third time to go cap in hand to his boss for a shift change but that didn't work either.

Why was it that we always struggled to raise teams for these kind of events. Surely the members of Wakefield Harriers and Leeds City would be bending over backwards to represent their clubs. They would surely pick their teams rather than recruit them. When I was first asked to represent Ackworth in The Kippax Rat Relays all those years ago albeit only in Team 'D', I was pleased as punch. Other people obviously felt differently which begged the question of why they had joined a running club in the first place if they were reluctant to represent it.

I received the phone call I had been hoping for when Gail Tombs said that Cathy Berry would run the fifth leg with her. This meant that I would have to fill in on Leg Three with Ian, and as he hadn't previously run any of the legs, I would have to reconnoitre it the next day. I had run Leg Three some years ago so would only run the parts of which I was unsure. But doing this on my own meant I could only run small sections as I had to park my car and run out and then back to the car. I completed this over two days on Thursday and Friday, not even thinking about how I felt or if I was tired. That week I had run more miles than Forest Gump and had still to run in the relay itself.

A phone call to Adrian confirmed he too had a full team but not before being given more grief. The guy who had needed to give himself a fitness test, and had been earmarked for Leg Six had thrown a wobbly and said that he would only be prepared to run a morning leg. That had meant more ringing around for Adrian and shuffling his pack. We checked mentally that everyone had their numbers and literature and Adrian was able to fill out the lists with our running order.

But as they say, "It will be all right on the night" or in our case on the day and what a glorious day beckoned turning into a scorcher particularly for the runners on the later legs. Our 'A' Team looked particularly strong with Charlie Lines and Andrew Jackson getting us off to a cracking start despite having to negotiate gypsy caravans and their fierce animals near Rothwell Sports Centre. They finished the leg in an excellent 4th place, one adrift of Rothwell. Whereas Rothwell were able to maintain the momentum, we gradually lost places but nevertheless finished in a very creditable 11th place with everyone playing their part. This bettered our previous best finish of 12th in 1995.

I was delighted with the 'B' Team we had assembled. Three former lady club champions, a husband and wife pairing and two bus drivers to bring us home on the last leg, were just the ticket. Despite finishing only 29th from 37 teams, we made a significant improvement on previous years and were only 17 seconds adrift of Ilkley who were one place in front.

With fifty miles under my belt the previous week, I was running on anger and adrenalin with little regard for how I felt. Despite having to dodge the clays at a pigeon shoot in progress, I belted along with Ian in my slipstream and together we made up six places on Leg Three, having a ding dong battle with the St Theresa's pairing. They sportingly called us back when we went slightly off route and we returned the favour later on. But we didn't anticipate having a sprint finish with two other pairs to see who could reach the changeover point at Thornbury first.

Probably due to the fact that our 'A' Team finished in a best ever 11th place and we managed to stay ahead of all the cut off times, Adrian claimed that all the hassle had been worthwhile. I somehow doubted it.

The previous year, race director Lionel Theobald of Kippax Harriers had set out early to run all six legs covering the 64 miles of the Leeds Country Way and had managed to finish before the presentations were made. He said that this had been easy when compared to organising the event.

With everything over bar the shouting, with the dust well and truly settled and confident of the fact that I would never put myself through this ordeal again, I inserted the following advertisement in the club newsletter, perhaps a little tongue in cheek.

Situation Vacant for highly motivated individual of strong energetic profile from a successful background to identify and establish opportunities using available resources. Must be innovative, adaptable and empowering, demonstrate a high level of tact and diplomacy while possessing enthusiasm and determination to deliver results. Negotiating and Team Building skills are important along with the ability to communicate at all levels, make decisions on your feet and 'Think outside the box'. The successful applicant must be able to ride setbacks, have the patience of job, bouncebackability and a bloody big crystal ball. No, the position isn't a Junior Executive for a Blue Chip Company. It's for a person to co-ordinate the Ackworth teams for the Leeds Country Relay in 2006.

CHAPTER 24

More Than A Monster

THE STUNNING scenery on the journey from Perth was suffi-
cient to hold my attention particularly near Pitlochry where
the train line runs through a deep narrow gauge. What had
been a pleasant journey was interrupted with a bang when a party
of schoolgirls boarded at Newtonmore. Those who didn't continually race through the carriage sat in obligatory pose with feet tucked
up on seat with one trying her utmost to tear the seat arm from it's
socket by opening and closing it with such ferocity. Others called
up each other on their mobile phones to while away the journey, no
doubt running up a hefty bill for Dad at the same time.

Nobody seemed to bother so I didn't and unperturbed I passed
away the remainder of the journey with my head buried in Paul
Gogarty's 'Coast Road'. At last the shoreline of the Moray Firth
came into view along with the imposing stanchions of the Kessock
Bridge, and we duly arrived in Inverness, dead on midday.

Rapidly turning into a grumpy old man, I held back to avoid being ploughed down by the schoolgirls. I cleared the ticket barrier,
sauntered along the concourse and through the door of the Royal
Highland Hotel. Adjoining the station, this would be a fine base
and ideal for my early train back to Glasgow on Monday morning.

My room wasn't ready so I hit the streets making my way to the
Ness Bank and Johnny Fox's Irish Pub, apparently voted the best
pub in Inverness. As I ordered a pint of the black stuff, the piped
music suddenly started with 'Irish Rover' followed by 'Dirty Old
Town' and 'Fairytale of New York', easily the best Christmas pop
song by a country mile. The busy waitress came over for my order
and I opted for a burger and fries with all the relish.

Shoppers came in here, mothers with children, businessmen and yes, drunks. Drunk No 1 was slouched at the bar in a woolly hat, denim jacket and plimsolls, aka The Edge of Rock Band, U2. Getting up from the stool his legs buckled and he wobbled and teetered the few yards to the door before more of the same out on the street.

I soon followed him, making my way towards the Victorian Market where I encountered drunk No 2 who approached with glazed expressionless eyes, before taking a swipe at a convenient wheelie bin and sending the cans, bottles and debris sprawling out across the pavement.

The Victorian Market is a close-knit maze of the typical shops you would expect in a market along with arts and crafts, knick knacks and a sizeable proportion of Charity shops. I left the Market towards the Bus Station where drunk No 3 was zigzagging along the pavement buffeting into the wall, into a bus shelter and clipping passers by in order to give his cigarette that elusive light. If people were like this before 1-00 clock in the afternoon, what would late afternoon and evening hold for the city. Wanting to get in on the act, I said to a woman, "I wouldn't mind a pint of what he's had". "Aye, why not" she replied.

The return bus fare for the 25 minute journey to Dingwall knocked me back £6-10 and really did knock me back! The Stagecoach bus approached the run on to the Kessock Bridge passing the wind-swept ground of Inverness Caledonian Thistle, arch rivals of my adopted team, Ross County.

On alighting, I followed the flow over the railway bridge and past the old jail to the ground. At £6-10 bus fare, £12 admission into the ground, £2 for a programme, £1 for a half time lottery ticket and £1 plus for pie and Bovril it was costing me a pretty penny. Just imagine having to fork out your well-earned dosh to support a premier club in England with inflated ticket prices. There's no wonder attendances are currently on the wane.

Despite this being my first home game for almost two years, (I had been to plenty of away games throughout this time), I still picked my regular seat with the same people sitting around me. The fat man with jam jar glasses, who's personal hygiene packed a harder shot than any of the County forwards, sat on the end of the row. Next to him were look-alike brother, look-alike wife and look-alike son. Between them they ploughed their way through packets of crisps, packets of sweets and packets of fags. Then there was the bushy bearded guy who would wait for a lull in the crowd noise before delivering his cryptic comments for maximum effect. There was the polite supporter who from time to time would voice comments such as "Nice play County" or "Good decision referee". Last but not least was the man who continually upped and left his seat to replenish his appetite for Bovril and pies and talking about pies it was half time and time I was going for mine.

Hoping to steal a march, I walked around the back of the terracing to the stall on the far side of the ground, but a queue had developed by the time I reached here and I was forced to listen to the confident banter of the Queen of the South supporters who's team lead 1-0 at this stage, very much against the run of play. There was a bitterly cold wind with rain in the air and I hoped that conditions would improve for the race next day.

No doubt buoyed by the fact that Queens had two men sent off in the second half, County threw everything but the kitchen sink at the opposition, duly equalised but couldn't grab a winner. The biggest cheer of the day came at the final whistle when an announcement confirmed that St Mirren had been beaten meaning the draw would send County to the top of Division One. Would the dream of Premiership Football and regular games against the old firm teams become reality. The 2,000 supporters drifted away happily, into the dusk and the drizzle.

Installed in the hotel and unpacked, I made my way through the city and onto the Ness Banks towards the Queens Park Stadium in order to register for the race. The river although shallow was flowing rapidly, obviously not deterring a couple of anglers who had

waded towards the centre to try their luck. The evening was bitterly cold and the walk was much longer than anticipated. A steady
trickle of people emerged from the opposite direction, most carrying plastic bags as if they were coming away from the registration.

A series of marquees in the centre of the running track formed the
race headquarters comprising registration, trade and charity stands
with the pasta party in a separate marquee.

With the Robin Hood Marathon and the Great North Run still in
my legs from recent weeks, my intention had been to transfer my
entry to the shorter River Ness 10K. But with the race apparently
sold out several weeks ago, they weren't getting rid of me so easily
and I would go in the marathon after all.

When I saw my book, 'Middle of the Packer' on sale at the
stand of Sports Retailer, Run & Become, I felt pleased as punch.
Introducing myself to proprietor Adrian Stott and thanking him for
selling copies, he told me that he would be present at tomorrows
race in the lead vehicle. I told him I would have a good look at the
vehicle before the start as that would be the last I would see of it
once the race was underway.

I felt tired just looking at a map of the point-to-point course on
the marquee wall. "What's the course like" asked a guy doing the
same as me. "It's the first time, I've run here", I said. "Some people
say it's hard and others say it's not too bad. Somebody said it was
hilly between 3 and 5 miles, someone said it was undulating most
of the way and somebody else said the main hills are from 16 miles".
"What I do know", I told him, "Is that it starts on higher ground, and
that the last four miles are flat. You'll just have to see how you find
it on the day". He seemed pleased with what I had told him and we
wished each other the best of luck for the following day.

In truth I hadn't even started thinking about the undulations on
the course and didn't particularly feel up for it. I would have to get
my brain into Marathon mode before too long. After buying half a
dozen rum truffles from The Inverness Fudge Company that almost
topped the scales, I meandered back to the hotel by way of a short

cut through a housing estate and across some playing fields. With my legs starting to feel heavy, I made the decision to catch a taxi to race start in the morning and with that I turned in for the night.

With the breakfast room closed at crack of dawn, I grabbed a yogurt and some biscuits from the station shop before heading towards the taxi rank. Requiring to go to Bught Park I asked the driver for Bute but after appearing to think about it for a while he said, " You mean Bucht". Even though the taxi appeared to be facing the correct way, the driver nevertheless spun the cab around and headed off in the opposite direction no doubt knowing a more effective and expensive longer route.

Runners and their families were heading towards the long line of coaches, poised for the considerable journey to the race start near Whitebridge. This must have been a good, one off contract for the local coach firms. Even though the front coaches had nicely filled, they still remained parked, so I had to walk some way along the queue to find one with available seats.

A woman standing on the grass stood looking at the guy occupying the seat in front of me and from time to time they would signal to each other or pass cryptic messages. What was all that about then? Lead by a police car with a flashing light, the convoy of coaches started to move and the woman started waving frantically at her spouse and then continued to wave as she walked.

No sooner had our coach moved forward than it stopped again to let on a straggler who came to sit next to me. He was from overseas, probably South America, and out of breath. When he eventually composed himself., he asked me if this was the bus for the 10K start. "Afraid not" I said, "It's for the marathon, you'd better get off." The runner in the seat behind obviously overhearing the conversation said, "He can do the last 10K for me if he wants". I sympathised with the guy as I have done exactly the same thing, while also being a long way from home.

The convoy of some forty coaches, headed back through the streets of Inverness towards the A9. Once on the dual carriageway they started to jockey for position, overtaking each other and playing cat and mouse. Our coach eventually moved up to number five in the pecking order behind the police car.

A guy walked down the aisle of the coach to talk to the driver. One wag commented, "Does he want the coach for the 10K as well". After talking to the driver he made his way back up the coach and negotiating the centre stairwell, disappeared into the toilet. At the time I thought rather him than me and I trusted the coach didn't suddenly brake, swerve or turn a sharp corner. As soon as he emerged and returned to his seat, a young lady made her way to the toilet, eventually coming out and looking pleased with herself. She was quickly followed by another woman and then a man and in all eleven such people followed in quick succession. What was the obsession with runners and toilets? Surely they could wait while we reached the start.

The constant stream to the urinal prompted the driver to make an announcement stating the toilet wasn't designed to take such hammer and would anyone else refrain from using it and try and hold on until we reached the start where facilities were sure to be much more plentiful.

We had turned off the A9 onto a minor road towards Fort Augustus and were travelling through beautiful moorland scenery. There were dense forests of pine with trees planted so tightly, they were vying with each other to capture the sunlight. Sheep grazed on hillsides and cows stood motionless on any available vantage point eyeing the procession of coaches and no doubt wondering what it was all about. Who needs to run a marathon when you can eat grass all day long. A boy and girl outside a holiday chalet waved frantically as we passed by.

The journey took about an hour and was in itself a mini scenic tour of the highlands that people on holiday would have gladly paid for. The trouble was, they were going to drop us off in the middle of nowhere and we would have to run back.

The start was on higher ground near Whitebridge and as the

coach slowed down, the driver announced, no doubt tongue in cheek. "Look what's over there in that field! Loads of Urinals." This was met with much merriment and a ripple of applause. An official in a yellow bib boarded the coach and gave instructions stating that everyone must use the portaloos and under no circumstances must anyone attempt to go elsewhere. He said that baggage must be placed in the numbered vans half an hour before race start.

The first man off the coach lit up a fag and when someone made a comment he said, "Well it's a bit difficult lighting up while I'm running. As well as the urinals there were tables from which ladies served tea, coffee and squash. All these were set out on a farm track against a backdrop of isolated heather moors and wilderness.

Although not as cold and windy as Saturday, the day was nevertheless chilly with spots of rain never too far away. A hot tea would hit the spot perfectly and I would worry about going to the loo later on. Despite instructions to the contrary, people still scaled barbed wire fences and meandered into the distance to pay a call. I hate using the portaloos in the knowledge a queue of people are waiting outside all chomping at the bit to go.

A girl had started to get ready by way of laying her kit out on the bonnet of a police car, needless to say the copper wasn't inside. I asked if I could share it and her North American accent prompted me to ask where she was from. "Wisconsin" was the reply, "that's right up top". I said that I had a good idea where all the states were but couldn't put them in Geographical order, but thought the nearest I had probably been was Minneapolis. She had run the Twin Cities Marathon there but enthused about the Grandmas Marathon run along the shore of Lake Superior. She preferred the scenic races to the big city events.

Having changed, vaselined, secured my number and chip and pulled on my bin bag, I wished her luck and handed in my luggage. I had left a fiver in my tracksuit pocket should I need anything at the end such as a taxi back to the hotel.

I took up a position some way back from the start line and a girl asked what time I was looking for. "Anything under four hours will do" I replied. "Then why are you standing in the 3-15 zone" she said. I told her I hadn't seen the time markings but as she had pointed it out I would move back slightly. I couldn't see a problem with people getting through the start but some of the back markers in the 1,000 strong field did actually take several minutes before they were underway. The girl had probably thought that an old bugger like me would never make it in 3-15, and she was of course correct. She had put me in my place so I retreated with my tail between my legs.

We were piped off to the accompaniment of 'Scottish Soldier' from the Lochaber Junior Pipe Band and started down a slight gradient. I felt slightly more upbeat about the race now and was sure I would be fine. I soon caught up with slower runners ahead but faster ones came through making a mockery of who starts where.

I soon hit upon a nice rhythm feeling comfortable, enjoying the stunning scenery and magnificent mountains and it was indeed a privilege to run in such beautiful surroundings. We quickly passed through Whitebridge where a pocket of spectators had gathered outside the hotel, making themselves heard. The next spectators were those who had alighted a Wallace Arnold Coach at a road junction to cheer us on. They appeared to be enjoying the enforced stop, having been caught up in a traffic jam at a road junction no doubt created by the race.

The first glimpse of Loch Ness was after five miles near Foyers where more spectators cheered us on our way through the village. At first the road perched high above the Loch but in places dropped down to the waters edge. There were many niggling little pulls to test the fitness but nothing too severe in those early miles.

Banter was friendly among the competitors and contributed towards the miles slipping by quickly and effortlessly. The same girl kept passing me before stopping to remove contents or adjust her bum bag. "Isn't it a beautiful morning" she said and I had to agree, with the cold wind and drizzle of early morning now giving way to almost ideal running conditions.

The views across the Loch from the higher ground towards Urquhart Castle were dramatic with rugged mountains in the distance. Occasionally we would run through dense woodland or through cuttings that would conceal the Loch but it would reappear through the trees with it's surface glistening like a silver tray. But there was no sign of the Monster, only the occasional small vessel taking advantage of the fine Autumnal conditions. This was altogether a far more uplifting experience than running in one of the big city marathons on crowded urban streets. There were caravans and chalets set in idyllic hillside locations as we passed through the next village of Inverfariagaig.

A guy of similar pace said that he was a duathlete, triathlete and adventure runner. He told me that he had recently completed a two-day event in Cleveland and remarked upon the steep climb out of the fishing village of Staithes. "I know it", I told him, "I stayed there at school camp". "Didn't Captain Cook live or work there?", he asked. Together we went through half way in 1 hour 43 minutes.

Sunday morning cyclists followed friends along the course but were also spontaneous in their encouragement for others too, while a couple of motorcyclists appeared to have dismounted in a lay-by and were enthusiastically cheering us on. This was indeed a stunning place to cycle and I sometimes wish I had done more of it over the years. A friend who had recently reduced his running due to persistent injuries had taken to cycling and planned a coast to coast ride and if successful, maybe a Lands End to John 'O' Groats. I couldn't help but be a little envious.

A pipe band and noisy spectators brought about a carnival atmosphere at Dores where the rugged and dramatic landscape changed to more rolling and much gentler. The long hill beyond seventeen miles was the most difficult on the course. Just when I thought I had made it with the familiar cry of "You're nearly at the top", another long drag presented itself around the next bend.

"This is the last big hill" said the runner alongside and he knew all about hills, living in the Lake District. His one previous marathon had been Langdale and if he had done that, then almost any other race would pose no difficulty. He was looking to run under three and a half hours and would certainly need to hold his running together if not quicken his pace.

I went through 20 miles in 2-45 and 22 in 3-03 still clipping along quite nicely and feeling fine. By 23 miles on the outskirts of Inverness I was hanging on for dear life being hardly able to put one foot down in front of the other. Crowds had started to line the pavements as we approached the capital of the highlands so I didn't wish to look too distressed. Runners with more training miles or those who had had obviously paced themselves better than I had, started to drift by in droves as I struggled to raise my game and get back on terms. A white marking on the road told me there was still 5K to go.

Announcements over the loud speaker at the finish could now be heard but the reality was that we still had to reach the bridge in the centre of Inverness before a final heartbreaking stretch, along the opposite river bank where I had walked the previous night. Here, hotels, smart guest houses and fine residential properties look over the river, so far removed from the bustling city centre of the highland capital.

A pocket of spectators encouraged me to keep moving and I responded with the cry of "How far is this bloody bridge". The bridge in fact came into view around the next bend of the river and as I glanced across, I could see runners streaming back along the far bank towards the finish. Soon I am on the far side myself, safe in the knowledge that I shall finish well inside my customary four-hour target.

The psychological effect of being in the final mile helps me to pick up the pace a little and I now start pass several runners. I press on alongside the endless playing fields of Bught Park, passing the Floral Hall and around two sides of the stadium. With spectators cheering from the grandstand to my right and a huge model of the Loch Ness Monster in the centre of the track, I resort to a sprint finish in order to head off the late bid of a lady Knavesmire Harrier.

The trill of the championship chip sounds as I cross the finish line carpet, a medal is placed around my neck and a particularly heavy goody-bag is thrust into my hand. What could possibly be inside, I wonder! Runners seated on benches indicate I must now remove my chip. I have great difficulty bending down but fortunately help is on hand. I apologise to the steward for tying the chip too tightly but he says that after fastening and unfastening shoes for his children, mine is a doddle. In some races, the plastic disc like chips are fastened with a band around the sock but the traditional ones are worn on the shoe and secured by the laces. These are worn to ensure you are given an accurate time from start line to finish.

Families are allowed to join the runners far too quickly after the finish and there is pandemonium with far too many people milling about. Still unsure on my feet, a dog licks my hand, which I don't like and I end up sitting on my backside after falling over a toddler. His father provides an outstretched hand to help me to my feet and apologises profusely. I didn't bargain for this lot after running twenty-six miles.

I collect my kit bag and grab a chair in the changing marquee. First of all I make sure my fiver and my mobile phone are still in there and then forage for my towel to wipe my face. The chap next to me is tracked down by his wife who says, "What are we doing now". I answer for him by saying, "He's sitting here for half an hour and doing nothing, like me". She didn't seem too impressed but I wasn't bothered. He eventually got up to go for a massage but returned saying the queue was too long.

An Italian sat to my left, introducing himself as Sandro and shaking my hand. He had run 3-59 and seemed well chuffed. "Did you have to sprint to beat four hours", I asked. "No not really he replied", "anyway I should gain a minute or so on my chip timing".

He said that it was his 24th marathon. He had lived here for seventeen years, had done three marathons back in Italy and had done London three times. He hated London saying there were far too many competitors.

Sandro's priority seemed to be to jettison all the items in his goody-bag, which were a tin of soup, a jar of pickle and a packet of pasta. There was little wonder the bag was so heavy. I turned him down on all three but other people gratefully accepted them. "I thought you Italians liked pasta" I said to him before too, jettisoning my pickle to lighten the load.

I walked past the 'Run and Become' stand where they still had some 'Middle of the Packers' on sale but the pile did seem to have been reduced. Well I hope it had! The queue for the Monster Barbecue was too long so I bought a tea and started the considerable walk back to Inverness, stopping here and there to have a look at restaurant menus.

Drunks numbers 4 and 5 were arguing hammer and tongs on the steps outside Johnny Fox's Irish Pub in the shape of a man and woman, both about forty years old. The hard as nails doorman just looked on not prepared to intervene. Inside the place looked to be heaving and having intended to come here for my meal, I would now give it a wide berth.

On the streets leading to the hotel, hard looking young men with fixed stares and glazed eyes were staggering around and mouthing off. At least if they were all in this state on Sunday afternoon, they wouldn't be out in the evening. I wouldn't bank on it!

I had intended to do any number of things in the late afternoon including a visit to the castle but once in the hotel room I slept like a baby for a couple of hours even before showering. I had a brief stroll or hobble and called for pie and chips before returning to my room to watch the soaps. This extended into 'Heartbeat' and I was unable to drag myself away until the end.

Wetherspoons was packed serving cheap beer and meals late into the evening but the crowd in here was orderly with many looking as if they had run the marathon or one of the accompanying races. The tell tale medals that several were still wearing, really gave the game away.

I moved on to The Phoenix, a traditional Scottish boozer with a large centre bar and small cubicles and alcoves, which was frequented by fictional detective 'Rebus' in one of the novels by Ian Rankin.

An earlier football game was showing and the clientele including myself and barman John numbered six. The others were drunk No 6 Pete and his Eastern European girlfriend with an accent to die for, who shall be named Petra. These two persistently argued but whereas Petra kept relatively calm, Pete continually flew off the handle. From time to time he would make a comment such as, "This is doin ma heed in" and would storm outside to cool off, only to return minutes later for more of the same. Throughout all of this, barman John read his newspaper and the two guys with Petra and Pete got up only to freshen their glasses. It appeared as if Petra had given up everything for Pete, who wasn't prepared to return the commitment.

I passed a group of youths staggering and singing and a gang of girls who's dress sense left little to the imagination on my way to Lauders. A disco was just winding down here and people appeared to be leaving to continue partying elsewhere. The streets were still busy with revellers as I turned in and this being on a Sunday evening at almost midnight.

I returned to the hotel to reflect on yet another eventful running weekend. When's the next one.

CHAPTER 25

The Best Dressed Runner

WITH FIREWORKS going off at all hours for a fortnight and bonfires a plenty over the last two evenings, perhaps a misty Sunday Morning would have been expected. But perpetual drizzle had put a dampener on the previous nights festivities, turning to heavy rain this morning and bringing with it a particularly strong wind.

Hardly the conditions to be running a ten-mile race but listening to 'Flashdance' in the car on the way lifted my spirits and I would be raring to go by the time we arrived. Standing water on the road near Knaresborough didn't particularly fill us with confidence as the rain continued to pour down. The car park in a huge field at Ripley Castle had started to cut up and later in the morning would resemble a quagmire. People sat motionless inside their cars somewhat reluctant to brave the elements, no doubt hoping the rain would ease. With almost an hour to the race start, there was still every chance.

As we reluctantly left the car dressed in cagoules, waterproofs and with umbrellas for extra protection, I tip toed across the field so as not to dirty my shoes. I had meticulously polished them as we intended to go for a pub meal afterwards and I didn't want them caked in mud. I quickly gave up on this mission as it became impossible. "You're looking smart", said Moira Lenaghan of Cross Gates Harriers, "aren't you running". "Of course I'm running", I replied, "I always look smart. I'm the best dressed runner on the circuit".

There was a sizeable queue outside the sit down urinals, but we ventured behind tarpaulin sheets to find two huge circular objects like giant lemon squeezers, with men relieving themselves on each of the four sides. These were about the best urinals I'd seen at such events. Far better than the eight stander at Walkington and much more effective than the sloping chute at Nottingham where tall men stood at one end with shorties at the other. I would tell our chairman Cyril that we could do worse than to hire these for our own promotion, the Wilkinsons Ackworth Half Marathon. I didn't have long to wait as Cyril was virtually the next person we bumped into. I told him about the superb urinals but he said that it would depend upon who could give him the best deal.

We wandered into the race headquarters on Ripley Main Street as much to avoid the rain as out of interest. People were browsing at a start list and with the names in alphabetical order by running club and I could see we would have a dozen or so competing today. The two guys next to me were obviously pretty useful athletes as they were quoting names of runners likely to be figuring at the sharp end of the race.

Roy produced a mat to stand on from his car boot and he and Ian were the first to change. They then returned to the warmth of the car, swapping places with me and Terry who provided a couple of black bin liners to keep us warm. After a token jog in which I felt remarkably comfortable, we made our way to the start.

Runners were generally facing in the opposite direction to the way I believed we would set off, but following much prompting from marshals and some shunting backwards and forwards, everybody generally settled down. This reminded me of one particular race some years previously, when everyone was packed in tightly and ready to go. They suddenly asked us all to turn around and face the other way, which meant the plodders were on the front row and the speed men at the back, and would have to fight their way through.

This would be the 22nd running of the popular Guy Fawkes Ten Mile Race organised by Nidd Valley Road Runners. The race had originally started out at Harrogate, had been run at Knaresborough for several years before finding a more permanent home at Ripley Castle, courtesy of the Ingilby family. According to my 'Big Book of races completed', this would be my fifth Ripley outing with three at Harrogate and four at Knaresborough under my belt, making this my twelfth Guy Fawkes Ten. Not bad at all!

With no microphone or loud haler available, the announcer struggled to make himself heard above the constant buzz of runners in conversation. The cries of Shush! Shush! helped make him a little more audible and one of his announcements was greeted with general approval. Apparently Jet.2. had donated two return tickets to any one of the eighteen destinations serviced from Leeds-Bradford Airport. These wouldn't be awarded to the race winner but instead would go to the 400th finisher. What a good idea and what a wonderful surprise for someone. Despite in excess of 800 runners registered, I rather hoped that I would come a little higher than half way, but who could tell.

I glanced around on overhearing a woman behind say, "I wish we'd get started, I'm going 'Stir Crazy'. What on earth did she mean? I'd heard the horrible Janice Battersby character use the same expression in Coronation Street recently. What was it all about? I was under the impression 'Stir Crazy' had something to do with jail, as in the film comedy of the same title with Richard Pryor and Gene Wilder. Maybe this woman had just come out of jail or perhaps she would get out of jail if she made it around the arduous course safely.

I believe the rain has eased a little, I believe the sky looked a little brighter and I believe the wind had dropped a fraction. It was time to jettison the bin liners which we duly threw over the sea of heads, towards the side of the road. Many people were doing the same with little regard for who, if anybody would pick them all up. On a cold morning at the start of a recent race, four of us undergoing this ritual had all tried to hit the same spectator with the tightly rolled up bags. Who says runners are supposed to be likeable and responsible people!

When keen photographer Terry removed his bin liner to reveal his hands, it became apparent that he would be running with his camera. This seemed a strange thing to do on a wet, miserable morning when surely all of his efforts should be channelled solely into running. Perhaps model and local celebrity Nell McAndrew was running. Terry had the hots for her and probably wanted to take an action photo, but he must have known what he was doing.

With all the firework jokes such as going off with a bang out of the way, we were off like rockets or more like damp squibs, along the historic Ripley Main Street. Some weaved around those in front to make up places while others were content just to sit back, bide their time and let the race unfold.

I followed the flow turning left along a gravel path inside the Castle grounds and with hardly room for everyone, I made use of the grass verge. Those ahead slowed with others walking as we passed through a narrow gateway and out onto the road. Some ran on the road with others on the pavement alongside a high wall, no doubt marking the perimeter of the castle grounds. I cut across the grass and onto the road, moving effortlessly.

There must have been a change to the usual course as I couldn't recollect previously coming this way. I drew level with Wakefield Harrier, Stuart Anderson. "I haven't come this way before" he said. "Me neither" I replied. Some years ago, Stuart, club mate John Bell and I had an almighty tussle in the later stages of this race. With all three of us here again today, could those events be recreated, or would I show them both a clean pair of heels.

At the bottom of what appeared to be a considerable climb, perhaps Stuart, and I for that matter began to wish we hadn't come this way at all. A sign indicated we were entering the village of Bedlam where an end stone terraced house with panoramic views and a for sale sign in the garden caught my eye. The last time a similar house had taken my fancy while I was out running, I had followed it up only to find the asking price to be 299K. However this particular property did have an outdoor swimming pool, albeit not much good in the frozen wastes of North Yorkshire.

I ran pretty easily up this long hill, gaining an insight into how the leaders must feel for most of the time. Then to my amazement the lead vehicle, a land rover complete with race clock and flashing lights, pulled out of a side road almost in front of me. With the runners strung out into the distance, the lead vehicle then proceeded to overtake all of these, no doubt attempting to catch up with the race leaders. I wondered what had gone wrong but I wasn't complaining as I only usually catch a glimpse of the lead vehicle at the start of the race.

The rain had eased considerably but it was still gusty as we turned into the wind again at Burnt Yates at the top of another testing little climb. The Guy Fawkes Ten is a hilly circuit with fine views over Lower Nidderdale but not the course for a personal best, although runners return each year for the challenge as was depicted by the large turnout today.

One of the few flat stretches brought a chance to catch my breath and to have a chat with the runner alongside who was a first timer here. He asked me if there were any more hills he should be aware of but wouldn't have welcomed what I had to say "To put it kindly", I replied, there's very little flat on this course".

At the start of the long descent into Birstwith, the giant golf balls of the U.S. Base at Menwith Hill were visible in the distance but quickly disappeared out of sight as we headed down the valley. Crossing the River Nidd for the first time, I held back a shade, in anticipation of what lay ahead.

The toughest hill on the course or any course for that matter is a steep side road running alongside St James's Churchyard. Some resorted to a walk almost immediately as I have done in the past, but this year I was determined to make it to the top while still running, although at times agonisingly slowly. One or two who were walking, appeared to be leaning into the hill and were still keeping up with me, while others were running even slower than I was. I adopted my own individual technique of counting to a hundred strides which has previously served me well. After repeating this process for eight or nine times, I at last made it to the top where the supportive marshal heaped praise upon everyone.

With legs like jelly, I staggered into a side road, but regained my rhythm once again within a couple of hundred yards, passing the five mile post in 37 minutes. Although this was by no means the end of the climbing, there were several useful descents and exposed sections where the wind fairly whipped us along, perhaps accounting for some of the quick times. I gained suitable momentum down the long incline into Hampstwaite, where stone houses and school buildings nestle alongside the village green. Perhaps I gained too much momentum as I was unable to grab hold of the cup that was held out to me at the drinks table, soaking the lady around her ankles and her feet. Turning round to apologise, I made doubly sure to hold onto the next cup that was held out.

Crossing the Nidd again at eight miles, there was much pandemonium on the far side of a hedge with dogs barking and cattle appearing to stampede up and down the field. Two cows obviously keen to get in on the act had managed to escape into the road and had joined the race for the last two miles. Terry was on hand with his camera of course, to capture the highlights.

Leaving the road for the final mile on a broad woodland track, the marshal at the gate shouted. "Get a move on, there's a bit of skirt behind you". The bit of skirt actually passed me in the woods but much to my disappointment was wearing shorts and a singlet, rather than a skirt and stilettos. No one else passed me as I tried to keep up with the 'skirt' and in doing so. I managed to make up a few places in the bargain. A furious descent and a tough little pull signified the end was in sight before a quick burst to tape, inside the castle grounds. In trying to hold off a fast finisher, I was able to sneak under one hour, fifteen minutes and was well pleased with my mornings work.

Terry was waiting at the finish, holding his camera and smiling, no doubt waiting to tell me about the cows. Roy joined us within a minute saying, "You must have run well, I couldn't catch you". Ian brought up the quartet still trying to get to grips with his multi-functional watch. His first words were, "What time did you do?".

Back at the car, Roy once again produced his magic carpet to stand on and we soon changed back into warm clothing from the boot of his car. I quickly bagged my wet running shoes and clothing, making sure I didn't dirty my newly awarded 'Guy Fawkes Ten' tee shirt. Using one of my running socks to polish my shoes, I heard voice say, "You can do mine when you've finished".

Looking up I saw a runner trying to avoid the puddles on his way back to the car, while at the same time, licking an ice cream cornet which seemed foolhardy on such a bitterly cold morning like today. "They're not my running shoes" I said, "They're my ordinary shoes, we're going to the pub. "You look smart" he said, "haven't you been running". "Of course I've been running", I replied. "I always look smart, I'm the best dressed runner on the circuit".

CHAPTER 26

The Abbey Habit

THE ADVENT of the computer somehow passed me by. Whereas others took to the concept like ducks to water, I was left trailing behind, forever struggling to catch up, just like I am in most races. While colleagues appeared eager to learn, I was unable to grasp the technology and the jargon. I remained far happier with the tried and trusted methods that had always served me well and the back of the fag packet culture.

I was put off on some of the early training courses I attended, when the tutors seemed to know little more than I did and could never get the equipment to work satisfactorily. Those who tended to excel were the people on twilight or night shifts who were able to spend time on a computer and lock themselves away for a couple of hours and do little else. I worked in an environment where I tended to be continually fire fighting, so got by with the minimum amount of knowledge required.

I was sent on a computer course close to home where they couldn't get the computers to work for most of the morning. I remember thinking that I would have been better out for a run as the centre was located on one of my regular routes. On looking back, I now wish I had shown more aptitude and enthusiasm as this surely cost me dearly both in job prospects and in monitory terms, over the years.

Only when I started to attend Adult Training Classes at The Joseph Priestley College did things start to shape up and computers become more meaningful. I was introduced to Databases which opened up a whole new concept. I would be able to log all the races I had done, and when I had completed this I would be able to produce lists of particular races, distances, best times and so on. I would join the ranks of the many anoraks who created lists of trains numbers, birds spotted, football programmes and many more. But unlike these people, I would actually be logging things that I had been a part of.

I was well aware that I had run 69 Marathons and somewhere in the region of 230 Half Marathons but hadn't a clue about the rest. On totting up, I knew I had passed the 600 race mark some years ago, but what the database told me was that The 2005 Leeds Abbey Dash would in fact be my 800th race. Launched in 1985 the Abbey Dash is the north's premier end of year road race and was voted amongst the UK's top five 10K's. The event is meticulously organised by Leeds based Abbey Runners in conjunction with the Help the Aged Charity.

This would be a fitting event to mark the milestone. It would be the 21st running of which I had missed only one. "Does this man never get injured", I ask. The year I missed out, I had entered as usual but had come down with a fairly severe cold. As late as race day, I had intended to run but my Dad pointed out that I would be foolish and a mug to do so. Not wanting to be called a fool and definitely not a mug, I reluctantly declined, missing out on what would now have been a full house.

It hardly seemed twelve months ago that Christmas shoppers in the centre of Leeds were bolstered by over 3,000 runners plus spectators in the 2004 version of the event. The early races attracted an entry of 1000 competitors, so this speaks volumes about the pulling power and continual growth of the event plus the resurgence of the running and fitness boom in the region..

The Abbey Dash as the name implies is a dash from Leeds City Centre to Kirkstall Abbey and back over a ten-kilometre course. Well a dash as far as those up front are concerned. Others are just content to better their previous time or to make it back safely. For most it constitutes their annual fitness test before the extravagances of the festive period kick in. Many are content to plod around to raise money for Help the Aged or their own nominated charity.

For several weeks now, runners, joggers and plodders alike had been commonplace on neighbourhood streets getting in vital training to give themselves the best possible chance on the big day. Drivers had been warned to avoid Kirkstall Road like the plague on Sunday morning and any of the other western approaches to the city for that matter.

The conditions on race day in keeping with most years were bright and crisp with a light wind in contrast to the torrential rain which blighted the 2002 event.

To ensure a good parking spot, I arrived in the city centre virtually changed albeit an hour before the start. I filled the time reading the newspaper and accompanying magazine, occasionally looking up at enthusiastic athletes already undergoing their own warm up routines. With half an hour still to go, competitors were jogging around Park Square, stretching against railings or generally milling around. I reluctantly aroused myself to finish race preparations by applying deep heat spray to my troublesome knees.

In the days when the race started at 11 'O' Clock, it would be usual to call for a pint afterwards, but the advent of the 9-30 start meant hanging around for the pubs to open. A club mate came up with the wonderful idea of having a full breakfast after the race which was something we had looked forward to on a couple of occasions. But with far more competitors today and Christmas shoppers to boot, it would perhaps be more sensible to get away quickly.

I acknowledge two of my clubs leading lady runners, Faye Banks and Christine McCarthy as they belted past in one of their warm up exercises. They then slowed down to jogging on the spot with a high knee lift. I decided not to follow suit and resumed a very gentle jog with Derek Mosby of Rothwell Harriers. A lady athlete from another local club came up from behind and pinched my bum which I thought was a nice gesture, a very nice gesture indeed. All of these runners are so friendly, well most of them anyway.

Local celebrity Nell McAndrew lead a mass warm up for competitors in Victoria Gardens. I can't help thinking that club mate Terry Minett won't be too far away with his camera.

Eventually a crocodile of runners are directed to the start in Little Queen Street. There are lots of familiar colours from local clubs and familiar faces. By posting out the souvenir tee shirts before the race, Help the Aged had obviously made a bold statement as hundreds of competitors would run in these creating a sea of yellow. Friendly banter takes place along with handshakes and the usual good luck messages.

Hoping to give a good account of myself I take up a reasonable position at the start. We soon edge forward towards Wellington Street and following last minute instructions and announcements, we are underway. We walk but suddenly break out into a shuffle and then into a jog, only to come to an abrupt halt. It takes me approximately 20 seconds to cross the start line but it will take others much longer. But no need to worry as accurate start to finish times will be posted for everybody, courtesy of the computer chip worn on the running shoe. Already the leaders are a couple of hundred yards ahead but we are soon jogging once again.

Past the Holiday Inn and through the traffic lights at the Yorkshire Post and for once I don't have to stop on red. The procession continues beyond Fridays Restaurant, at times eight, ten or a dozen abreast, strewn across the carriageway. Those from further back are trying to make up for lost time by squeezing past, cutting in or generally forcing their way through. I glimpse Brian Dodd and wonder how the hell he is so far ahead? He must have started on the front grid alongside Mick Walsh. I exchange pleasantries with Paul Smith before Terry Minett passes me clutching his camera as I guessed he would be.

I complete the first K near Yorkshire Chemicals in a touch below five minutes. Am I doing alright or do I need to pick up the pace or ease back slightly. 'Bus Drivers Wanted' on a poster, not a bad vocation on a morning like this. I could certainly use one of those mean machines from Eddie Wright Motorcycles, as we go under the viaduct for the first time and past the 2K marker.

McDonalds and Pizza Hut are on the left but I need fast feet at this stage, not fast food. Past the Esso Service Station and I feel to be running on empty. A sign on a billboard says Carrington Curtains – 2 Miles and it could be curtains for me if I don't get a second or third wind soon. Kosovans and other nationals at the car wash have put down their buckets and sponges to watch the race unfold as we approach Kirkstall Lights. Who can fail to notice the familiar black and yellow logo of the William Morrison Supermarket who are responsible for yet another new road layout here.

The magnificent marshals wave us through the lights and up the incline. Who says this course is flat! The flashing light of the lead motorcycle approaches from the opposite direction with one guy well in front and a sizeable group battling it out in arrears. They don't look to be going much quicker than I am!

With runners now solid on both sides of the road, a pocket of spectators signifies the turn into the Abbey grounds. I mind the step here, before a welcome downhill towards the riverside. Last year we were treading water here, but better conditions preside today. A friend Paul, my very own spectator, shouted words of encouragement plus a cryptic comment about having to work hard to run off the pies. We had been to watch my adopted team, Ross County at Queen of the South the previous day and had perhaps overindulged a little on the refreshments. A gentle slope beyond the 5K marker and we are directed onto the other side of the road by the Abbey House Museum for the return trip to the city.

Runners are still coming through thick and fast towards the Abbey but the glare from the low sun prevents me from picking out anybody in particular. I ease down the gentle slope past West End House and John Holt Funeral Services. I'm dying on my feet but hope I won't require him today. Up the gentle gradient past George 1V pub, before the long disheartening stretch towards the railway viaduct.

Past the 7K marker near Kirkstall Valley Primary School but still the viaduct doesn't appear to be getting any closer. Marshals have their work cut out as impatient drivers try to edge their cars into gaps from the many side streets.

Loads of eating places line the route here, such as Fat Chops Café, Kirkstall Fried Chicken and Sheesh Mahal. The thought of food keeps me going for the moment. Le Raj Restaurant will open shortly. More shops include the Fireworks Factory, who have had much to answer for in recent weeks, Freedom Divers and Snakes 'n' Adders which puts an immediate spring into my step. Plenty of pubs such as the Rising Sun and Cardigan Arms but they aren't open yet and no time to stop anyway.

At last the viaduct is reached and a sign says H. M. Prison- 1 Mile. With only 2K to go, I might just get out of jail in time. Yorkshire Television is beyond the grass verge and the car parks and I wonder if any of their presenters are running today.

I'm not in the frame by the time we reach the Northern Snooker Centre and totally exhausted at Charlie Browns. I hope the fire engines aren't suddenly required to answer an emergency call as we pass the forecourt at Kirkstall Fire Station.

With the job almost done, I dig deep for one final effort up the nasty little slope to Westgate Point. I free wheel down the other side between the Law Courts and the Town Hall Tavern and it's all plain sailing from here.

I keep going up the slight incline towards the Town Hall, where the appreciative crowd treat every finisher like a champion, as the clock ticks towards 43 minutes. Through the check out funnels with medal, goody-bag, flyers and application forms for the next races thrust upon me. The inquest begins over a drink on the Town Hall steps as to what went well or how it all went horribly wrong. Some are elated with others understandingly disappointed. I am delighted with my run for 505th place which was completely out of the blue and only slightly slower than my first Dash almost twenty one years ago. More handshakes and farewells take place. Well done everybody! Haste ye back next year.

Making my way back to the car, runners are now coming through thick and fast with the finishing chutes full to bulging. As I am changing an elderly couple ask to see my medal and say well done. I exchanged banter with the girl parked behind who has run a similar time. She say's that on getting home, She'd sit in front of the fire, turn the heat up full blast and stay there all day getting up only for hot drinks.. Now what a good idea! I tell her that when I get home, I might just go out for a run. After all, I was born to run!

CHAPTER 27

How To Win Friends And Influence People

A NUMBER OF years ago, my boss at the time saw fit to send me on The Dale Carnegie Course in Effective Speaking and Human Relations. The course was aimed at developing self confidence and to get along with others within ones family and in social and occupational relationships. It was also designed to increase ones ability to communicate ideas, to build positive attitudes, increase enthusiasm, reduce tension and anxiety and to enhance ones enjoyment of life.

Presumably his idea was to bring me out of myself particularly in meetings in which I was required to represent the factory, to contribute more, stand my ground and perhaps more importantly, come across professionally to others.

On enrolling I was presented with three rather large books. 'How to win friends and influence people', 'How to stop worrying and start living' and 'The quick and easy way to effective speaking'. I was also given several supplementary pamphlets including 'Six ways of making people like you', 'Showing how to break the worry habit' and 'Teaching mental attitudes that lead to inner security and happiness'.

The course took place over twelve weeks on Thursday evenings from 6-30 to 9-30 and the first few sessions were extremely heavy going. There were people of all age groups and from all walks of life ranging from the superbly confident at one end of the spectrum to nervous wrecks at the other, with some travelling considerable distances to attend. It was all plain sailing for one or two who had probably enrolled purely as something to fill the long winter evenings. Others appeared to be slightly out of their depth including a young lad from Castleford who had suddenly found himself promoted to foreman within a small building firm and his boss presumably thought the course would knock him into good shape. 'He talked fondly to me about their lass and his new babby. I saw myself as sitting somewhere in the 'Middle of the pack'.

The intensity of the course soon whittled the number of students down from somewhere in the high twenties to a more manageable fifteen or so. I knew, or at least thought I knew one of these guys from a previous life but he jumped ship before I could actually decipher if he was one and the same. What a waste of money, presumably in most cases for the companies who had paid hefty fees for the course only to see their delegates drop out after only a couple of weeks.

During the first session we had to speak on a topic for a minute, two minutes the following week and three minutes the next. They taught us a sure method of remembering names and I was required to stand up and recite as many of my classmates as possible. Each week we started with a simple warm up routine as they do in the Japanese workplace. This entailed simple exercises with lots of chanting and handshakes. We were then asked in turn to talk about anything exciting that had happened to us, which in my case were usually the running events in which I had taken part.

Discussing the course and it's content back at work, colleagues were at a loss to understand what I was doing there with some saying that it sounded like a load of old rubbish. But I looked upon it more positively and while I can't say that I looked forward or relished attending each week, I got to the stage where I didn't mind.

Over the twelve weeks, the leaders portrayed ideas on how to make people like you, how to be a leader, how to criticise and not be hated and a whole range of other interpersonal concepts. Each week the leaders nominated the best and most improved students who were awarded the prestigious Dale Carnegie pens. Some received several of these over the duration of the course while I managed to win only one. I believe this aspect of the proceedings was slightly stage managed in order to build everyone's confidences.

On the twelfth week, those still standing were awarded certificates. On the thirteenth week we visited a restaurant in Leeds for a meal and drinks, where the conversation ebbed and flowed into the small hours with everyone displaying their new-found confidences and interpersonal skills. I made a couple of friends hopefully for life on the course and still keep in touch with them.

One of the concepts of the course of which I decided to put into practice was making conversation to total strangers on trains, buses, planes or anywhere the occasion arose. While I found some people to be not particularly receptive, others would readily chat away and I've had interesting conversations with strangers that have lasted for the duration of what would have otherwise been long and arduous journeys. Dale Carnegie emphasised that the most important part in the art of conversation is the listening element rather than the speaking, and I would like to think that I have developed into a good listener.

The idea of making conversation to total strangers in London would not apparently go down too well as they apparently frown upon people who interrupt their boredom and misery, perceiving them to be nutters. However I'll put this theory into practice on the tube when I am next in the capital.

When I semi retired in 2003, I started running on a morning at roughly the same time and on similar routes, so quickly became a recognised figure on the streets. One particular day I decided to incorporate one of the Dale Carnegie principals into my morning run to freshen things up slightly and to add a little interest. I would make a point of speaking to fifty people as I went about my hour long run, if only to say good morning. I can imagine people thinking that I am not training particularly hard if I can take time out to talk while others tell me I am running too quickly if I can't.

After all, acclaimed writer Pete McCarthy travelled across Ireland in pursuit of bars bearing his name and writer comedian, Dave Gorman travelled the length and breadth of Europe in search of other Dave Gorman's. My task would be much quicker and far easier and I would know if I had succeeded within an hour.

The March morning was bitterly cold as I closed the gate to be immediately spotted by No1, Norma the Crossing Warden. "You're not wearing shorts on a morning like this"?, she said. "Sure am" I replied. No 2. Woman taking cheeky boy to nursery. "Mummy, he's always jogging" said the boy, "He's always jogging". "Not always", I replied. No 3. "Good Morning" to lady putting displays outside general store. No 4. " Good Morning" to Day Carer, Barbara, in Sheltered Housing Complex. I just caught the tail end of her asking the lady if she wanted a fish bringing for lunch as she left the house.

No 5. "Good morning" to attractive Oriental Girl at Bus Stop who returned a nice smile. Must come this way more often at this time. I would now set myself a challenge within a challenge and see how far I could run before the bus passed me. No 6.Spoke to Lady dog walker but no reply was forthcoming. No 7. Spoke to local plumber getting out of his van. No 8. Acknowledged Security Guard in Sentry Box outside motor auctions. That must count! No 9. "Good morning" to Community Police Officer on the beat.

I turned down the steep hill towards the canal where people would be thin on the ground but surprisingly spoke to No 10, a lady hanging out her washing and No 11, a walker striding out purposefully with backpack and a cane. I bagged three in one go around the next corner where I was greeted by a yellowy green liquid running down the middle of the road and three Yorkshire Water Officials in bright luminous industrial bibs, Nos 12,13 & 14. The men were reasonably attired for the job they appeared to be doing but the woman was in a business suit and stilettos. "What a nice colour I said". " Isn't it" replied the woman. "Has somebody dumped it", I enquired? "No it's a dye, were doing an experiment" she replied. Who says running is boring!

Along the canal towpath, I spoke to No 15, a birdwatcher peering through binoculars but his reply was slightly muffled. Three youths in school attire obviously playing truant shouted taunts from the opposite bank with the safety of the water between us. I should have crossed at the lock gate and run back up the far side to bang all their heads together but I was on a mission and will discount them from my tally. No 16. A man waved while steering his narrow boat 'Nettle' away from the bank, no doubt giving it a run out ahead of the summer season. "It's been a long time since that moved", I shouted and he nodded in an agreement. No 17. "Good morning" to a workman dredging the canal. No 18."You must be daft coming out in this weather", I said to a fisherman pulling his tackle into position on a small trolley. "I'd be daft not to" he replied. "It's either this or sitting at home with the wife".

Leaving the canal and joining the road, someone in a passing car who I didn't recognise, tooted their horn and waved. I duly acknowledged and will take this as No 19, and still only twenty minutes into the run. I am well on target.

I soon spot and catch up with No 20, a lady jogger and as I pull level, say to her. "Never mind looking at your watch, get a move on". "I will do if you'll pull me along" she replied. The invitation was far too good to turn down and so we ran along together chatting away and putting the world to rights. Not surprisingly I lose track of my counting and have to recap when we go our separate ways. I bid "Good Morning" to No 21, a young woman leading a crocodile of schoolchildren in luminous bibs and No 22, a school crossing warden who rarely speaks but this morning, grudgingly condescends to grunt a reply.

No 23 is a dustman on his daily round, No 24 is the guy who walks to work while reading his newspaper and No 25 is an official from the Highways Agency, gazing through a camera mounted on a tripod. "Did you get a good one of me" I call, but he didn't appear to see the funny side. I cut through the petrol station forecourt and spot No 26, a familiar face filling his car at one of the pumps. "

I could do with topping up", I shout across to him.

Turning into secluded Farrar Lane, Richard, No 27, blows the horn of his Post Office Van to acknowledge me, and John, No 28, a fellow runner with Rothwell Harriers, winds down the window of his van and I stop briefly to chat. Another John, No 29, mine host at The New Mason's Arms, bids me "Good Morning" while out taking his dog for a walk and collecting his newspaper.

Into the grounds of the De Vere Hotel and Golf Course, I bid "Good Morning" to No 30, a young man starting his hotel shift, No 31, a grounds man on his grass cutter and Nos 32 & 33, two golfers pulling their trolleys through the woods between holes. A guy coming towards me who runs with a dumb bell in each hand is No 34 and a lady dog walker is No 35. I know they'll both speak to me as they do regularly.

Returning through Rothwell I shout across the road to No 36, Kevin, a neighbour who emerges from the sandwich shop. Subconsciously I think I'll try to beat him home but won't now as I momentarily stop and talk to No 37, Faye who asks if I am doing the Marathon. "Yes, but I could do with a new pair of knees", I reply. I bid No 38, Mrs McElroy "Good Morning", no doubt on her way to morning mass.

Propped upon it's stand by the side of the road is a smart looking motorcycle, which in fact turns out to be a Harley Davison. As I approach, a taxi pulls up and No 39, a young man appears to settle his fare with the cab driver before walking across to the bike. "You're lucky" I said. I was just about to get a ride back on that". "You may as well take it for the hassle it's giving me", he replied.

No 40, Charlie is a Wakefield Wildcats supporter so I stop for a few minutes to discuss the fortunes of his team. No sooner am I up and running again before I'm stopped by No 41, Colin who asks how my training is going for London. I bid " Good morning" to No 42, a young lady at the bus stop on her way to work in a High Street travel agents, her smart tell tale uniform somewhat giving the game away. "You're running the opposite way today" she remarks.

How am I doing" I shout to No 43, Pauline who obviously didn't hear me properly and says, "I'm alright thanks". I tell Nos 44 & 45, The Watchtower ladies that I can't stop to talk now, as the end is almost in sight.

Some action at last in the shape of a prang at a busy road junction with a W.P.C. struggling to keep the considerable tailback of traffic flowing in three directions while another officer appears to be taking statements from the two unfortunate drivers. A cyclist, No 46, mounts the pavement to avoid the congestion and says, "I wouldn't use my car at this time of day if they paid me". I nodded in agreement with a couple of accidents I suffered in the morning rush hour immediately springing to mind.

But I save the best until almost last in the shape of No 47, a youth who clearly out of sorts staggered across the road, puffing away on a foul smelling roll up and depositing substantial mouthfuls of saliva onto the pavement. "There's no wonder you're guzzling", I said, "smoking that thing". 'How not to win friends and influence people".

I pause to cross the road by a group of people who are awaiting a coach. "Where are you going?" I ask. "Lincoln Market", responds one of the ladies who shall be No 48. "Will there be room for me", I say. "You've got to book in advance", she replies. Some people just have no sense of humour.

I see No 49, the lady with the Alsatian from a distance. She allows her dog to manoeuvre into position, cock it's leg and piddle down the side of my well looked after, environmentally free, green wheelie bin which is out on the pavement awaiting collection. "Not against my bin please", I shout, "Not against my bin". No reply was forthcoming as she attempted to drag the beast away.

Better news when No 50, the postman hands me two letters as I reach my gate. The first is from British Red Cross thanking me for a donation but asking for a further one. The second informs me that I have won a copy of, 'The Great North Run – The First 25 Years' book, in a competition. I'd rather set my heart on one of the limited edition prints portraying the runners crossing the Tyne Bridge but I mustn't grumble. So I had successfully completed the challenge along with a nice surprise at the end. "What next" I ask myself.

CHAPTER 28

Burns Supper

WHEN I printed a form for The Dumfries Marathon from the excellent John Schofield web site and handed it to the club's resident marathon man Roy, after one of the Wednesday evening training sessions, the last thing I expected him to do was fill it in and send it off. Not only did he do this but he went ahead and booked his caravan into a nearby site for a couple of nights on the corresponding weekend.

As the March date loomed ever closer and thinking along the lines of 'Another fine mess you got me into' I thought I had better show willing and go along and do the race with Roy. Due to various commitments, I had done little running leading up to the event with only three runs in January and little more in February. It would have been twelve weeks since my previous race, the longest period between races since I first started to put myself through this regular punishment back in 1983.

A couple of longer training runs in which I broke no pots but at least had managed to run for a couple of hours, filled me with a little more optimism but I realised I would be in for a long hard struggle come the day. Horrendous weather two weeks previously had seen the cancellation of the Stranraer Half Marathon in the same region and only a week before the race, a heavy overnight snowfall had brought Glasgow city centre to a standstill. With no real improvement in the weather, there was still a chance that I may have been able to get out of jail.

But there would be no such luck as the weather improved in that final week providing a bright and cold morning on race day. I opted to drive there and back in the day which I reckoned would take me three hours each way. The best-laid plans were thwarted when I found the slip road from the A1 onto the A66 at Scotch Corner to be closed with a diversion in place. Had the weather deteriorated overnight and had the snow returned to block the road and save the day. The answer to these questions was no, as the diversion through several picturesque villages and along quiet country lanes soon brought me back onto the A66, heading for the high ground and beyond to Penrith and the M6.

One of the advantages of travelling on long car journeys alone is that you can play otherwise little used CD's and listen to them all the way through rather than just picking out your favourite tracks. On this journey, my music was 'The very best of Simon & Garfunkel, Tales from New York'. I only had cause to sing out aloud once, honest, to 'If I could'. Real title 'El Condor Pasa'. You know the one! 'I'd rather be a sparrow than a snail'.

I'd travelled these roads many times, more recently to watch my beloved Ross County at Queen of South in Dumfries. I knew the town layout pretty well so was quietly confident of finding a place to park near to the start of the race, which would be outside the main police headquarters. This would be a first for me regarding race starts and was sure to be an arresting experience.

I'd started a race outside a railway station, I'd started a race in the car park of a fire station and run an entire race in the confines of a power station, but never started from a police station. Better ensure my tax disc is valid and my tyres have the legal depth of tread! Sorry boys, only joking. You do a wonderful job really!

With a huge funfair in place on the riverside car park, I began to regret not having a plan 'B' when my mobile suddenly rang and I pulled over to the side of the road as you do. Roy was calling to say he was parked and almost changed while I told him I was within striking distance of the start.

People were already limbering up and doing their stretches as I pulled into the car park opposite police H.Q. with still half an hour to go. Roy soon joined me and we finished changing and undertaking last minute preparations before taking a gentle jog in pursuit of a toilet which turned out to be the municipal conveniences in the town centre. Most of the runners must have had the same idea as a sizeable queue had developed. With a chill in the air but with the watery sun threatening to emerge, I unusually opted for three layers of clothing with a long sleeve tee shirt, a short sleeve one and my club vest on top and I chose to wear gloves. The race would finish in Dock Park on the waterfront so we were required to hand in our baggage, which would be taken there and hopefully be waiting for us in four hours time or thereabouts.

It became apparent that this would be only a small field, some two hundred strong at an estimate. There were the usual suspects for these sort of races, 'Excuse the pun', in the shape of '100 Marathon Club Members' and other such organisations. I noticed a pocket of athletes from the hosts, Dumfries Running Club while there were those from Annan & District and Border Harriers from just down the road. Represented from further a field were Shettlestone Harriers and the quaintly named Troon Tortoises. I spotted one runner in the Blue and Gold of Beverley A.C. from East Yorkshire.

Last but not least were the tell tale tattooed arms of Brian Mills of Leominster, a man with over five hundred marathons to his name. What a fantastic achievement! Just imagine, a marathon every week for ten years or a marathon every other week for twenty years. How many pairs of running shoes must Brian have gone through in this time let alone how many knee replacements and new pairs of feet. How much money did he spend on entry fees, travel and accommodation?. He could have done far worse for his money. He could have supported a premiership football team.

Dumfries which derives it's name from Dum Fres, the fort of the Frisians, nestles on the banks of the Nith and is spanned by five bridges, the earliest dating back to 1426. But it was Scottish national poet, Robbie Burns who brought Dumfries to international fame, spending the last five years of his life in town as an exciseman. His former home in the appropriately named Burns Street is now a museum.

Some weeks earlier on my way to a football match, I had sat in the no smoking section on the balcony in The Robert the Bruce pub, close to where the race would start in the town centre. As people down below had lit up, I'd watched the smoke gradually rise until it had gradually engulfed our section. This would be the last weekend before the 'No Smoking Policy' took effect in Scotland so those wanting to indulge in future would have to huddle together in small pockets on the pavement outside.

County somewhat fortuitously beat home side Queen of the South that day, with a goal in the final minute. As the home side restarted, I found myself uncharacteristically standing up and screaming at the referee to blow for time. "Has your watch stopped" I yelled, or "Have you lost your whistle". Some weeks later we travelled to see County at nearby Gretna, the previous seasons Scottish Cup giant killers. We couldn't even purchase a Scotch pie there which is part of the reason for going to a Scottish game, if not the only reason. Gretna should have had points deducted for not selling Scotch pies.

The Dumfries Marathon was a one off race organised by Dumfries Running Club to celebrate their 25th Anniversary. It would follow parts of the Solway Estuary and the picturesque Nith Valley on a predominantly flat route. Looking at the distant hills, some still with a covering of recent snow, this seemed in all probability, very unlikely.

Following the usual last minute instructions, and with no bumping, boring or jostling for position, we were soon into our stride moving steadily through the deserted and gently undulating streets, into the suburbs and quickly onto country lanes. We took precedent over a long line of cars queuing to enter a roundabout, with the drivers no doubt thinking, "Why the hell did I pick today" or "Why did I come this way". A railway level crossing beckoned but we passed below the track by way of a subway with the slope up the far side making my lungs work hard.

I noticed signposts for Annan, Dalton and Mouswald where Roy had parked his caravan. He could have saved himself time and passage by joining in at this point. Running together at this early stage and with one eye on the mountains that appeared to be moving ever closer, I remarked to Roy that they surely wouldn't find a flat course around here.

Today was one of those days that come along, in my case all too often, when every bone in my body was aching, my calves were tight, my knees were hurting and my thighs appeared to be rubbing tightly against my shorts. When I pumped my arms to try and gain suitable momentum, they hurt too. I even looked down at one point to make sure I had my shoes on the correct feet. It felt as if all the different parts of my body were working against each other.

I had opted for an old pair of trainers as my new ones weren't yet broken in, and these appeared to be hitting the ground very heavily and awkwardly. I wasn't happy either, with my choice of three layers of clothing and at the drinks station at ten miles, I chose to jettison the short-sleeved tee shirt, reluctantly handing it to one of the officials. It'll be waiting at the finish for you he said, which was a nice gesture but the way I felt, I wasn't confident about making it so far.

I thanked my tee shirt for past services, like you would do if you discard an old tee shirt, pair of socks or shorts. (Or is this only me). I wasn't happy about leaving it so far from home but I'm sure the nice man would look after it.

My mind wandered to a recent early morning run on an out of the way farm track. I was well attired to combat the cold with woolly hat and gloves when I saw a couple of schoolboys walking towards me, in tee shirts sporting their school logo. They were nowhere near their school or a bus stop to their school and it was perishing. "If you're bunking off, I'd go home and get wrapped up" I said. Needless to say, the reply to my sound piece of advice had been none.

This part of the course ran through low-lying farm country hugging the Solway Coastline. Cows and sheep grazed in fields behind neatly trimmed hedgerows bordering straight country lanes. If the seas around these islands raised by several feet in the decades ahead as is predicted, I'm sure the land in these parts would come under threat. From time to time there would be a driveway leading to a farm, a plantation, a large house or a caravan park and at some of these places, small pockets of spectators gathered to urge us on.

Salt marshes and mud flats come together along this estuary to form neither land nor sea. The marshes provide a playground to huge flocks of barnacled geese which were almost wiped out, half a century ago. It was across these sands that Mary Queen of Scots said her last farewells before crossing the Solway to the sanctuary of England. Today the shifting sands provide a dangerous workplace for cockle pickers, legal or otherwise.

We ran through small villages and hamlets, namely Clarencefield and Ruthwell. This village owes it's fame to the Ruthwell Cross, one of Scotland's finest dark age monuments. This stands in an annex to the village church and is 18' high. The cross has portions of an Old English poem, 'The Rood Lay' inscribed upon it with scenes depicting the life of Christ. A commemorative service to mark the anniversary of Burn's death is held at Brow Well, close to here.

Despite my discomfort, I had been holding my place but from ten miles I really had to tough it out with a constant stream of runners now starting to overtake. I completed the half marathon in 1 hour 53 minutes but was slowing badly. The pain from my knee was transferring to the rest of my leg and shooting up the body to my neck. I tried changing my running style in order to nurse my knee but this proved to be fruitless and must have made me look silly.

The race was well organised and a credit to Dumfries Running Club. The many marshals around the course and the helpers at the drinks tables all appeared to be enjoying their day and were most appreciative of the runners. I wouldn't hesitate to return should they stage the event again and hopefully do myself justice. The

dozens of runners who were now passing me, were most supportive with their comments and words of encouragement.

We approached Bankend over a bridge crossing Lochar Water
with a testing little pull and a sharp left turn through the village.
"This is where the Half Marathon starts", said a runner about to
overtake me," Have you done it"? "No, but I wish I was doing it
today", I replied. A man and a woman drifted by effortlessly and
we exchanged pleasantries. She looked remarkably fresh and I suspected she was pacing the guy around part of the course and had
only just started. "Next time I'll invest in a new pair of knees", I remarked. "Next time, what next time, there won't be no bloody next
time", he laughed and I just grimaced.

I passed a mother and daughter standing by their car in a lay-by
for the umpteenth time, obviously waiting for dad to appear. "You
must know some good short cuts" I said and they both smiled.
The next time I saw them, Dad must have passed me as he was
standing with them by the road-side tucking into a Mars bar or
similar.

Still runners passed me by but not with the same regularity. One
guy had a style between a walk and a hobble but he was still moving quicker than I was. Others leaned to one side, leaned forward
or shuffled while others alternated between plodding and walking.
I wondered what this lot made of me. At least I hadn't succumbed
to a walk but I could remember the days when I had walked at
least half a dozen times in a marathon and finished an hour quicker
than I was likely to do today. "It comes to us all", they would tell
me, "It comes to us all!

A guy of stocky stature picked me off with the running style of
a pit bull terrier. His shaven head, sporting the obligatory earring
seemed to be growing out of his shoulders with no noticeable neck-
line but with bulging muscles on his arms and an array of tattoos.
He was stereotypical of the many pub doormen seen in almost any
town each weekend. If this guy could beat me, it was perhaps time
to call it a day.

Then the unthinkable happened and I started to home in on a runner ahead or at least I thought it was a runner. At first he appeared to be a speck on the horizon but gradually became bigger until I realised it was definitely another runner and I would eventually pass him. I caught a further two competitors who shall be named Tam and Rab and who were in a similar state of disrepair to myself.

They were from Greater Glasgow, had never run the Great Scottish Run as it was too expensive and had never run the Edinburgh Marathon for similar monitory reasons. They claimed to have run a 50K race in Fife where they had been force fed with endless plates of neeps and tatties for an entry fee of only £5. "Did I know if there was any food on today"?

The final miles were along the Nith Estuary through the villages of Glencaple, Sheerington and Kelton, where spectator support was sporadic but enthusiastic though there would no doubt be a endless wait between runners coming through at this stage. I appeared to climb gradually as the roads became busier towards the outskirts of Dumfries, still managing an agonisingly slow shuffle with each mile now taking almost twelve minutes. The balance was somewhat redressed when marshals at a roundabout directed me left, down a long hill towards the waterfront. Kingholm Quay comprised a series of boathouses and shipyards with some that appeared to have seen better days.

Glancing back at the final drinks station and approaching the last mile, a runner was just coming onto my radar but I was determined to hold onto my lowly position and not be caught again. As in many of these races, I somehow mustered the elusive speed that had deserted me for the last ten miles and as I entered Dock Park, I must have looked more like a three hour man rather than a four and a half. The endless stretch along the straight tree lined path seemed cruel at this stage, but with my rediscovered speed, the finish line banner and changing marquees quickly came into view and I crossed the line in four hours and plenty of minutes.

"You don't look too happy" said Roy who had thoughtfully waited for me at the finish but I started to feel much happier when I had changed and was sitting drinking my soup and eating a sandwich. Had I finished much later in the day it could have doubled as a 'Burns Supper'. Rab and Tam who finished a couple of minutes further back would have been delighted at the catering arrangements.

Not so for race winners, John Kennedy of Clydesdale and Dawn Richardson of Quakers would have their prizes safely tucked away by now and be well on their way home.

I bumped into Rab and Tam again, wandering aimlessly around town. "Do you know where the car park is", asked Rab,"We seem to be lost". "It's this way", I said. "I don't think it is" he replied, so we headed off in our separate ways.

When Roy brought application forms for the Mablethorpe Marathon some weeks later, I told him to go just away. I then said I'd think about it. And that's just what I did, thought about it. Well probably next year!

CHAPTER 29

Streets Of London

*I*CAN REMEMBER walking through the dimly lit streets in the early hours with a couple of mates singing Ralph McTell's "Streets of London". After a night out in Pontefract in the early seventies, my car had run out of petrol on the way home and we were making our way to a late night garage in the hope of filling my can. Little did I know that in years to come, I would run, jog and plod those streets of London on several occasions.

I retired from Marathon running for the first time in 2000 after bowing out in style at the Twin Cities Marathon from Minneapolis to St Paul in America's Mid-West. But for reasons that no doubt at the time seemed to make sense, I was persuaded, bullied and cajoled out of retirement on several occasions. Throughout this period I managed only one or two marathons a year but through lack of fitness, dodgy knees and lethargy, I usually struggled to break four hours.

At Leicester in 2003 on a murky day, the hilly country lanes, hilly main roads and hilly suburbia really sorted me out. The race started and finished at Mallory Park Motor Racing circuit and much to my disappointment, ran nowhere near Leicester's widely acclaimed Golden Mile. I spent the first part of the race trying to establish if England had beaten France in the Rugby Union World Cup Semi Final.

A year later after the Belfast Marathon, I once again announced my retirement to running friends and colleagues alike and this time there would be no turning back. In the race I had the struggle to end all struggles with my knees killing me, even after I had resorted to walking. This was more the pity as despite the wet and miserable conditions, the course was a varied mix of city, parks and suburbs with enthusiastic and supportive crowds to cheer us on.

A marathon relay was being held in tandem with the main event and from time to time close to the changeover points, runners who had completed their stint were being taken back to the finish on coaches. I would see the runners with their mornings work completed, enthusiastically chatting away as the coaches came past and I vowed to be on one of these coaches myself, at the next changeover point.

But this never happened and buoyed by talking about Arsenal and other football issues to a fellow struggler, we somehow miraculously managed to run the final two miles, albeit painfully slowly. I failed to gain a place for the next London event so decided to put marathon running on the back burner for the time being.

However in the weeks leading up to London, my enthusiasm was rekindled as several club members who would be running there had started to talk about the big day. As I would no doubt be watching the proceedings on television, I decided to do my own long run on the day before the race. I set out at crack 'o' dawn, running on tow paths, through housing estates, through fields and along country lanes. My knees were hurting at ten miles but towards the end of what I logged as an eighteen mile run, I was motoring along without a care in the world.

Similar enjoyable runs throughout the summer without repercussions, prompted me to enter two Autumn Marathons. I ran comfortably under four hours in each and with it, restored my enthusiasm for marathon running once again. A successful application for London 2006 would mark my seventieth marathon and had me thinking along the lines of the Marathon 100 Club once again. Five a year for the next six years would see me successfully reach the target well before my sixtieth birthday.

From time to time at races I would bump into 100 Club Members, Steve Edwards and Wally Oakes who have hundreds of successfully completed marathons to their name. They would ask how many I had done and the total had hardly changed over recent years. A friend who shall remain nameless had found out about the 100 Marathon Club after completing about thirty. He told his wife that he wouldn't mind having a go for it. "The best of luck" she said, "But expect your bags to be packed long before you reach that target".

I was accepted to the London Marathon for the first time in 1988 after several refusals, but only after appealing. My appeal was up-held but I wasn't notified until mid February which meant training had to be sandwiched into a couple of months.

Along with neighbour Graham Callaly and his brother Tom, we completed our long runs, I finished two half marathons at York and Scarborough in reasonable shape and with a week to go felt really up for it. The short Wednesday evening training run was meant to keep things ticking over for the big day but instead ended in disaster as I appeared to have nothing left in the tank. Graham kept pushing ahead, but had to stop and wait or jog back for me.

We travelled to London, but I felt out of sorts even walking around steadily sightseeing. On Saturday evening I had a jog in Hyde Park and after a couple of hundred yards, needed to stop and walk. On race day morning, I returned my entry to the Tower Thistle Hotel, phoned home to say, "Don't look out for me on the telly", and duly took up my position as a spectator on Tower Bridge.

I spotted both Tom and Graham and moved on to Lower Thames Street at about 22 Miles into the race. I sat on a wall and saw Denmark's finest, Henrik Jorgenson come through well clear of the pack. As the runners came through thick and fast and the specta-tors began to build, I moved to stand closer to the pavements edge. "You're not supposed to stand there" said a guy who had been sit-ting on the wall. Taking my frustration at not running out on him, I replied, "Don't be so stupid, If you want to see the race, then get up off your arse!".

After seeing Graham and Tom safely past and one or two others who I was able to spot, the sheer multitude of runners became almost a blur. I retired to a hostelry in the Square Mile for a pint and a sandwich. Guess what was on the telly? Yes, the Marathon.

The downside of not running meant I was unable to collect the sponsorship money from those who had pledged. However some people were both generous and sympathetic towards me saying I deserved the money anyway so the upside was that I raised the measly sum of £37 for The Prince of Wales Hospice in Pontefract.

I had often been critical of those who carried their number over to the following year with no real intention of doing the race anyway but was happy to make use of this facility myself, securing a place for 1989. Again my preparations went smoothly until a Thursday evening a couple of weeks before the race. I had started my short run when the heavens opened. The rain turned to sleet and then to hail and I can remember the hailstones bouncing off my cheeks.

I enjoyed my shower that evening so much the better, was able to stand the red hot water and fair started to glow. I went out for a drink and can remember getting a real fug on before my whole body started to itch. The next morning I was covered in spots which the doctor diagnosed as Chicken Pox. Determined not to let the curse of the London Marathon strike again, I had a few days off work but was soon out pounding the pavements once again.

I travelled with Graham and Kevin Toolan to the capital by train. We made our way to the race registration which was held in a marquee outside The Royal Festival Hall on the South Bank. A torrential down pour prompted us to make a detour into a pub for a pint and a sausage sandwich. On Friday evening we met up with Kevin's brother and enjoyed several more pots, not the ideal preparation with only a day to go before the marathon.

On Saturday afternoon we saw Charlton Athletic take on Manchester United, a couple of seasons before the Reds golden era. I told these two not to shout anything which would attract attention to ourselves but Charlton had some quick players up front and after only a couple of minutes, one of these was upended inside the penalty box. I immediately rose to my feet screaming for a penalty. The referee duly obliged, Charlton scored from the spot and won the game 1-0.

1989 marked the advent of ADT as the main event sponsor taking over from Mars. On Blackheath Common I bumped into an old school friend, Brian Gater who I knew had played rugby but had never associated with running. We wished each other well for the long journey ahead. I suspected there would be many others out there like Brian, taking part to raise money for good causes. I would be running this year for The West Yorkshire Ambulance Appeal and had in the region of £700 riding upon my success. A minutes silence took place for those killed in the Hillsborough disaster before we were sent on our way. Even though I felt sluggish throughout, the atmosphere was terrific and running with Kevin for most of the way, I thoroughly enjoyed the experience.

After being rejected for all those years, I surprisingly secured a place again for 1990. The race started in torrential rain with drizzle for most of the journey. This time I was able to enjoy the race and take in much more of the surroundings particularly the new developments in Docklands. I ran well for most of the time finishing in a creditable 3-35, relishing the stretch through Admiralty Arch and along The Mall where runners were met with a wall of noise.

In 1993, I secured a club entry and on a windy day took six minutes to pass through the start. I ran for most of the way with Mick Eaton who has since, sadly passed away.

I used the 1995 race as a long training run ahead of the 35 mile, Two Oceans Marathon in South Africa with the intention of just easing myself around. I became a bit blaze about the whole thing and if anyone asked what I expected to do I would say. "Oh, I'm just using this as a long training run". Well, long training run or not, I suffered cramp around twenty miles, and had to walk several times before coming back to finish strongly.

After the 1997 event, editor Richard Hancock wrote in the club newsletter. Andy Bennett had a fine run staying over a minute clear of a pack of Ackworth Road Runners who were engaged in their own private race. It's little things like this that make it all seem worthwhile.

2000 was a complete disaster when I struggled from start to finish. I never felt comfortable and would have dropped out at half way had there been a half marathon option. I was continually being overtaken in the later stages by a stream of runners and from time to time, those who recognised me would give a tap on the shoulder or turn around to provide encouragement. Andy Timson of Rothwell Harriers urged me to stay with him for the final few miles but after a couple of hundred yards, I wished him well and once again had to drop off the pace. It just didn't happen for me that day and I finished in a shade over four hours.

And so the 2006 Flora London would mark my seventieth marathon for which I would be better prepared, have more training miles under my belt and would give a good account of myself. For reasons unknown, none of these requirements fell into place and sore knees and irritating niggles prevented me from doing those all important long training runs.

But all was not lost as with a month to go, I would use the tough Spen Twenty race at Cleckheaton as my important work out for the big day. However on race morning, I opened the curtains to a covering of snow with more beginning to fall. The weather forecast was grim, the race would be held on higher ground close to the Pennines and may not even take place. So I chickened out, got suitably attired setting out on an earlier run closer to home. Despite wearing gloves, my finger ends ached and throbbed for most of the journey and felt as if they may drop off at any point. My knees stiffened and my calves tightened before I called it a day after a couple of hours. I would need a miracle to get around comfortably at London.

With a mile to go on one of my final training runs before the Marathon, I caught up with a fellow runner near 'The Jawbones of Whale' at Rothwell. Honest! I had played football with this lad in a previous life but had never associated him with running. He said he was part of an eight man team from a local pub, running for Cystic Fibrosis.

I knew a couple the guys he mentioned who were part of the team but didn't know Stuart Oldroyd. "You know Stuart" he said. "Is he from the big Holdroyd family in Woodlesford?". "No". "Is he one of the Carlton 'Rhubarb' Oldroyds?". "No". "Is he a tall guy with glasses?". "No, you'll know Stuart", he said.

The following day, the girl in the bank asked me if I was running. I told her I was. "Stuart Oldroyd's running, isn't he", she asked. "Apparently so", I replied. The lady at the chemists said more or less same thing as did the assistant in Greggs. The girl in the fish and chip shop asked if I was running and said she knew one or two who were. "Stuart's running", she said. "Stuart Oldroyd"

And the same happened the next day too. Everyone seemed to know Stuart Oldroyd and knew that he would be running in the marathon. He even assumed Christian name only status like Davina, Elton or Delia. Somebody on the train down mentioned Stuart was running as did someone at the registration who said he was actually in the building, there and then. Being so popular, he must have really been coining in the sponsorship money.

The Marathon was a minor distraction that I could have well done without on what promised to be a hectic but enjoyable weekend. As I entered the Excel Building where the race registration would take place, the Marathon signature tune from the film 'The Trapper' struck up, stopped and then suddenly started again. The lulls in-between it playing were like bliss.

Signs above the long rows of tables indicated where I should register. Some of the numbered zones had no takers but there was a considerable queue where I was required to wait. The girl in front told me she was nervous. "About registering" I asked, "Or about the race. "Both", she replied, "What will I have to do. "Well you'll have to sign your form and they may ask you a question such as your telephone number. It's to prevent people passing on their entries to somebody else". This didn't seem to appease her as she seemed terrified.

Her friend who was a bundle of energy joined us, having already registered in another queue and said that it was her first marathon. "Well you'll be alright running in those" I said looking down at her high-heeled boots, as you do. "Oh I'd be able to get round in these", she giggled, "I run everywhere in them. We all wished each other luck and moved on. I saw the girls later and they said they were OK now after having loads of freebies thrust upon them.

From the humble beginnings of a marquee on the South Bank, the registration had evolved into big business over the years. Apart from the wide array of sports and fitness stands, there were those from manufacturers, charities, medical organisations and others depicting anything remotely to do with running. An enthusiastic sales girl attempted to explain to me that it surely made sense to sign up for her all singing and all dancing credit card. I told her I was happy with the ones I had and so she moved on to another un-suspecting punter.

The young lady at the Beirut Marathon stand told me I would be safer walking around there on an evening than in Central London. I bet they told Terry Waite that too!

"Is it the up route or the down this year" I asked the guy at the Comrades Marathon (56 Miles) stand. "It's up" he said. "So that means it will go up in the 2010 World Cup Year". "That's correct he replied". "Well sign me up for then" I said, "I'll use tomorrows race as my first long training run. I had often considered the Comrades but somehow couldn't imagine myself putting in all of those train-ing miles. If only!

There was no time to kill as I had a football match to attend. A man on the Docklands Light Railway was dressed up like a Christmas tree with his number already pinned in place and ready to go. Why do they do this?

I put my map reading skills to the test on the London Under-ground on discovering the Central Line was closed west of

Shepherds Bush. Five trains later and a considerable walk brought me to Loftus Road minutes before kick off. My cause wasn't enhanced when I caught the train in the wrong direction at South Kensington and had to hop off at the first stop and backtrack. There wasn't much to choose between QPR and Watford. After scoring a goal, a home player took his shirt off in celebration, was booked, was booked again and then sent off. He didn't take too kindly to this, kicking a bucket and then kicking the side of the dug out on his walk towards the tunnel. The game was exciting but the skill level poor. I remember thinking at the time that If Leeds United couldn't beat sides like this, they wouldn't deserve to be promoted. They neither couldn't, didn't or weren't..

No time to waste as I had to meet a friend to see a show. I had seen 'Les Miserables' previously but Rebecca was far easier on the eye than the incumbent I had been with on the previous occasion.

Race morning beckoned and after an early breakfast, I flagged a taxi down on the street. Les and Gary were already waiting at Charing Cross where the three of us caught the train to Greenwich for a first glimpse of the Cutty Sark, before ascending the steep hill to the red start in Greenwich Park and on to the blue start at Blackheath.

Persistent drizzle meant sheltering in the PG Tips marquee before taking up our places in Block 5. It took some time to cross the start line and even longer to find running space. I became stuck behind a man with a collection bucket, two ladies out for a Sunday stroll and a guy with a huge backpack with a St Georges flag sticking out. Why do these people start so far forward?

At two miles, dozens of runners suddenly decided to swerve in front of me in order to have a pee behind some railings in Charlton Park. Don't any of these runners have any race etiquette. I was now starting to run on angry and began to press along quite nicely, interchanging places with a Giant Sausage. All was going well until one guy without warning, suddenly veered across my bow to give an appreciative youngster by the roadside a slap on the hand.

Beyond the suburbs of Charlton and Woolwich, the open spaces of Greenwich made for a welcome change with The National Maritime Museum set back on the left and The Royal Naval College in spacious grounds to the right. Turning towards the Cutty Sark, I smiled and tried to look good for the masses of spectators and for the TV cameras. The pubs in and around Greenwich are of a nautical theme with names such as 'Gipsy Moth', 'Admiral Hardy' and 'Spanish Galleon' and some of the streets, Jamaica Road and Trafalgar Way have seafaring names too.

I could hear the spectators behind encouraging Gordon Ramsey but would have thought it more appropriate for some to throw rotten eggs and tomatoes at the controversial celebrity chef. Some ran with names across their vests and were duly picked out for applause while many ran in the colours of their nominated charities.

Throughout the years, the race has become extremely charity orientated which is no bad thing. The down side however is that run of the mill club runners who are unable to achieve a qualifying standard time, but support local races up and down the country on most weekends, find it difficult if nigh on impossible to secure an entry. The respective arguments will no doubt linger on for many years to come.

A fellow runner states that he is sick of pounding the straight monotonous roads and is looking for some turns. His wish is granted as we soon cross the suspension bridge leading to The Surrey Quays. A pleasant suburban stretch brings with it the ten mile post displayed by an archway of balloons which I go through in eighty-two minutes. I hope I feel as strong as this at twenty miles.

Turning onto Tower Bridge, the wall of spectator noise is deafening, and I receive a timely boost by way of some encouragement from a marshal who I recognise as a member of Knavesmire Harriers, the York based running club.

Through half way and into Narrow Street, running the opposite way to previous years, passing luxury apartments, attractive mews town houses and 'The Prospect of Whitby', riverside pub. Along

Limehouse Causeway towards The Isle of Dogs, there are brief glimpses looking out across the huge river bend.

I've seen this area evolve over the years with pristine developments and futuristic skyscrapers replacing derelict barren land. We cross bridges over quays and creeks where luxury yachts are moored alongside rusting barges. There are glimpses of the Canary Wharf Building and the Docklands Light Railway who's driverless trains run on huge stilts. More pub names depicting the areas maritime history in 'The Oporto' and 'Star of the East' and one depicting the present by way of 'The Rogue Trader'.

As marathons go, I'd run a good fifteen-mile race, struggled to twenty but had then decided to hoist the white flag. My knees were starting to ache, I was having regular flashes of pain and after prolonging the inevitable for as long as possible, I eventually succumbed to a walk at a drinks station. The runs became shorter as the walks became more frequent and much longer.

The masses of spectators lining The Embankment were fanatical in their support and encouragement with some sounding horns and others shaking rattles or beating on tins. They congregated on every bridge, wall or any available vantage point and I was only sorry I couldn't have performed better at this stage. I felt like a punch-drunk boxer swaying from side to side rather than a well trained long distance runner.

In those final six miles I must have at least doubled my finishing position. I was overtaken by batman, spider-man, superman, half a dozen Dennis the Menaces and a load of Ginger Jocks. The giant sausage sizzled past, obviously cooking on gas. Under Blackfriars and Waterloo Bridges, the huge sweep of the river opened up before me towards the Houses of Parliament and The London Eye.

Why couldn't we go up Northumberland Avenue to Admiralty Arch as we had done in years gone by, cutting off the corner? Why isn't the marathon twenty-five miles which would be a far more sensible distance? Why is everyone looking so fresh when I am having an almighty struggle.

Encouraged by club mates in the crowd and with Big Ben out of the way along with my four hour target, I manage to gain some respectability by running all the way along the tree lined Birdcage Walk. As Marshals move me to one side of the road in order to keep the pedestrian crossing points flowing, I realise the end is now in sight. I find a spurt from somewhere running down the Mall with the backdrop of Buck House to finish in a shade under four and a quarter hours. I am somewhat disappointed but relieved to have finished.

Club mate, Teresa Williams greeted me on completing her first marathon and saying "Never again". Highlight of the day was having my photograph taken at the finish with Ann Bath of Kippax Harriers.

After an ice cream and a quick shower back at the hotel, I hit the streets again in search of 'The Pontefract Castle' pub in Marylebone. I spotted two runners already in there, proudly wearing their medals and why not. While watching the football on telly, I dropped into conversation with a guy, told him I had done the Marathon and he said that he thought I looked about thirty-eight years old. "Let me know when you want another pint", I replied.

The same guy went on to say that he was an unlicensed boxer but I hadn't to mention it to his girlfriend as she didn't know. "Won't she know if you get knocked about a bit", I asked. "I lay low at my brothers for a week or so after fights", he replied.

On Monday I climbed the 500 plus steps to the top of St Paul's for disappointing views on a murky day, not particularly recommended after the Marathon. I watched photographers with cameras held aloft, snapping away as the armoured van sped into the law courts. "Who was in there?", I asked.

"Dun no was the reply".

"Will you have got a good shot?".

"Probably not"

After a spot of people watching in Paternoster Square over a cappuccino, I headed to 'The Prospect of Whitby' a pub on the marathon route where I met a friend for lunch. The sun had finally emerged and there were fine views across the river from our vantage point in the beer garden.

In the afternoon I revisited Greenwich, called at the Shakespeare Globe Theatre and did two floors out of seven at The Tate Modern. I can't say I'm particularly into Jackson Pollock or Tracey Enim. Club mate, Jane Lingard's works at The Wakefield Art Gallery are far more my cup of tea.

I caught the riverboat to Westminster obtaining a freebee when the clippie couldn't get his machine to work. I strolled up Whitehall, through Trafalgar Square and Covent Garden before calling for a well earned Guinness at 'O'Neil's'. After running a marathon, I felt as though I had walked a marathon today. But there was no time to lose as I had to be changed and out again to meet an old work colleague for a drink.

Back home and out on my first run, Norma the school crossing warden told me Jim O'Neil had run 3-20, Tina's husband about four hours and Stuart Oldroyd 4-35. I didn't know him but well done to him anyway!

I'm safe in the knowledge however that I'll do far better next time when I take it more seriously and do more training. On a positive note I raised over £1,000 for The Alzheimer's Society.

CHAPTER 30

What Do You Think Of Tony Blair?

THEY SAY bad luck generally comes in threes and they certainly did for me at a time when I could have least done without it. On the Monday before the Stockholm Marathon, I found the passenger foot well of my car awash once again following a deluge of rain. This was at least the seventh or eighth time this had occurred in my two-year tenure ship of the car, the upside being that any passengers were able to have a foot bath. I drove to the dealers, told them the car was no good to me in this condition and asked them nicely to sort it out. By midweek, they were confident they had done the trick, this time by replacing the windscreen.

Then my washing machine broke down, the necessary part wasn't available and so the mechanic promised to repair it on the Tuesday after Stockholm. Then on Thursday, the day before I was due to fly out, I discovered yet more water in a downstairs cupboard, tracing it to the cylinder in the upstairs airing cupboard. The plumber came almost immediately, located the pin-prick leak but couldn't do anything major until the following week. He reckoned It would be OK if I stuffed towels up against the leak.

After changing the towels or at least ringing them out on a half hourly basis, I realised that going away and leaving the situation would be somewhat foolhardy. I contacted the Airline as soon as the desk opened on Friday morning and explained my predicament. I told them I definitely wouldn't be able to make the 10-00 clock flight and so the kind young lady offered to transfer me to the evening service, free of charge if I confirmed with her later on. After watching people in similar situations throw tantrums on the

TV airline documentaries, I was pleasantly surprised and couldn't really see what all the fuss was about.

The next job would be to commandeer the plumber before he went to another job, even if it meant dragging him out of bed, He understandably was none too impressed, but after a little gentle persuasion, he agreed to drop in mid morning and drain the cylinder. He in fact started to do this but then disappeared onto another job, leaving me to keep the water flowing by sucking through a tube. This brought the memories flooding back of when I had to drain the petrol tank of a car after inadvertently filling it with diesel. He returned sometime later to remove the cylinder giving me ample time to make the evening flight.

Walking through the considerable corridors towards the arrivals hall at Arlanda airport late on Friday evening, I studied the posters of celebrities welcoming passengers to Stockholm. Among the many TV personalities and statesmen, I recognised footballer Henrik Larsson, athlete Carolina Kluft and golfer Annekka Sorenstam.

The futuristic Arlanda Express railway station resembled one of those nuclear bases carved out of rock where Bond villains such as Blofeld or Zorrin launched their deadly attacks to take over the world. But despite the impressive state of the art decor and the boast that I would be whisked into the heart of the city in twenty minutes, the train failed to materialise.

So after a further delay, I arrived at the hotel reception desk shortly before midnight, was allocated my room and unpacked in a jiffy. Among my many phone calls this morning had been one to the hotel advising them of my late arrival and asking them to hold onto my room.

My one question on returning to the reception desk ten minutes later was, "What time does the bar close?" The porter more or less told me they would serve while ever people were in there so I kept my fingers crossed and took to the streets.

Stockholm is little different from British cities on a weekend with revellers in high spirits, drunks tottering around unsteadily and people shouting out the odds. One guy guzzled a huge ball of saliva hitting the pavement inches away from my foot, nothing new there. They were indeed still serving when I returned to the hotel bar, so I was able to have a nightcap, reflecting on the half day I had missed due to my urgent plumbing requirements. On hindsight, this may have well been a blessing in disguise as I hadn't had the opportunity to walk myself to a standstill the day before the race or inadvertently drift into a drinking session.

At breakfast on Saturday morning, a young man whom I had spoken to in the elevator the previous evening parked himself at my table. He had asked if I was doing the marathon so knew we both had common ground. He said that he was living in Germany where he worked as a physical fitness instructor but was originally from the Kurdistan region of Northern Iraq. He told me that if he returned there, suddenly demonstrating the action of a knife slitting his throat.

As I anticipated, it wasn't long before he asked the inevitable question. "What do you think of Tony Blair". Trying to stay diplomatic as always and not particularly wishing to go down this route, I replied, "It's perhaps time we had a change of leadership". I left him to finish his breakfast but not before we had wished each other well for the race.

My priority would be to register for the Marathon, which I had planned to do on Friday afternoon. Registration took place in an ice hockey stadium next to 1912 Olympic stadium and reached on the impressive underground network. The registration wasn't as large as it's counterparts at some of the big city races, not quite as crowded and by no means as intimidating as the London Marathon registration on a busy Saturday morning.

Among the usual stands connected to running and sport in general were those promoting other Scandinavian races. The man at the Aland Marathon stand, an island in the Baltic Sea, twixt Sweden and Finland did his utmost to persuade me that it surely made sense to run in his race. Maybe in years to come when I had a little more time on my hands.

Runners were arriving fast and furious as I left the campus, many perhaps to register but others no doubt for the race start at 2-00pm. On arriving back at the hotel, I had little time to change and complete the numerous small tasks in readiness for the race. I remembered to write my name and details on the reverse side of the running number, so the paramedics would know who I was if I keeled over en route. I then packed the huge plastic bag provided to store my kit while I was out pounding the streets.

The underground train to the stadium was busy with my carriage full to bursting, further enhanced when a young couple boarded at an intermediate station with a pushchair resembling a gun carriage. Everyone packed tightly together, at which point I noticed that some of the people were carrying the large plastic bags, each personalised with individual names. Kennett Svensson, a good traditional Swedish name, kept toppling into me whenever the train jerked or came to a halt.

Runners and their supporters streamed onto the platform but then hit a bottleneck on reaching the escalators. When the long corridor eventually emerged into the daylight, everyone looked up at the bright yellow ball in the sky. Conditions would be indeed stifling.

Changing was in a series of marquees but most people opted to finalise their preparations outside on grass, on benches, on walls or in the small grandstand. I grabbed a bottle of water which was in abundant supply and decided to pick out a shaded area in which to change. Music was blasting out from a disco and in-between each record, many of which were British, the announcer conveyed information about the race, the course and individual good luck messages.

Strangely, nobody appeared to play any Abba music in Sweden. They hadn't been particularly revered in their homeland despite being one of the countries biggest exports and their music in many quarters was considered to be naff. I saw Abba in February 1977 at Manchester Free Trade Hall. One newspaper at the time claimed them to be crass, glib and contrived but I wouldn't hear a word of it. I considered them to be up there with the best. Funnily enough, Abba are now portrayed in some quarters as having been cool.

I sat on a grassy knoll and started to read the race programme with sections printed in Swedish, Finnish, English and German. This was the 27ᵗʰ running of the Stockholm Marathon and 52 runners had completed the lot. Of the 17,200 competitors, 8,500 were overseas including over 5,000 from Finland and 479 from Great Britain.

Among the previous winners were former London champion and Olympian, Hugh Jones who had twice been victorious here along with Kevin Forster, Dave Clarke and American running legend Bill Rodgers. Ingrid Kristiansen, three times and Grete Waitz had both been victorious for Norway in the ladies event. All these statistics held my interest until it was time to apply vaseline and to hand in my luggage.

Making my way over to the huge outside storage compound, I contemplated the fact that rain would be welcome for runners out on the course but not for the baggage which would become soaked. There was no pleasing everybody. Suddenly I stopped in my tracks. Was it?, it couldn't be. Yes it definitely was schoolchildren singing on the melodious chorus of 'Grocer Jack' by Keith West that was booming out over the amplifiers. I stood on the spot until it had finished. Where had they unearthed that one from?

I joined the sizeable queue that would lead to the various coloured start zones where we would assemble. The masses of competitors appeared to be waiting for someone to give the signal for a small gate to be opened. Above the gate was a prefabricated podium or gantry of scaffolding, where two guys stood. They were obviously in charge and judging by the smiles on their faces and the banter exchanged between the two of them, they were apparently relishing this responsibility.

I spoke to a young man who was wearing a similar George Cross Vest to mine along with his Swedish wife or girlfriend. They told me they had applied for the London Marathon but had been expected to pay a fee merely for the luxury of an application form. They hadn't bothered and wouldn't apply in future.

He casually asked "What do you think of Tony Blair?". On my last visit here, everyone seemed to be interested in my opinion of Sven Erickson but this time it was Tony Blair. Following our showing at the recent World Cup it would be debatable who ranked as the least popular. But would 'Call me Dave' or 'Call me Steve' shape up any better. Only time would tell!

Eventually everyone edged forward with hundreds of people moving in from the sides only to compound the difficulty of passing under the small gantry. Once at the other side we completed a U Turn and signs indicated passage to the respective colour zones. I would start in Yellow Zone behind Red and Blue. Green and black would start further back. Some started to break rank ducking under the tape, across the grass and scrambled up the banking onto the road.

Once in the starting enclosures, there was ample room to warm up, stretch or move around. Looking around I realised that individual names were also printed on running numbers as well as kit backs. Standing next to me was Maria Velasquez. Surely she was the woman who played the love interest parts in old cowboy films, in some as a Mexican senorita and others as an Indian squaw. Many different films but always the same actress. On second thoughts, the actress had probably been Maria Vasquez.

Maria indeed said that she was of Mexican origin but now a Swedish National. She looked serious and was keen to start as the typed bracelet attached to her wrist depicted, displaying her anticipated projected kilometre time splits. I had seen a stand at the Race registration where these were available and I now noticed that several people were wearing them. These were all well and good but with so many people in front and the inevitable delay through the start before getting into our stride, we would be playing catch up almost immediately.

Following announcements and speeches, we were walked forward before settling into our starting positions and were soon underway to a lively rendition of the 'Tritsch-Tratsch Polka by Johan Strauss, an excellent choice I thought.

The opening few hundred yards alongside the stadium were stop – start until we made a big left turn into the wide tree lined boulevard of Valhallavagen. Now there was more walking than running taking place as everyone competed for the tiniest chink of space. Imagine the start of The London Marathon, The Great North Run or any of the large mass participation events, only this appeared to be twice as congested.

I brushed shoulders with fellow competitors, clipped ankles and came to an abrupt halt on several occasions when I crashed into the person in front. Surely it hadn't been like this on my previous visit in 1990 but that day there were only 11,000 runners. For every two competing then, there was an extra person today.

Progress was painfully slow through the residential Ostermalm area with the first kilometre post reached in only 12 minutes. To my right, the adjacent road was also full to bursting with runners but they at least appeared to be making some headway. With this in mind, dozens of runners made the switch cutting across gardens and flowerbeds to reach the far carriageway. Others made the better choice of using the footpath through the gardens between the parallel roads scattering spectators and families out of the way a little sharply.

Those who had switched carriageways had wasted their time as the two roads soon merged bringing the brief momentum to an abrupt halt. We headed across the open grassland of Gardet, with industrial units to the north and the huge concrete broadcasting tower rising above the trees.

Even if progress was slow, there was a feel good factor about the quiet, leafy, gently undulating lanes of Djurgarden. Most of the cities better museums are in this long green island including the open-air museum, Skansen and the Vasa Museum, home to the vast warship.

Screams of laughter and music in abundance could be heard as we ran past Grona Lund, the amusement park on the waterfront. Above the tree tops and buildings I could see punters who were fastened into rows of seats, being slowly elevated to the top of one of those tall towers only to be hurtled back down to the ground again. I envied these people and often wished I had the nerve to join them but I didn't have a head for heights. I didn't do 'Big Rides', high balconies, escalators on the outside of buildings, lighthouses and the likes.

But I was confident that I would do in the years ahead and would overcome this fear. I would ride on the 'Big One' at Blackpool, and 'The Corkscrew' wherever that was. I would ride in a hot air balloon, complete a parachute jump, well maybe not, and even climb the ladders at home to clear my guttering.

With several kilometres out of the way and more room to manoeuvre freely, we left Djurgarden behind for possibly the most rewarding section of the course along the waters edge. Strandvagen is lined with luxurious 19th century residences with some of the cities most prestigious addresses. The outlook on the left is of ferries and pleasure boats gently swaying, some serving the larger islands of the archipelago. Many were flying the blue and gold Swedish standard and I suspected they would still be doing so after the forthcoming World Cup Tournament had finished.

Larger ferries docked along Skeppsbron overlooked by the immense Royal Palace. Narrow passages and alleyways lead up the hillside to the labyrinth of tight cobbled streets and quaint squares, which constitute Gamla Stan, The Old Town.

A carpet is crossed signifying ten kilometres completed, in a rather pedestrian 55 minutes. My four-hour target was looking slightly dubious even at this early stage with the humid conditions draining away both my energy and my confidence.

Large crowds gathered at Slussen where the huge locks transfer craft of all descriptions from Lake Malaron to The Baltic Sea. I notice the Katarina Lift with it's observation platform as we approach the ramp into an underpass. I look up at the many enthusiastic spectators lining the wall side and wonder what shape I would be in when I came round again in two hours time.

The next stage is below the Soder Cliffs with the water to the right hand side and the crowds not quite as dense. Those sitting aboard the luxury pleasure craft lend their support from time to time in-between drinking beer and wine or generally partying. They were clearly having a better time than we were. If I was really struggling on the second lap, I wondered if I could commandeer one of these vessels to whisk me across to the far shore to save myself time and passage.

Despite not feeling up to scratch I was nevertheless enjoying my first overseas event in three years. Little extras such as the sweets, chocolate bars handed out at the feed stations made these races special. They even had pickled gherkins but I passed on this opportunity. Stewards with huge rubber rakes cleared away the mountains of discarded cups and debris near the water stations ensuring the route was kept cup free.

The Island of Langholmen came into view with the double spanned Vasterbron beyond, connecting Sodermalm with Kingsholmen where we would run. The incline leading to the bridge felt like a mountainside but levelled out towards the crest. There were many strugglers and several walkers on the bridge and I was at least able to take some satisfaction at the amount of places I made up. At this stage I vowed that I would run up here on the second lap come what may. From this lofty vantage point, the views over the parapet of the waterways and the city made the climb seem worthwhile.

At the start of the descent, I exchanged pleasantries with a fellow Brit, dressed out in Union Flag attire and we wished each other well for the rest of the journey. The descent to the far bank returned one or two painful twinges to my knees, reminding me that the persistent problem wouldn't seem to go away.

At the next water station there were music and pom- pom girls.

The announcer called out Number 3491, Andrew Bennett, England. This put a much needed spring into my step but not for long. I wondered how had he recognised me, but then I realised he must have taken my name and number from the programme.

Along the waterfront at Kungsholmen, spectators called out to the runners from neighbourhood bars and youngsters held out those big rubber hands for runners to give them the high fives. I mainly resisted the temptation but succumbed as three nubile young women held out their giant gloves in anticipation of being slapped.

The imposing Stadhuset, the City Hall is in the distance but surely if I took a left turn up any of these side streets, I could have saved myself a few kilometres and some time in the bargain. If I had done that, I may have missed one of those magic carpets that are designed to produce split times and to detect cheats, so for the time being I would put my head down and soldier on.

Around the corner from the City Hall is Kungholms Kyrka, another striking building and a couple of further dog-legs bring us onto another pleasant stretch alongside a waterway. More boats are moored here, the vast number being all the more surprising when you consider Sweden's short summer season. We ran under a couple of bridges and then slightly uphill onto Fleminggaten, one of the cities main thoroughfares and shopping streets.

Spectator support is sporadic along here with most pedestrians just going about their everyday business but a group of Latino youths wearing baseball caps back to front lent their support, some of the comments I suspect being a little tongue in cheek. I grabbed a cup of Maxim Electrolyte Red from one of the drinks tables and deposited the cup handily for one of the men with rubber rakes. I grabbed the sponge from the pocket of my shorts, dipped it into one of the huge water vats and freshened my face. I tried to run close to the buildings to secure as much shade as possible.

A right turn brings a welcome downhill over the railway goods yards and past the Metro Station at St Eriksplan. Odengatan redresses the balance with a long drag through pleasant suburbs before I spotted the twin brick towers of the Stadium signalling the completion of the first lap.

I couldn't comprehend and certainly didn't relish running a second circuit particularly the way I felt and the way I was moving. I began to regret the fact that I wasn't wearing a cap as the sunrays started to beat down on the top of my balding pate. With thirteen miles completed, the masses of runners had thinned out considerably but the course nevertheless remained pretty hectic.

The second time through Djurgarden is by a slightly different route with the many testing pulls sapping my strength and the inclines playing havoc with my knees. We ran over bridges and by pockets of traditional clapboard Swedish houses and with my stride continuing to shorten, each kilometre post reached was like a minor victory.

At times like this I would start to think of my heroes and how they would have coped in this situation. Of Joss Naylor who would train on the Fells for five hours after tea and of American Ultra Distance runner Dean Karnazes. He covered 199 miles over two days and nights and when fatigue set in and he believed he could go no further, he would concentrate on running to the next lamp post or bush and then to the one after that and so on.

The picnics and barbecues were now in full swing on the luxury yachts moored along the Sodermalm waterfront so there was little hope now of lift to the far shore. Bronzed men with shades perched on top of their heads and traditional blonde girls raised their glasses to the constant stream of runners as music blasted out from below the decks.

I had vowed to run all the way up the Vasterbron for a second time and I managed to do so albeit very slowly. A car had somehow found it's way onto the course and was weaving first to the right and then to the left in a vain attempt to negotiate the runners. This didn't go down too well as people banged on the sides, on the roof and generally hurled abuse. With the car well out of the way and hopefully off the course, sirens could be heard moving ever closer and pretty soon an ambulance manoeuvred it's way in and out of the runners, probably answering the call of a runner in distress further along the route.

A group of soldiers complete with back-packs, eased their way past making it all look too easy. The accompanying sergeant barked out orders and encouragement ensuring they all stayed together and that nobody dropped off the pace. This reminded me of the TV programme back home, 'Bad lads Army'. The drill sergeant with the peak of his cap squashed against his forehead and almost covering his eyes would scream at one of the recruits who was only standing an inch away from the end of his nose. But even the strugglers in this platoon were doing better than me.

For some inexplicable reason, I found that I was able to pick up the pace in the final kilometres and in doing so was able to overtake the soldiers as we entered the stadium. I missed out on my four-hour target once again by several minutes, perhaps rueing the fact that if only I had got my act together and picked up the pace a little earlier, found that elusive short cut or commandeered a boat.

A young girl placed a remarkably heavy medal around my neck and I followed the flow of finishers to collect a tee shirt and a drink. I was dreading having to bend down to unfasten my shoe lace to remove the computer chip, but fortunately help was on hand. I noticed many of the lady competitors had been presented with a rose which I thought was a nice touch.

I returned to the stadium the next day to see the finish of the junior races. The smiles, excitement and determination on the faces of the younger runners was a joy to watch as they approached the finish. Why hadn't they organised events like this when I was a youngster. As in the marathon, many of the juniors wore the yellow and blue of the national team, some with the names of their stars, Ljungberg or Larsson emblazoned across their shoulders. Just like England in the World Cup several weeks later, the Swedes had not played to their full potential with peoples favourite Larsson blasting a penalty over the crossbar against Germany.

So after walking myself to a standstill, it was back home the next day to fix my plumbing and to climb the ladder and remove the debris from my guttering.

CHAPTER 31

Playing Gooseberry

HE FIRST time I visited Egton was to stay with Alison's family over a long weekend. I had met Alison while on holiday in Great Yarmouth back in the late seventies and was sure this would be the real thing. I had left work early on Friday afternoon in order to get there for teatime.

This would be a real adventure for me in my clapped out Austin 1100 and it would be on a wing and a prayer as to whether I would actually make it. But 'Clapped Out' rose courageously to the challenge enjoying the many steep inclines and descents over The North York Moors and into what is now termed as 'Heartbeat Country'. Darkness was falling as I reached Eskdale but I could still make out the contours of the high rolling hills above the village.

I had the impression Alison's parents were distinctly pleased to see me, her younger sister blushed shyly while her kid brother raced around the house without a care in the world. On Friday evening we attended one of those superb dances in the village hall where people of all age groups joined in to the wide variety of music. There was a generous buffet with the likes of Ginger Beer and Dandelion and Burdock served from large pitchers.

Everybody knew everyone else and throughout the evening I was introduced to countless people. The group of young men propping up the bar probably wondered who the jerk was with Alison.

Activities seemed to revolve around village life and on Saturday morning we visited a fete and sale of work in neighbouring Egton Bridge which nestles among lush water meadows in the valley bottom. Pretty stone cottages overlooked the rivers northern bank near to the railway bridge carrying the Whitby to Middlesbrough line through the gorge. St Hedda's Church, one of several in the area bearing that name was built in 1860.

I had drinks with Alison's family at The Postgate Inn, named after Father Nicholas Postgate, one of England's last Roman Catholic martyrs. He was hung at York during 1679 for baptising a child into the Roman Faith. The remoteness of these villages allowed Catholicism to survive throughout the reformation.

On Saturday evening, Alison introduced me to Whitby's nightlife, showing me off to more friends when we visited several pubs around the picturesque harbour. We shared a taxi home with another couple as the last bus up the valley departed very early. On Sunday I put 'Clapped Out' to through it's paces once again as we visited some of the picturesque coastal villages, namely Staithes, Sandsend and Robin Hood's Bay, all reached by steep approach roads. We drove the quiet roads over the vast heather landscape, slowing from time to time to allow safe passage to sheep who of course keep the moors in check by nibbling away and preventing the spread of bracken.

On Sunday afternoon, Mrs Alison cooked a generous roast dinner after which I said my farewells and promised to return in the not too distant future. This regrettably never happened. The reason being was that I wasn't prepared to forgo playing football for the occasional weekend. After all, if I did this, somebody would step into the team and I might not be able to win back my place. Any young man worth his salt had to have a place in a football team.

If only I'd known what I know now. On Saturday's I'd have been able to sell knick knacks from the boot of 'Clapped Out'. I'd have then progressed to selling them from the boot of more reliable van. I'd have then progressed to a market stall, then on to an emporium and then a high street store.

I'd have had a luxury home, luxury car, luxury villa and a luxury wife. I wish I'd never even joined a football team, there was so much that I could have done with my time and so much I had missed. After all, we were only twenty-two angry young men kicking a bladder around a park shouting ridiculous comments such as. "Well played my son" and "Nice one fella" as well as giving the man in black maximum grief.

On a glorious Sunday morning in June, some thirty years later, I made that same journey using generally the same roads but this time in my more reliable Ford Focus. Taking the Whitby road out of Pickering, hikers were out in droves around the huge natural amphitheatre, 'The Hole of Horcum. I passed the legendary Saltersgate Inn where the peat fire is reputed never to burn out and The Fylingdales early warning station where the giant golf balls have now been replaced by what looks like a giant block of cheese. A couple of coaches that were slowing down the traffic thankfully turned off to Goathland, home of the sixties TV drama 'Heartbeat'.

I took the next side road over remote moorland getting that 'On top of the world feeling'. I occasionally slowed down for the odd hiker, a cattle grid and dozens of stray sheep. A steep descent into Grosmont, terminus to The North York Moors Railway provided picturesque views across the valley. An equally steep climb out of the village made me wonder how 'Clapped Out' had coped all those years ago as even Focus was starting to struggle now.

As the road levelled, a tell tale 'Beware Runners' sign reassured me I wasn't too far away from Egton and another indicating 9K as I approached the village told me I was almost there. A marshal directed me into a field that doubled as a car park, just as the juniors were finishing the Fun Run.

The Egton Road Race or Gooseberry Run is so named after the important summer event in the area where competitors from neighbouring villages and further a field exhibit their hairy fruits with some of the winning entries apparently as big as plums. The distance of the race would be approximately 10 Kilometres. Although I had previously been aware of the event, it had usually clashed with others around with this being the first year I had made a concerted effort to make the start line.

Athletes were already jogging around and limbering up, perhaps not advisable to overdo it on a scorching hot summer morning. Starting to panic, I asked the guy in the next car if the start was at 11-00 'O'clock. "No, 11-30" he said, "I was too early". So with time to spare, I wandered back into the village which comprised a series of stone cottages set back from neatly trimmed grass verges around a series of road junctions. There was a War Memorial, two pubs, 'The Wheatsheaf' and 'The Horseshoe' and a garage under an archway which I vaguely remembered from my previous visit.

I entered the cricket field which served as race headquarters and noticed a printed sign outlying all the do's and don'ts with one line dissuading the flying of model planes or similar craft. The impressive cricket pavilion had been opened in 1992 by actor Ian Carmichael. A friendly young lady served me cakes and asked for a small donation. Was she Alison? No, perhaps too young. I wondered if Alison still lived in the village, what she was doing now or if she would be watching today? I bought tom-bola tickets from one of several stalls with proceeds directed towards the Mortuary Chapel at St Hilda's Church and the British Air Ambulance Service.

I crossed the road carefully negotiating the marshals who were checking in Fun Run stragglers and returned to my car to get changed. With the temperature already at 25C, I was glad this would be a relatively short race. My thoughts went out to those who were running in the 'Thirsk 10' later today when the temperature would undoubtedly soar and to several I knew who were taking part in the Edinburgh Marathon.

Changed and ready to go, I jogged to the edge of the field where the land fell away steeply and looked over the green valley to open moorland, beautiful and wild and beyond towards the North Sea. I felt privileged to be running a race in such an ideal setting.

The race director or chap in charge called the runners forward to give last minute instructions and advice. He said that it was more important to stay safe and enjoy the race, than to go hell for leather for a personal best, perhaps sound words on a day like this. The field which I estimated to be no more than 200 strong, appeared to comprise mainly locals, although there were a sprinkling of club vests with a contingent from local club, Loftus A.C. I spoke to a runner who I recognised sporting the colours of his club Baildon, who said that he didn't feel up to the task ahead. To show my support for England at the World Cup in Germany, I would run in my George Cross vest, although I noticed several others doing the same.

Eavesdropping in on another conversation, a runner said to a marshal, "Didn't you fancy doing it this year". "You must be joking", he replied, "Never again ". Surely it couldn't be so bad but my Baildon colleague informed me that last years conditions were just as warm as today.

A guy with long hair and a pleasant face, who I would have considered 'Eye Candy' had I been a woman, appeared to be local as he attempted to help the marshals stop the flow of traffic, before taking his place on the front row. After the familiar call of three two one, we were underway running back towards the village and turning sharp right where a signpost indicated Guisborough – 17 Miles.

I could see the lead car not too far ahead and perhaps twenty men and one lady in front of me. Despite the lofty location of the village above the valley, the course wasn't too severe with several long drags and one sharp hill on a hair pin bend tackled both out and on the way back. The route was pleasant with the roads flanked by dry stone walls enclosing fertile fields and occasional woodland. I could imagine fictional detectives, Bellamy and Ventress trundling down these country lanes in their sixties style Ford Anglia, hotly in pursuit of burglar bill in the TV series 'Heartbeat'.

The descents provided the opportunity for panoramic views across the deep wooded heart of Eskdale with patchwork fields, villages, tiny hamlets and remote farm buildings with the higher moorland bereft of trees, all enhanced in the glorious sunlight.

With a different throw of the dice, I may well have been living in this glorious part of the world today.

I soon started to pick up places as many of the runners had set off too quickly in the hot conditions and were already beginning to fade. I overtook 'Eye Candy' who was flagging badly, before setting my sights on the runner in front wearing the maroon and gold of Loftus. To my amazement he started to walk and I soon caught him. But he responded positively overtaking me, before finding the need to walk again when I passed him once more. This happened on several occasions before I was eventually able to shake him off. Surely it was obvious that a steadier pace would have served him better in these arduous conditions.

This race was typical of those village events that are organised with pride and passion and where everyone pitches in to help. The course was superbly marshalled with officials sometimes in places where there was no particular need. There were four drinks stations, crucial in the extreme conditions and everyone provided encouragement and had a smile for the runners.

At 5K, completed in a shade below 24 minutes, a marshal indicated there were twelve people in front of me which seemed very encouraging. I had recently finished 18th in a low-key race at Bramham Park near Leeds and with many more lofty placings to my name, I may start to develop nosebleeds. With those ahead well strung out and with my stride shortening, it would be doubtful if I could pick up any further places. I did manage to pass another runner before the finish, again worse for wear but was caught by a competitor who came through finishing strongly. I assume that I did finish in 13th position, not bad for a supposed 'Middle of the Packer'. Who knows, next time I may even make the top ten!

Running comfortably below five minutes each, the final country kilometre was one of those irritating stretches that was not only long but seemed endless too. Slowing badly and feeling tired, I circumnavigated the village, returning to the finish on back roads. I could hear the announcer for some time before turning onto the main road where I could see the yellow bibs of a group of marshals in the distance. With nothing hinging on the race or my time and with no other runners either in front or behind, there was no need for the customary sprint finish. I was able to coast home to the finish inside the cricket field, enjoying the final moments so much the better.

A girl obviously becoming carried away with the proceedings poured water over my head and around my shoulders which although welcome, was a little over the top as she continued to do so even after I had indicated enough was enough. Her colleague hung a small medallion around my now soaking neck, and I moved on to a table for a well-earned cup of water.

As I sat there, the next runner finished to receive the water over the head treatment, followed by the run-walk-run man. He said the hot conditions had affected him early on, he hadn't run in the heat this year and he had struggled badly. We shook hands and hoped to see each other again.

Crossing the road where more finishers were now starting to trickle through, the chap in charge said to me, "You'll have lost two stones today, running in that heat". "If only", I replied, "I'll enjoy my roast beef and Yorkshires all the better". "I hope you do" he said, "You deserve it" and as an afterthought he added, "See you again next year".

CHAPTER 32

Charity Begins At Home

IN THE absence of any coaches being organised by the local running clubs, I chose to travel to the 2006 BUPA Great North Run by train. The internet time table informed me there would be a train departing from Leeds at 6-30 am, but while purchasing a ticket some days previously, the timetables within the station concourse didn't show this. The girl in the ticket office assured me the train was a special and would in fact run. She told me a day return to Newcastle would set me back £42 but advised that by purchasing day returns from Leeds to York and York to Newcastle, I would save £14 and wouldn't even have to change trains.

The train was packed to the rafters but two minutes before departure time, two guards came around placing tickets into the slots on top of the seat rests to indicate these places were reserved. This prompted a mad scramble as people tried to claim their rightful seats. "Isn't it rather late to be doing this" a lady asked the guard who came up with the superb reply of, "No, not really". I was fortunately unaffected by all of the movement and stayed where I had been sitting for the past twenty minutes.

The guy next to me was running for Cancer Research and we chatted about the prospects for the race. When he asked which Charity I was running for, I told him I wasn't. His wife or partner who was sitting across the aisle and had apparently been listening in on our conversation said in a refined Oxbridge accent, "But surely, isn't that a number wasted". Trying to keep my cool but privately seething, I replied. "Wasted number, this is the 22nd time I've run this race and I can't keep returning to the same people each time to ask for sponsorship. I was sponsored in the London

Marathon so can't go again cap in hand to these people. Besides, they all know I can easily run thirteen miles so don't really see it as a challenge for me any more".

That appeared to appease her at least for the time being so I asked how many times she had run here. "I've run the Race for Life but I haven't run at Newcastle before. You ran last year, didn't you Toby? These people got their comeuppance when they had to move seats at York as another game of musical chairs ensued when more people boarded the train and attempted to claim the seats they had booked. My new colleague irritatingly bounced a toddler on his lap for most of the journey, occasionally breaking off to walk him up and down the aisle. More people were packed in at Darlington but the train couldn't take any more passengers at Durham.

With over two hours to kill in Newcastle, I bought a tea in the station and sat down to read a book. I returned for a top up if only to listen once again to the assistants singing Geordie accent. Competitors and their supporters spilled off the trains, some already stripped for action with their numbers secured in place. As I watched and studied these people, the vast majority were sporting vests or tee shirts of mainstream charities with others wearing the colours of lesser known ones. I would be running in my Ackworth club vest, would stand out like a sore thumb and started to feel decidedly guilty and self conscious.

I thought about this at length and concluded that over the years I had raised more than my fare share for various charities and appeals. I had standing orders for a couple of charities, had recently sent £50 to the Sudan Appeal and had just paid my final instalment of £500 staggered over several years to the Leeds Cathedral Restoration Fund. If I had decided to run for a charity today, then I would have been spoiled for choice with almost two hundred listed in the Race Guide.

I followed the flow of people along Grainger Street passing the massive Earl Grey monument towards Town Moor. I stopped to talk with friends Elizabeth and Geoff Mort who were on their way to grab a carbo-loading MacDonald's before doing battle. Some years previously, this couple had dressed as bride and groom for the race to celebrate a wedding anniversary and were handing out champagne to friends of which I was one of the lucky recipients. We wished each other well and I moved on.

A dozen or so men looking decidedly worse for wear, appeared ahead of me from a doorway over which a sign read, 'Hostel'. They were all resplendent in matching black and white Newcastle United shirts. One of their number told me they had all decided to buy them yesterday afternoon on the spur of the moment, but after a Saturday lunchtime drinking session and night on the 'Toon', they weren't really up for the challenge today.

I sat on a seat in a churchyard to write a postcard to friend John in the form of a poem about the Great North Run. "What do you think to this" I said, reading out the verses to a girl on the next bench who was starting to change into her running kit, so chuffed was I with my efforts.

The stream of competitors turned into a tide along Northumberland Street and through the University Campus bolstered by more people emerging from every side street. I purchased another tea at a stand in Claremont Road. At this rate I would be awash with tea, running on tea and would soon need a pee.

Stopping to talk to a friendly face in Stuart Whittall of Rothwell Harriers, he told me that each year he pledged would be his last Great North Run but wouldn't be able to bring himself to watch it on TV if he wasn't running.

D.J. Alan Robson was interviewing people from his vantage point on the footbridge over the Central Motorway. He picked out passing competitors, one who I noticed was impressively dressed as a Roman Centurion. All of these people were running for charities and were telling him the amount of money they hoped to raise. And then all of a sudden while talking to one particular runner, he announced. "That's as good a reason as any for running. He's running because he likes to run. Best of luck to you Sir". So I wouldn't be the only person who wasn't running for a charity and this made me feel a whole lot better.

Picking a spot on the grassy embankment in which to change ready for action, I discovered my trouser seat to be covered in a white gunge which had probably found it's way there when I had sat down to write the postcard. Try as I may, I couldn't remove it and just succeeded in spreading it around even more. From having all the time in the world, I was now running late and would have to get a move on in order to make the buses that would be transporting the baggage to South Shields. More bad luck came my way while trying to squeeze in my belongings, the zip to my bag broke which resulted in me having to secure it with safety pins. These things usually happen to me in threes, what would be next?

Despite reading the considerable amount of race literature, I had forgotten the time the baggage buses departed. Somebody told me ten to ten while someone else said ten past. There was one thing for certain, I would have to hurry. Hundreds of people were coming away from the buses leaving me very much swimming against the tide, but I eventually made it depositing my bag on bus No 12. Now all I would have to do was make sure I didn't forget that number!

I took a more leisurely stroll back towards the Red Zone where I would line up. Security was tighter than in previous years with high metal fences erected alongside the respective blocks and competitors numbers being rigorously checked as they entered through a gate. This would deter people rushing down from the embankments to join in at the front as soon as the race started or would it? I moved towards the front of the block but saw nobody who I recognised. The start line banner still appeared to be some way forward and it would take perhaps a couple of minutes to cross the line.

I wore a black bin liner over my tee shirt and vest primarily to keep warm but also to prevent the hundreds of charity runners from noticing my club vest but I had no need to worry. In this section there were many people who had returned to run year upon year, so as well as the many charity vests, there were a fair selection of club vests too,

Starting to perspire, I jettisoned the bin liner as the runners packed tighter together. Some 50,000 entries had been accepted which was in stark contrast to an evening race I had done some weeks earlier at Laxton in East Yorkshire, where 61 competitors had done battle. Earlier in the summer I had run in a race with a field of only eleven where I finished a rather miserable eighth. I wouldn't have expected to see the likes of Toby and his spouse supporting these sort of events.

The wheelchair race started to great applause followed by the elite ladies in which top British Athlete Jo Pavey was making her half marathon debut. The announcer then introduced the elite men who were expected to figure at the sharp end of the race but I was too far back to see any of these. With the helicopters almost stationary overhead and the tension starting to build, the 2006 Great North Run was soon underway.

Nothing happened for a few seconds but we were soon jogging only to come to an abrupt halt once again. Several walks and shuffles later, it had taken a minute and a half to cross the start line but at least we now appeared to be moving freely. Some runners obviously irritated at the delay were going flat out, looking for the narrowest of gaps to squeeze through and taking their fair share of chances. There were those who kept moving from side to side weaving in and out, only to see their progress come to an immediate halt as they hit a wall of human flesh. Others were quite prepared to plod along, bide their time and let their race unfold.

I appeared to be pressing along quite nicely and feeling pretty comfortable until my third piece of bad luck of the day occurred barely a mile into the race. Entering the first underpass, I glanced around before moving out to pass a couple of slower runners. As I moved out to overtake them, the guy in front of me decided to do exactly the same thing and I crashed into him, staggered for what seemed an eternity before eventually hitting the ground. But I was up again in a flash only to go back down again as another runner caught me, knocking me onto the floor once again. It's times like these when I could have done with a rear view mirror.

As I rather reluctantly picked myself up again and got underway, I felt like one of those lottery balls that had been pinged here, there and everywhere or perhaps more descriptively like a sack of spuds. And all of this before I had passed Carol Vorderman and friends who were walking the race for the late Richard Whiteley. The hit record, 'I get knocked down, but I get up again' flashed through my mind and would have been a rather appropriate title for the chapter.

This was by no means the first time I had taken a tumble while running but it was certainly the most high profile. I fell at exactly the same place on successive Saturdays while out on training runs so took care to avoid that particular route for a while. I also hit the deck at the start of a Wednesday evening run when fifteen or so, squeezed together on a narrow pavement and I was the unlucky one who clipped the heel of a runner in front. However on this occasion I was humbled by the number of people around me who asked how I was and enquired of my well being. I had come away from the fall practically unscathed apart from a grazed knee.

Feeling all shook up, I can remember little about the next miles. I remember crossing the Tyne Bridge and looking across at the other bridges spanning the river. I remember the lively rock band on the roundabout near Gateshead. I remember looking up to see the Red Arrows on their first fly past and I remember the magnificent crowds and the many children holding out their hands for the high fives. I can also remember thinking that to my knowledge the course hadn't changed in all the years I had run here but somehow they kept managing to squeeze in a couple of extra long hills.

A signpost for Pelaw brought back memories of the film classic 'Get Carter' when Michael Caine came out of the door of the seedy B & B, holding a rifle while wearing nothing more than his birthday suit. The two gangsters who had come to sort him out retreated into the street where the Pelaw Majorettes were strutting their stuff.

Having shaken off my stiffness, aches and pains, I reached the eight mile post in a shade below an hour but the gradual climb up John Reid Road proved to be my undoing as it has been in so many other years. After so much climbing, the descent comes all in one mad rush down the knee jarring Coast Road Bank. There still appeared to be as many runners around me as when I had taken my fall in the tunnel but with the camera gantry at the finish now in my sights, I tried to pick up the pace in the final stages.

A sign said 800 Metres to go, then 600 and then 400. "This is cruel" said a guy who looked to be struggling badly. I turned onto the grass and with barely 50 Metres to go, I would just miss my 100 minute target.

As I walked down the hill towards Baggage Bus No 12, the spectacular coastline unfolded with the hundreds of parked cars and dozens of buses in the foreground, the buildings in the town and Tynemouth Priory on the headland beyond. Changing back into my grotty trousers in one of the sizeable marquees, a fellow runner came to my rescue when he provided me with a magic wipe to remove the persistent gunge.

Looking to make a quick getaway and stay ahead of the flow, I walked along Ocean Road towards the Metro Station eating a haddock out of the paper that I had so been looking forward to since Mile Five. As I walked, I continually looked skywards as the Red Arrows once again performed their magic, flying in formation along the coastline, before peeling off and once again regrouping for further flypasts.

The sheer volume of families and spectators streaming from the Metro was staggering albeit now two and a half hours into the race. Why had these people left it so late when most of the runners would have completed by the time they reached the finishing area? The best laid plans were thrown into disarray when the first train filled and departed while I was still queuing outside in the street. The next train quickly filled so I had to make do with the third.

People who had almost certainly run the race boarded the train at the next two stations, Chichester and Tyne Dock. How had they arrived there so quickly? Meanwhile, two guys wearing finishers tee shirts joined the Leeds train at Durham. They must have known some good short cuts or had hitched a lift.

The enthusiasm and camaraderie of everyone involved was what perhaps stood out for me on the day. The officials at the start, marshals on the course, the people in the check out funnels, those handing out the goody bags and drinks and even the bus drivers and staff at the Metro Station all went out of their way to be supportive and friendly making the day so much more enjoyable.

My run of bad luck continued on arriving home. Mum had taken a fall resulting in her been hospitalised for several weeks. I lost a cheque and had to request a duplicate and also misplaced a credit card, which mysteriously turned up, some weeks later in an obvious place. I must have looked there at least five times but not before first cancelling it and then requesting a replacement. But worst of all, two shite hawks had left their calling cards all over my front window unless it was the same one that had returned again.

CHAPTER 33

Making Up The Numbers

A WORK COLLEAGUE at the time told me he was taking part in a local fun run as part of a ten-man team of Sunday footballers from his local pub. Apparently there would be fifty quid prize money, cans of beer and lots of other goodies for each of the first ten, ten-man teams to finish. He regularly kept me informed on the progress of his training which constituted laps of a football pitch, followed by pints of foaming bitter, no doubt a pint for every lap completed. Being much acclaimed by my work mates for my running prowess if not for my work contribution, I had a strong conviction at the back of my mind that as the big day grew ever closer, I would somehow be roped in.

Sure enough with the race only a couple of weeks away, my mate admitted they were struggling to raise ten runners. Our boss at the time who had one 10K race under his belt had been signed up and it surely made sense that I should do the same. I told him I definitely didn't want to run as you do, but made the grave mistake of telling him that if they were still short at this time next week, then I would help him out. Unfortunately by doing this, I had more or less booked my place but I suppose that one tiny part of me was saying that I was dying to run.

The Examiner Fun Run was dubbed as Forty Furlongs, which was a roundabout way of saying that it was five miles. It was organised by Huddersfield Rugby Club in conjunction with The Pennine Marathon in which I had struggled on a scorching hot day several years ago. There was a funfair, a barbecue, hosts of sideshows along with both Mens and Ladies five a side football, which was already underway when I arrived at the Waterloo Grounds. Proceeds from the events would go towards several local charities.

I quickly located my new team- mates who resembled a bunch of mis-shapes rather than a team of footballers, let alone a team of runners. A couple of them thanked me profusely for turning out obviously believing that I was to be their big white hope and salvation but they were probably a little disappointed on seeing me in the flesh. Introductions were quickly made and I was given a red football shirt to wear which sported the logo of a local building firm, obviously the team sponsor, emblazoned across the chest with the number 7 on the back.

I recollected my Sunday footballing days when team, shirt and ball sponsors were almost unheard of at that time. My team had managed to secure sponsorship from a local Travel Agent who had then seen fit to leave dozens of clients in Benidorm with no money, no hotel or no means of getting home.

One of my team- mates was of bunter-esque proportions and had done well to fit inside the figure hugging football shirt, let alone make it safely around the five-mile course. Another guy who like me had been roped in at short notice said that he was the father of one of the players, he used to do a bit for Longwood Harriers in his younger days but hadn't run in a number of years. Another footballer was pulling frantically on one of those never-ending roll ups as if this were his last request before facing the firing squad. My work mate was frantically filling in our team sheet after establishing who had turned up and ensuring the all important ten men were present.

The Fun Run would start ten minutes ahead of the marathon and announcements being made indicated we should be making our way towards the assembly area. The bumper field numbered six or seven hundred in my estimation but probably not quite a thousand. Supplementing the usual batmen, supermen, fairies and cavemen with clubs were four girls in huge Fosters Lager cans joined together as a four pack, a group of pirates pushing a galleon on wheels with jolly roger flag hoisted and a giant Oxo cube on legs. Last but not least was a rosy- cheeked Bo peep with a real live sheep, which also sported a race number.

There were many wearing tee shirts with firms names who were probably going in the team competition, many like ourselves in football strips, lots of youngsters but only a few serious athletes wearing club vests.

My team assembled together somewhere in the middle of the pack, this no doubt a new experience for most of them. One or two of my new found friends appeared to be extremely confident, others talked away appearing none too bothered at what lay ahead while one guy appeared to be bag of nerves. Billy Bunter had already started to perspire heavily before a stride was taken in earnest. "You should be nearer the front", said one guy, obviously not wanting the masses to impede my blistering start. "I'm alright", I replied, "It'll sort itself out soon enough".

And sure enough it did within half a mile or so along Wakefield Road with some of those in front, beginning to rue their early break-neck speed already being reduced to a steady jog. I passed many youngsters who had set off too quickly although others were going well and were still holding their own. Bo peep must have got off to a flyer but had now stopped for running repairs by the roadside. Although she appeared to be quite willing, her sheep appeared to have thrown in the towel.

Regular runners like myself are on a good hiding to nothing in these events, being expected to do well but often being criticised for doing too well. But today was slightly different being part of a team and I was determined to do my best and to give my all.

At Aspley near the canal basin, we turned left into Somerset Road for the long and arduous drag towards Castle Hill, probably the highest point in the area. This climb would be difficult for the experienced runners in the field, let alone the occasional fun runners and the many juniors taking part. I passed a couple of my leaner looking team mates, urging them on, wishing them well and telling them the worst was nearly over but as we rounded the next bend, an equally challenging long drag presented itself ahead. Many had now succumbed to walking which wasn't an option for me and I began to easily pick up places.

The drink at the top of the hill provided by raucous fancy dressers really hit the spot on the warm day, setting me up nicely for the long descent down Fenay Lane. I really went for it on this stretch, making up more ground, passing youngsters who were still going strongly, gaining valuable time and really starting to enjoy myself. Turning into Penistone Road at the bottom, I soon caught the former Longwood man who was now beginning to struggle as we exchanged words of encouragement.

Police on point duty held up the traffic at the busy road junction giving priority to the runners and I kicked on the gentle gradient turning into the Rugby Ground to complete the final 100 yards. Spectators were noisy and enthusiastic along the final run in putting those at higher profile events to shame. When I had finished the marathon on this very same stretch some years ago, almost everyone had gone home. I decided there and then that I would be back to do the Examiner Fun Run again.

I finished in a lofty 48th position in a shade below 37 minutes and was first man home for the team. They couldn't have asked for more than that, could they? The former Longwood man was several places behind with the two lean and mean footballers our next counters. My workmate and my boss were somewhere in the middle of the pack with Billy Bunter bringing up the rear in a shade under an hour and starting to perspire like a tap.

I said my goodbyes as the two lean guys were being press-ganged into the five a side football while my other team mates appeared to be drifting into a drinking session as they waited for the outcome of the results.

Back in the workplace on Monday, my colleague was ecstatic at our third placing in the ten- man team event. He said that now they knew what it was all about, they would return next year with a better, stronger and fitter team with more training under their belts. Now where have I heard that before?

CHAPTER 34

Strange But True

ONE OF the advantages of reaching the ripe old age of forty in the early nineties, well probably the only advantage was the fact I could run in the Barnsley Classic Veterans 10K and hopefully after successful completion, I could change into warm clothing, call for a pint and still be in time to watch the start of the open race. More recently, the race has been staged at Royston on the outskirts of Barnsley but in those days, it was held on a hilly two-lap circuit in and around the Town Centre.

The regular large field had assembled on Peel Street with a sizeable crowd to see them on their way. There was the usual sprinkling of International Athletes, former Internationals and some fairly useful Africans too. As some of these undertook their own impressive individual warm up routines, I thumbed through my programme to see who was who.

Race Director Max McNally was here, there and everywhere, busying himself as always with last minute preparations. I'm sure they placed cardboard cut outs of Max on street corners around the route, so great was his presence. In one such race he had the audacity to tell me not to run on the pavement.

More and more athletes made their way into the start area, which was beginning to fill up nicely as the minutes ticked by. One could sense the tension start to build as final instructions were conveyed over the loudspeaker.

Amidst all of these scenes, a tall rangy lad sporting the blue and red vest of organising club Barnsley, remained in a passionate clinch with his girlfriend or spouse, against one of the crowd control barriers, seemingly oblivious to everything that was going on around him. With late arrivals now rushing to take their places at the start, the two of them still kissed on.

"Put her down, you don't know where she's been" came the cries followed by, "If you're running, you'd better get a move on". The lad clearly didn't relish the challenge ahead on a bitterly cold Autumnal afternoon and perhaps would have rather stayed where he was, pressing up against her warm body for the next hour or so, and who could blame him.

In the nick of time, he gave her a final kiss on the lips, at least for the time being and sprinted towards the front, jostling and bumping into spectators on his way.

With the race soon underway, and all of the runners now safely on their way towards Dodworth Road, most of the crowd seemed to spill into the race headquarters for a tea or simply for a warm against the radiators.

Back out on the pavement, it seemed no time at all before the flashing lights of the lead car turned the corner into the precinct with an open top bus carrying the mayor resplendent in his chain of office, the press and other dignitaries. Two motorcycle outriders in close attendance, lead the runners who were about to complete the first of two laps.

Mr Kenyan was in the lead by the width of a vest ahead of Mr Ethiopian but in the chasing pack and hanging onto these two for dear life was the local lad, much to the delight of the partisan crowd. He had obviously got his pre race preparations absolutely spot on.

Even though the lad understandably faded on the second tough circuit, he was still well placed in a particularly strong field. The lad was in fact a runner of some distinction who formed part of a successful Barnsley team who won many team prizes and competitions throughout the early nineties.

For the purpose of this article, the man in question shall be known as Tommy. Tommy had apparently been a pretty useful track athlete in his younger days but even though he still possessed a fair turn of speed, nowadays he was little more than a plodder in the distance events.

They said Tommy wasn't a full shilling but what I do know is that he had a foul mouth. In one local race, he swore at a pedestrian who reported him by making a mental note of his number. I told him to watch his tongue in the clubhouse one night after training and threatened to call a bobby. I can't stand bloody swearing! Tommy never seemed to have enough money for a drink. Feeling sorry for him after one particular race, I stood him a pint which he quaffed instantaneously rather than pacing himself, only to then go and sit on the coach declaring he was skint.

Tommy was always on the lookout for lifts and sometimes would start walking to local events, continually turning around to see if any passing cars would stop to pick him up or could be potentially flagged down. On training nights there would be a collective sigh of relief as Tommy left to go home but on dark nights he would hang around outside the clubhouse and make his move for a lift as soon as he saw unsuspecting punters getting into their cars. One member had felt so put on by Tommy that he had started parking his car several streets away.

One night as I walked down Horsefair in Pontefract, Tommy startled me when he called from the window of some adjacent premises to ask if the latest club newsletter had been mailed out yet?

The incident I am about to relate to occurred on a warm July evening at one of the 5K Summer Handicap Races organised annually by my club. The slower runners would set off first with the faster ones going last. I would set off somewhere in between. If the handicapper's calculations were spot on, then everyone should have finished almost together which didn't tend to happen too often. Points were awarded in the order we finished with bonus points for those who beat their handicap time and so on. The race started at the boating lake in Pontefract Park, with a small loop across the centre of the park followed by a larger circuit inside the rail of the racetrack used by the ambulances and officials to follow the horses and jockeys around at race meetings. The finish would be parallel to the winning post on the race circuit.

Tommy turned up in working clothes saying he hadn't known the event was taking place but had come on the off chance of arranging a lift to a race on Sunday. He nevertheless registered and was one of the first to start, rolling up his newspaper and tucking it into the back pocket of his jeans. Didn't he trust anyone to look after this for him or did he think they might read it or even walk off with it?

Just as with his drinking habits, Tommy had no sense of pacing himself in these shorter races, setting off at breakneck speed and soon disappearing out of sight. When my turn came to start, I quickly passed a couple of runners on the short loop and proceeded to overtake runners at regular intervals around the long back bend. I started to pick off those who were among the first runners to set off and was certain no one as yet had come past me.

At the back of my mind, I realised I hadn't passed Tommy, knew he was still out there somewhere but still didn't have him in my sights. As I hit the four-furlong marker, I could see there were no runners ahead of me unless they had already finished. At three furlongs from home I glanced around to see Jonathon Routledge in pursuit but still some distance behind. Another look over my shoulder at two furlongs indicated he was gaining ground but barring a catastrophe, he wouldn't catch me now.

With Jonathon still hot on my heels, I crossed the finishing line in 20-58, to a small ripple of applause from the organisers and from anyone else who had gathered to see what was happening. It only became apparent some time later that I had in fact won the race or at least I had been first past the post. When I asked about Tommy, I was at first told that he had done the small loop twice, then he had got lost and finally that he had packed in.

In the only race I have won in my life or the only race I am ever likely to win, Tommy deprived me of the opportunity to cross the line with my arms held aloft, to punch the air in celebration and to chant, "Here we go, here we go, here we go!

Everyone who has taken part in a race will have encountered problems when they need to pay a call of nature before the start. The higher profile the event, the greater the difficulties would be with long queues and insufficient toilets resulting in a mad dash to make the start on time. I usually try to go before leaving home which tends to serve me well, leaving me in need of only the urinal. But there are those of us who still need a cubicle as the start time approaches, no matter how many times they have previously been either at home or at the venue. Ladies of course have no choice in the matter unless they are prepared to squat down in the bushes and in many of the town centre events, there are no bushes to speak of.

I will describe the following incident exactly as it was explained to me. A competitor entered a toilet cubicle before the start of the race at a sports centre. He completed his chores only to find there was no toilet paper. My problem is that I usually can't find the end of the roll and only succeed in pushing it round and round inside the holder.

A pair of tell tale feet told him there was somebody in the next cubicle so he asked them if they were able to pass some toilet paper underneath the partition. They duly obliged but when he put his hand underneath to accept the paper, the person got hold of his wrist, unfastened his watch strap and consequently removed his watch. In a state of disrepair and hearing the door of the next cubicle open and close quickly, there was nothing he could do apart from probably shout, "Stop thief". He had been well and truly caught with his trousers down.

I suspect the theft was spontaneous rather than planned but this would be no consolation to the runner who wouldn't now be able to check his time splits, perhaps the least of his worries. I suppose the lesson to be learned is obviously to check for toilet paper when you enter the cubicle. But failing that, if you do have to ask your next-door neighbour for help, reach for the paper with your non watch wearing hand.

Putting bladder and bowel movements to one side for the time being, another problem to beset runners prior to the race is what to do with car keys. This of course is no problem if friends or family have travelled with you, with one exception in my case when my Dad locked the keys inside my car while I was out pounding the roads in Bridlington. If you are on your own or with running chums, this presents a dilemma. Do you hide them somewhere about the car, run round with them or give them to the runner likely to be the first man back.

In the early days when all of this was relatively new, along with most other runners I would place my keys under a wheel arch or wrap them in a cloth and push them inside the wheel hub. Other people no doubt had their own preferred secret hiding places on their own particular vehicles which no doubt served the purpose. This worked well until I heard about one such person having his car stolen from a field after the race had started and with the stewards having probably been called away elsewhere. Another incident entailed a friend having to call out the RAC after his coat had been stolen from the changing room along with his car keys and the money in the pocket.

I've assisted people in looking for lost keys on the ground beneath their cars, have jogged back down the course to look for keys and even given people a lift home after training for a spare set.

Some races provide a box or a lock up for the safe keeping of keys but these are few and far between. Other runners I have known have sounded out a none running club mate to foist their keys onto but this selfishly puts the onus onto that person to wait for the runner at the finish and more often than not, to track him down. At one such race, I had so many sets of keys thrust upon my person that I felt like a Christmas tree.

So while most runners tend to run around with car keys in a pocket, others secure them to a shoelace while some merely carry them in their hand, which must be a little tedious. I usually secure my keys inside a pocket or inside the waste band of my shorts using two or three safety pins. If a travelling companion is likely to finish ahead of me and arrive back at the car before me, I take a spare key along and give it to him to run round with. On the rare occasions when my key has worked loose, I've heard it fall to the ground and have been able to stop and retrieve it.

All was well with this arrangement until a couple of years ago when I ran the Netherthong 10K from a picturesque village in the Holme Valley near Huddersfield. The designated car park was a short walk from the village in a field, flanked by dry stone walls. I had secured my keys inside the waste band of my shorts as usual, had completed the race and was pretty satisfied with how I had run.

Making my way back to the car park, I was discussing the merits of the race and our respective performances with a fellow competitor. As we approached the field, I started to fiddle about with the safety pins in my shorts to release the keys without particularly concentrating. The upshot was that there were no keys there. Out of habit while running, from time to time I would automatically feel for my key to make sure it was safe, but I couldn't remember doing this today and if I had done, I didn't remember when.

I jogged back to the Primary School where the race had finished looking to the ground, just in case the keys had become dislodged when I had started to fiddle about with the safety pins. I asked at the school if any keys had been handed in which they hadn't. I was asked what I'd done with them, when I last had them and a host of other questions, which at the time seemed rather trivial.

I returned to the field looking up and down the various rows of cars with no luck and starting to panic, I made my way back to the school. The officials couldn't have been more helpful. They asked around, made an announcement at the presentation and a lady even drove around the course to see if she could spot them by the side of the road, all unfortunately to no avail. I was even offered a lift home to retrieve a spare set but would have to make my own way back by public transport.

Finally they opened an office to enable me to use a telephone to call the RAC, my mobile of course being inside the car along with my RAC membership card. I answered the necessary questions to verify who I was and fortunately there was a breakdown truck in the area, which they assured me would be here within half an hour. Because my car was in what I had described as a tufty field, they indicated that this may pose a problem for the recovery vehicle.

I thanked the people at the school for their support and updated them on the situation before once again returning to my car, which was now all on it's lonesome in the field. Suddenly I felt a twitch followed by a moving sensation in my nether regions. I looked down to see the elusive keys emerge from down the leg of my shorts and fall to the ground. They had obviously become unattached from the safety pins and become lodged in the lining of my shorts and I hadn't felt a thing.

Feeling mightily relieved, I let myself into the car, changed quickly and once again returned to the school but not before heading off the RAC vehicle at the pass. I told the people who had put themselves to considerable trouble on my behalf that the panic was over. Telling a white lie, I said I had found the keys in the field near my car not daring to mention they had been stuck in the lining of my shorts all the time.

A few weeks later with the dust settled, I wrote to thank the organisers at Netherthong and sent a small donation towards their funds. This happened several years ago but the memory came flooding back when I recently received my RAC renewal offering a £25 no call out discount on my next membership.

Whenever I am asked about my first race, I usually say it was The 1st Five Towns Hospice Half Marathon from Pontefract Park in May 1983. On recollection my first race was in fact as a teenager in an inter schools cross-country race back in 1967 or 1968. By finishing sixth or seventh in the trial, I had gained selection to the eight – man team to compete against three other local schools.

I was chuffed to bits on gaining selection, not that it had been too hard as many pupils either skived off, tossed it off at the back of the field or stopped on the way round for a smoke. Prefects were placed strategically close to a holly bush making sure we all scrambled through on each lap, emerging prickled, bleeding and dishevelled. Cycling several miles on my paper round each evening appeared to build up my strength for such events, so gaining selection had been no real problem.

The event would be run at Outwood Secondary Modern and unlike the cross – country circuit at my school, would leave the grounds and include several local roads and tracks. A mate who lived nearby offered to cycle with me around the course so that my preparation would be spot on for race day. The bonus of gaining selection was appealing if only for the opportunity to leave school early and have a couple of hours away from the classroom. There were no free periods, revision time or staff training in those days.

The Juniors started first followed by the intermediates in which I would run. What seemed like a huge lap of the playing fields was tackled at breakneck speed before we headed out of the school gates and onto Potovens Lane with our top runner, Bob Howe al-ready having built up a sizeable lead. My tactic in those days or the only tactic I knew was to start quickly and hang on for dear life, usually losing places in the final stages.

Heading into Grandstand Road where cockfighting and other pursuits took place in bygone days, I was nicely placed somewhere in the middle of the pack and feeling pretty comfortable. On the first real cross- country section some distance from the school, a group of spectators comprising older pupils and ruffians held out a bike to my dismay, which the runner immediately in front of me gratefully grabbed. Mounting it and wobbling all over the place before eventually steadying himself, he pedalled furiously through the mud appearing to make up a dozen or so places before dismounting and dumping it by the side of the path, several fields away.

By the time we reached Grandstand Road on the second circuit, I had almost caught up with this lad again only for the ruffians to once again hold out the bike for him which they had obviously retrieved from further down the course. This time I could make little impact on him, losing several places on the arduous final circuit of the school grounds.

With all the competitors from the various schools using the same changing rooms and showers, nothing was said about this at least for the time being. On congregating outside to watch the finish of the senior race, the marshals started to trickle back from their various positions out on the course.

Among these were the group of older pupils and ruffians with a toothy little squirt, his face covered in freckles pushing the tell tale bike with the frame, spokes and tyres all covered in mud and in need of a good clean. Needless to say, there wasn't a teacher to be seen. These ruffians looked particularly rough and the pupils with them looked hard as nails with a couple of them appearing to know one or two of our lads. So understandably, the incident was brushed under the carpet and nothing was ever mentioned about it to my knowledge.

I have lost count of the number of times I have looked down around me at the many pairs of ankles, feet and trainers, while I have been waiting for the race to start. I've seen fat calves, thin ankles, hairy legs, tattoos, the lot, you name it. Has everyone remembered to fasten the micro-chip to their running shoes. They all seem to have secured it to their right shoe but I've fastened mine on the left. Will it make a difference?

Perhaps of more interest is the wide range of footwear. Some tatty, some dirty, some old, some new, some pristine, some cheap, some back of the market, some upmarket. One club member would always buy the latest innovative top of the range running shoes, wear them a couple of times, decide they weren't to his liking and pass them on to colleagues at a much reduced price. There were no takers however for his ground breaking Nike Sock Racer.

While waiting at the start of the Robin Hood Marathon, a friend glanced down to discover he was wearing the wrong shoes and not the tried and trusted pair he had worn during all of his long training runs but it was too late to change them.

My only clanger in almost twenty-five years of running occurred at a local 10K event. My heart sank when I discovered I was wearing a previously discarded pair of trainers that were down at heel, scuffed and torn at the toe and green in places through using them for gardening. How I hadn't noticed this while I was putting them on, I don't know. I was probably too busy talking. We were lined up and ready to start so there was little I could do but go for it. They would be uncomfortable, I wouldn't be able to run properly in them and the toes of my socks would be black bright

But this old pair were 'Go Faster Shoes' and they rose magnificently to the challenge slipping through the gears effortlessly and responding each time I asked for more. They were probably smarting at their early retirement and were out to prove a point. After a life of mowing the lawn, cutting the hedge and trimming the borders, they were probably eager for some more action.

CHAPTER 35

The Long Run For Home

O N REACHING the crest of the bridge spanning the York Bypass, I could see the magnificent grandstands at the race course, the fields with neatly parked rows of cars and the clock tower of the Nestle Rowntree building where the time was edging just beyond half past eleven. When I had arrived at the scene some two hours earlier, the wheels of my car had propelled an avalanche of mud skywards as I tried to gain purchase on the soggy ground. My trip to the car wash several days ago had now proved to be fruitless.

One particular marshal was none too impressed when had I left my allocated parking space in search of terra firma and as others soon followed suit, she started to wave her arms around frantically. I felt a little guilty in hindsight as I've manned race car parks myself and had this done to me on several occasions. I wondered if my car would become submerged while trying to make my exit or would I aquaplane away to safety. With the Royal Ascot meeting recently switched to York and other prestigious meetings held at the track throughout the year, the management could surely have done far worse than to direct some of the proceeds towards upgrading the car park.

The Brass Monkey Half Marathon had once again been meticulously organised by Knavesmire Harriers with places selling out over several days back in September. For many it constituted their first serious workout of the year and for others, the first long training run in preparation the London Marathon.

The race is run predominantly on flat, fast country lanes with only the inclines to road and railway bridges as a hindrance and in keeping with this time of year, parts of the course are prone to icy cross winds. The enthusiasm and support of the marshals and those concerned provided a feel good factor when perhaps it would have been far more appealing to remain within the confines of a warm bed for a couple of extra hours. Fortunately the high winds and torrential rain of recent days had held off at least for the duration of the race, but conditions were bitterly cold and I was glad to have had the sense to run in my woolly hat and gloves. In truth I felt no warmer now than when I had started.

As half marathons go, I had run a good ten mile race but the usual lack of training miles and some painful twinges coming from my knees had caused me to slow badly in the final stages with a trickle of runners now starting to pass me by.

With the impressive gates to Bishopthorpe Palace and the twelve-mile marker now behind me, I started the long run for home but I would have to pick up the pace again if I were to break my 100 minute target. Club mate John Faulkner eased past having obviously paced himself far better than I had and we exchanged words of encouragement as he pressed on ahead. Martin Sanders, one of the elite runners at our club had jogged back down the course to encourage some of the stragglers and in passing had told me that he had finished in an excellent fourth position. He turned around to run with John, no doubt thinking he could pull him along over those last few hundred yards but John gave him little encouragement saying, "Go away Martin, I'm alright". Not particularly civil, I thought!

This was my 244th half marathon and with three more in the pipeline, I would be in with a shout of reaching 250 by the end of 2007. What chance would I have given myself in reaching that milestone back on that May day at Pontefract Park all those years ago when I lined up as a nervous novice, perhaps two stones heavier than I am today and wearing makeshift kit. This year would also see me pass the 900 race mark given a favourable wind at my back.

But would my legs hold out sufficiently to achieve 100 Marathons and would they provide me with one final push in achieving my long time goal to run in The Comrades Marathon, the South African Distance Classic. With that one under my belt, I would be sure to go to the long winding roads in the sky a happy man. Would I hang around for long enough to run in 50 different countries, would I ever beat Roy Young again and would I ever break 40 minutes in a 10K race.

One of the running magazines had recently reported on 58 year old Terry Lonergan, owner of the Complete Runner shops who recently ran his 100th consecutive sub 40 minute 10K race and I haven't even managed one to my name. Terry once told me that he had won a prize in a race many years ago and was awarded with a cigarette lighter for his efforts. Those were the days!

As I entered the racecourse with 200 yards still to go, everyone around me appeared to pick up the pace and I responded by somehow managing to find the elusive speed that had deserted me over the last three miles. Rounding the final bend and spurred on by the enthusiastic crowd, I managed to hold off a couple of fast finishers by the width of my vest. Unfortunately the race clock had already passed 1 hour 40 minutes and so I had missed out again on my intended target.

But there will always be another target, there will always be another day and there always be another race. Hopefully there will be many more races.

TO PURCHASE A COPY OF ANDREW BENNETT'S
FIRST BOOK

'MIDDLE OF THE PACKER'

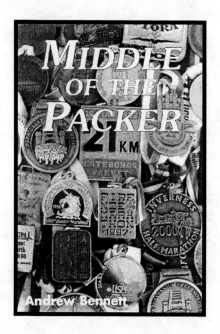

Contact Serendipity. 0845 130 2434

£10-00 PLUS £1-50 P & P.

ISBN 142513147-6

9 781425 131470